Teach...
Inspire...
Lead...

With REA's PRAXIS II® ParaPro Assessment test prep, you'll be in a class all your own.

D1452044

We'd like to hear from you!
Send your comments to info@rea.com.

Research & Education Association

The Best Test Preparation for the

PRAXIS II®

ParaPro Assessment
(0755 and 1755)

Mel Friedman, M.S.
Rena Grasso, Ph.D.
Carol Hunter, M.A.
Laura Meiselman, M.S.

Visit our Educator Support Center at:
www.REA.com/teacher

For updates to the test and this book visit: www.rea.com/praxis/parapro.htm

Planet Friendly Publishing
✔ Made in the United States
✔ Printed on Recycled Paper
Text: 10%   Cover: 10%
Learn more: www.greenedition.org

GREEN EDITION

At REA we're committed to producing books in an earth-friendly manner and to helping our customers make greener choices.

Manufacturing books in the United States ensures compliance with strict environmental laws and eliminates the need for international freight shipping, a major contributor to global air pollution.

And printing on recycled paper helps minimize our consumption of trees, water and fossil fuels. This book was printed on paper made with **10% post-consumer waste**. According to Environmental Defense's Paper Calculator, by using this innovative paper instead of conventional papers, we achieved the following environmental benefits:

Trees Saved: 4 • Air Emissions Eliminated: 832 pounds
Water Saved: 787 gallons • Solid Waste Eliminated: 246 pounds

For more information on our environmental practices, please visit us online at **www.rea.com/green**

Research & Education Association
61 Ethel Road West
Piscataway, New Jersey 08854
E-mail: info@rea.com

**The Best Test Preparation for the
PRAXIS II® ParaPro Assessment 0755/1755**

Printed in the United States of America

Library of Congress Control Number 2009927262

ISBN-13: 978-0-7386-0412-1
ISBN-10: 0-7386-0412-7

The competencies presented in this book were created and implemented by Educational Testing Service. For individual state requirements, consult your state education agency. For further information visit the PRAXIS website at www.ets.org. PRAXIS II® and The PRAXIS Series™ are trademarks of ETS®.

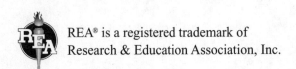

REA® is a registered trademark of
Research & Education Association, Inc.

About Research & Education Association

Founded in 1959, Research & Education Association is dedicated to publishing the finest and most effective educational materials—including software, study guides, and test preps—for students in middle school, high school, college, graduate school, and beyond.

REA's Test Preparation series includes books and software for all academic levels in almost all disciplines. Research & Education Association publishes test preps for students who have not yet entered high school, as well as for high school students preparing to enter college. Students from countries around the world seeking to attend college in the United States will find the assistance they need in REA's publications. For college students seeking advanced degrees, REA publishes test preps for many major graduate school admission examinations in a wide variety of disciplines, including engineering, law, and medicine. Students at every level, in every field, with every ambition can find what they are looking for among REA's publications.

REA's practice tests are always based upon the most recently administered exams and include every type of question that you can expect on the actual exams.

REA's publications and educational materials are highly regarded and continually receive an unprecedented amount of praise from professionals, instructors, librarians, parents, and students. Our authors are as diverse as the fields represented in the books we publish. They are well-known in their respective disciplines and serve on the faculties of prestigious high schools, colleges, and universities throughout the United States and Canada.

Today, REA's wide-ranging catalog is a leading resource for teachers, students, and professionals.

We invite you to visit us at *www.rea.com* to find out how "REA is making the world smarter."

Acknowledgments

We would like to thank Larry Kling, Vice President, Editorial, for his editorial direction; Pam Weston, Vice President, Publishing, for setting the quality standards for production integrity and managing the publication to completion; Diane Goldschmidt, Senior Editor, and Alice Leonard, Senior Editor, for pre-flight editorial review; Kathleen Casey, Senior Editor, for project management; Christine Saul, Senior Graphic Artist, for cover design; and Rachel DiMatteo, Graphic Artist, for post-production file mapping.

We also gratefully acknowledge Alison Minion for copyediting, DataStream Content Solutions for typesetting, the Editors of REA for proofreading, and Terry Casey for indexing the manuscript.

About the Authors

Mel H. Friedman, M.S. has a diversified background in mathematics and has developed test items for Educational Testing Service. His teaching experience is at both the high school and college levels.

Rena Grasso, Ph.D. has taught Writing at all levels (first-year to graduate school) at various colleges and universities for more than twenty-five years. In addition, she is currently tutoring students (middle school through high school) as well as adults, including both native speakers and ESL professionals seeking to improve both work-related writing and to pass the TOEFL exams. Dr. Grasso's experience includes professional grant writing and a range of technical and business writing formats. She has also written essays and articles on history, the arts, and political topics as well as reports and policy studies on educational issues. Rena Grasso holds an M.A. in Language Studies from Boston University and a Ph.D. from SUNY/Buffalo in Literature and Psychoanalytic Psychology.

Carol Hunter, M.A. is a former History and English teacher, staff developer, literacy resource teacher, and consultant in Albuquerque and San Diego City Schools. She also taught at The University of New Mexico, Chapman University, The College of Santa Fe, and Santa Fe Community College. She has an undergraduate degree in liberal arts, and an M.A. in History from The University of New Mexico. While working for San Diego City Schools, she received a Peer Coach Certificate from San Diego State University.

Laura Meiselman, M.S. has taught math to both regular and special education students in public and independent schools in New York for over 15 years. She has two master's degrees from Bank Street College of Education, one in Special Education and one in Math Leadership. She is the author of two books: *Tic Tac Math: Grades 5–8* and *What's Your Angle?* And *9 More Math Games*, published by Scholastic, Inc. She lives in the Hudson Valley with her daughter. When she's not doing curriculum writing or test preparation work, Laura can be found doing yoga, taking cooking classes, or reading.

CONTENTS

Introduction

ABOUT THIS BOOK

If you're looking to secure certification as a paraprofessional, many states and districts require the Praxis II ParaPro Assessment. Think of this book as your toolkit to pass the test. It will help take the mystery and anxiety out of the testing process by equipping you not only with the nuts and bolts, but also, ultimately, with the confidence to succeed alongside your peers across the United States.

We at REA have put a lot of thought into this, and the result is a book that pulls together all the critical information you need to know to pass the test. Let us help you fill in the blanks—literally and figuratively! We will provide you with the touchstones that will allow you to do your very best come test day and beyond. In this guide, REA offers our customary in-depth, up-to-date, objective coverage, with test-specific modules devoted to targeted review and realistic practice exams complete with the kind of detail that makes a difference when you're coming down the homestretch in your preparation. We also include a quick-view answer key and a competency-categorized progress chart to enable you to pinpoint your strengths and weaknesses.

ABOUT THE PRAXIS SERIES

Praxis is Educational Testing Service's (ETS) shorthand for Professional Assessments for Beginning Teachers. The Praxis Series is a group of teacher licensing tests that ETS developed in concert with states across the nation. There are three categories of tests in the series: Praxis I, Praxis II, and Praxis III. Praxis I includes the paper-based Pre-Professional Skills Tests (PPST) and the Praxis I Computer-Based Tests (CBT). Both versions cover essentially the same subject matter. These exams measure basic reading, mathematics, and writing skills and are often a requirement for admission to a teacher education program.

Praxis II embraces Subject Assessment/Specialty Area Tests, of which the Praxis II ParaPro Assessment is a part. Most Praxis II examinations cover the subject matter that students typically study in teacher education courses such as language acquisition, school curriculum, methods of teaching, and other professional development courses. However, the Praxis II ParaPro Assessment is expressly for prospective and practicing paraprofessionals; it measures both skills and knowledge in reading, mathematics, and writing as well as the ability to apply those skills to the classroom.

Praxis III is different from the multiple-choice and essay tests typically used for assessment purposes. With this assessment, ETS-trained observers evaluate an instructor's performance in the classroom, using nationally validated criteria. The observers may videotape the lesson, and other teaching experts may critique the resulting tapes.

Who Takes the Test?

Thirty-five states require the Praxis II ParaPro Assessment, which fulfills the mandate of the *No Child Left Behind Act of 2001* (NCLB). In order for a person to qualify as a paraprofessional, one must:

1. complete two years of study at an institution of higher education; or
2. obtain an associate's (or higher) degree; or
3. meet a rigorous standard of quality and be able to demonstrate, through a formal State or local academic assessment, knowledge of and the ability to assist in instructing reading, writing, and mathematics (or, as appropriate, reading readiness, writing readiness, and mathematics readiness).

When and Where Can I Take the Test?

ETS offers the Praxis II ParaPro Assessment paper-based test four times a year. The paper-based test requires pre-registration. The Internet-based test does not require pre-registration but is administered only in participating school districts throughout the year. Contact your district's administrative office for availability in your area.

How Do I Get More Information on the ETS Praxis Exams?

To receive information on upcoming administrations of any of the Praxis II Subject Assessments, consult the ETS registration bulletin or website, or contact ETS at:

Educational Testing Service
Teaching and Learning Division
P.O. Box 6051
Princeton, NJ 08541-6051
Phone: (609) 771-7395
Website: *www.ets.org/praxis*
E-mail: praxis@ets.org

Special accommodations are available for candidates who are visually impaired, hearing impaired, physically disabled, or specific learning disabled. For questions concerning disability services, contact:

ETS Disability Services: (609) 771-7780
TTY only: (609) 771-7714

Provisions are also available for examinees whose primary language is not English. The ETS registration bulletin and website include directions for those requesting such accommodations. You can also consult ETS with regard to available test sites; reporting test scores; requesting changes in tests, centers, and dates of test; purchasing additional score reports; retaking tests; and other basic facts.

PRAXIS Pointer

Work quickly and steadily. Avoid focusing on any one problem too long. Taking the practice tests in this book will help you learn to budget your precious time.

Is There a Registration Fee?

To take a Praxis examination, you must pay a registration fee, which is payable by check, money order, or with American Express, Discover, MasterCard, or Visa credit cards. In certain cases, ETS offers fee waivers. The registration bulletin and website give qualifications for receiving this benefit and describe the application process. Cash is not accepted for payment.

Can I Retake the Test?

Some states, institutions, and associations limit the number of times you can retest. Contact your state or licensing authority to confirm their retest policies.

HOW TO USE THIS BOOK

What Do I Study First?

Read over REA's subject reviews and suggestions for test taking. Studying the reviews thoroughly will reinforce the basic skills you will need to do well on the exams. Make sure to do the practice questions in this book so that you will be familiar with the format and procedures involved with taking the actual test.

When Should I Start Studying?

It is never too early to start studying; the earlier you begin, the more time you will have to sharpen your skills. Do not procrastinate! Cramming is not an effective way to study because it does not allow you the time needed to learn the test material.

FORMAT OF THE TEST

Whether you take the paper test (0755) or the computer-based version (1755) of the test, the test consists of 90 multiple-choice questions across three subject areas of reading, writing, and mathematics. Approximately two-thirds of the questions in each subject area focuses on basic skills and knowledge and one-third on the application of those skills in the classroom For the computer-based version you need only a beginner's level of computer skill. The test runs on an Internet browser, so if you have surfed the web, you can take the computer-based test. .

Content Category	Approximate Number of Questions	Approximate Percentage of Exam
Reading Skills and Knowledge	18	20%
Application of Reading Skills and Knowledge to the Classroom	12	13%
Mathematics Skills and Knowledge	18	20%

Content Category	Approximate Number of Questions	Approximate Percentage of Exam
Application of Mathematics Skills and Knowledge to the Classroom	12	13%
Writing Skills and Knowledge	18	20%
Application of Writing Skills and Knowledge to the Classroom	12	13%

The multiple-choice questions assess a paraprofessional's knowledge of certain job-related skills and knowledge. Four choices are provided for each multiple-choice question; the options bear the letters A through D. The exams use four types of multiple-choice questions:

1. The Roman numeral multiple-choice question

2. The "Which of the following?" multiple-choice question

3. The complete-the-statement multiple-choice question

4. The multiple-choice question with qualifiers

The following sections describe each type of question and suggested strategies.

Roman Numeral Multiple-Choice Questions

Perhaps the most difficult of the types of multiple-choice questions is the Roman numeral question, because it allows for more than one correct answer. Strategy: Assess each answer before looking at the Roman numeral choices. Consider the following Roman numeral multiple-choice question:

The following tasks are all asked of third grade students during a unit on multiplication.

I.   Sort 20 counters into four equal groups
II.   Solve x × 5 = 20
III. Multiply 4 × 5
IV.   Draw a picture of 4 plates, each with 5 cookies

Which of the following shows the tasks correctly ordered from the one involving the most concrete to the most abstract thinking?

    (A)   I, II, III, IV

    (B)   II, III, IV, I

    (C)   IV, I, II, III

    (D)   I, IV, III, II

In reviewing the questions, you should note that you may choose two or three answers by selecting (A), (B), (C), or (D). The correct answer is (D) because it includes four correct statements. When teaching a concept such as multiplication, it can be beneficial to students to begin with the more concrete tasks and lead up to the more abstract. Task I is the most concrete because it asks the students to physically manipulate the blocks. Task IV is more abstract because it requires students to visualize and illustrate the concept of grouping. Task III is even more abstract because it requires students to do problem solving by just using numbers and symbols. Task II is the most abstract because it asks students to solve the problem with an unknown. Therefore, (D) (I, IV, III, II) is the correct answer.

"Which of the Following?" Multiple-Choice Questions

In a "Which of the following?" question, one of the answers is correct among the various choices. **Strategy:** Form a sentence by replacing the first part of the question with each of the answer choices in turn, and then determine which of the resulting sentences is correct. Consider the following example:

Which of the following instructional approaches does the passage describe?

> This approach attempts to facilitate students' language development through the use of experiences, rather than with printed material alone. After participating in an event or experience, the students, with assistance from the teacher, make a written record of it as a group.

    (A)   Sight word

    (B)   Whole language

    (C)   Think aloud

    (D)   Language experience

Using the suggested technique, one would read:

    (A)   Sight word approach attempts to facilitate students' language development through the use of experiences, rather than with printed material alone

(B) Whole language approach attempts to facilitate students' language development through the use of experiences, rather than with printed material alone

(C) Think Aloud approach attempts to facilitate students' language development through the use of experiences, rather than with printed material alone

(D) Language experience approach attempts to facilitate students' language development through the use of experiences, rather than with printed material alone

Read all of the options. By substituting the various choices into the sentence the correct choice becomes obvious, (D) language experience. The Sight Word method (A) to reading instruction involves exposing students to lists or cards with words commonly found in beginning reader books. Whole Language (B) refers to an approach to literacy instruction which values holistic and authentic experiences with literature. During a Think Aloud (C) the teacher models, explains, and describes how to apply a literacy strategy successfully.

Not all "Which of the following?" multiple-choice questions are as straightforward and simple as the previous example. Consider the following multiple-choice question that requires reading a passage:

> Language not only expresses an individual's ideology, it also sets perimeters while it persuades and influences the discourse in the community that hears and interprets its meaning. Therefore, the language of failure should not be present in the learning environment (i.e., the classroom) because it will have a prohibitive impact on the students' desire to learn as well as a negative influence on the students' self-esteem. *The Oxford English Dictionary* defines *failure* as "a fault, a shortcoming, a lack of success, a person who turns out unsuccessfully, becoming insolvent, etc." We as educators might well ask ourselves if this is the sort of doctrine that we want to permeate our classrooms. Perhaps our own university axiom, *mens agitat molem* ("the mind can move mountains") will help us discover if, indeed, the concepts of failure are really the types of influences we wish to introduce to impressionable new students. Is the mind capable of moving a mountain when it is already convinced it cannot? One must remain aware that individuals acquire knowledge at independent rates of speed. Certainly, no one would suggest that one infant "failed" the

art of learning to walk because she acquired the skill two months after her infant counterpart. Would anyone suggest that infant number one failed walking? Of course not. What would a mentor project to either toddler were he to suggest that a slower acquisition of walking skills implied failure? Yet, we as educators feel the need to suggest that student A failed due to the slower procurement of abstract concepts than student B. It is absolutely essential to shift the learning focus from failure to success.

Which of the following statements best conveys the meaning of the passage?

    (A)   Learning is something that happens at different speeds and is, therefore, natural.

    (B)   Instructors need to be sensitive to students' individual needs.

    (C)   Instructors need to shift the educational focus from failure to success in learning environments.

    (D)   Failure is a potential hazard in the classroom and should be avoided at all costs.

The answer is (C). The passage suggests that education today is based primarily on failure and negative reinforcement and that, in order to create a more productive and positive learning environment, the emphasis must shift to success.

Strategy: Underline key information as you read the question. For instance, as you read the previous question, you might underline or highlight the sentence: "Therefore, the language of failure should not be present in the learning environment (i.e., the classroom) because it will have a prohibitive impact on the students' desire to learn as well as a negative influence on the students' self-esteem." This sentence gives you a hint of the thesis, and therefore the meaning of the passage. The highlighting will thus save you time; saving time is helpful when you must answer 90 questions in two hours.

Complete-the-Statement Multiple-Choice Questions

The complete-the-statement multiple-choice question consists of an incomplete statement for which you must select the answer choice that will complete the statement correctly. Here is an example:

The repetition of an initial consonant sound is an example of the literary device known as

    (A)   metaphor.

    (B)   personification.

(C)   alliteration.

(D)   denouement.

The correct answer is (C). With this type of question your strategy should be to eliminate answer choices you are certain to be wrong, thus reducing your choices.

Multiple-Choice Questions with Qualifiers

Some of the multiple-choice questions may contain qualifiers—words like *not*, *least*, and *except*. These added words make the test questions more difficult because rather than having to choose the best answer, as is usually the case, you must actually select the opposite. **Strategy:** Circle the qualifier. It is easy to forget to select the negative; circling the qualifier in the question stem is a flag. This will serve as a reminder as you are reading the question and especially if you must reread or check the answer at a later time. Now consider this question with a qualifier:

Which of the following is NOT characteristic of Italian Renaissance humanism?

(A)   Its foundation is in the study of the classics.

(B)   Intellectual life was its focus.

(C)   It was noticeable in the artistic accomplishments of the period.

(D)   It was based on learning and understanding about what it means to be human.

You are looking for the exception in this question, so you want to compare each answer choice to the question to find which answer is not representative of Italian Renaissance humanism. Humanism is *not* learning and understanding, nor is it the study of being human, so (D) is the correct answer. Humanism was an intellectual movement based on the study of the classics. And, artistic accomplishments of the period did reflect the characteristics of the Renaissance.

New question formats will, at times, appear on the Praxis II ParaPro Assessment. If such a new format question appears on the test you are taking—don't panic! You have the tools you need to succeed. Simply follow these steps:

1. Read the directions thoroughly.

2. Read the question carefully, as you would any other question.

3. Decide what you should be trying to determine.

4. Look for the details that will help you answer correctly.

You will receive answer sheets, similar to the ones in this volume, on which you will fill in you response: (A), (B), (C), or (D). As the previous example questions have shown, there are four options for each of the multiple-choice questions; questions with more than one correct answer may use Roman numerals. Individual test items require a variety of different thinking levels, ranging from simple recall to evaluation and problem solving.

> **PRAXIS Pointer**
>
> Don't make questions more difficult than they are—there are no "trick" questions or hidden meanings.

You should spend approximately one-and-a-half minutes on each multiple-choice question on each of the practice tests—and on the real exams, of course.

The reviews in this book will help you sharpen the basic skills needed to approach the exams and offer you strategies for attacking the questions. By using the reviews in conjunction with the practice tests, you will better prepare yourself for the actual tests. You have learned through your coursework and your practical experience in schools most of what you need to know to answer the questions on the test. In your classes, you gained the expertise to make important decisions about situations you will face in the classroom. The reviews in this book will help you fit the information you have acquired in practice into its specific testable category. Reviewing your class notes and textbooks along with systematic use of this book will give you an excellent springboard for passing the Praxis II ParaPro Assessment.

SCORING

The numbers of raw points awarded on the Praxis II ParaPro Assessment is based on the number of correct answers given. Most Praxis examinations vary by edition, which means that each test has several variations that contain different questions. The different questions are intended to measure the same general types of knowledge or skills. However, there is no way to guarantee that the questions on all editions of the test will have the same degree of difficulty. To avoid penalizing test takers who answer questions that are more difficult, the initial scores are adjusted for difficulty by using a statistical process known as equating. To avoid confusion between the adjusted and unadjusted scores, ETS reports the adjusted scores on a score scale that makes them clearly different from the unadjusted scores. Unadjusted scores or "raw scores" are simply the number of questions answered correctly. Adjusted scores, which are equated to the scale ETS uses for reporting the scores are called "scaled scores." For each edition of a Praxis test, a "raw-to-scale conversion table" is used to translate raw to scaled scores.

Unfortunately there is no way to predict how many questions answered correctly on our practice tests will correspond to the scores of the actual exam. As discussed above, each test is a different edition and, therefore the questions on one edition may be slightly easier than the questions on another. Hence the conversion tables are adjusted for the level of difficulty on different tests in order to make the versions of the tests more equitable, and there is no way to predict which version of the test you will be given.

The easier the questions are on a test edition, the more questions must be answered correctly to earn a given scaled score. The college or university in which you are enrolled may set passing scores for the completion of your teacher education program and for graduation. Be sure to check the requirements in the catalogues or bulletins. You will also want to talk with your advisor. The passing scores for the Praxis II tests vary from state to state or district. To find out which of the Praxis II tests your state requires and what your state's set passing score is, contact your state's education department directly.

Score Reporting

When Will I Receive My Examinee Score Report and in What Form Will It Be?

ETS mails test-score reports six weeks after the test date. There is an exception for computer-based tests and for the Praxis I PPST examinations. Score reports will list your current score and the highest score you have earned on each test you have taken over the last 10 years. Along with your score report, ETS will provide you with a booklet that offers details on your scores. For each test date, you may request that ETS send a copy of your scores to as many as three score recipients, provided that each institution or agency is eligible to receive the scores.

STUDYING FOR THE TEST

It is critical to your success that you study effectively. Throughout this guide, you will find Praxis Pointers that will give you tips for successful test taking. The following are a few tips to help get you going:

- Choose a time and place for studying that works best for you. Some people set aside a certain number of hours every morning to study; others may choose to study at night before retiring. Only you know what is most effective for you.

- Use your time wisely and be consistent. Work out a study routine and stick to it; don't let your personal schedule interfere. Remember, seven weeks of studying is a modest investment to put you on your chosen path.

- Don't cram the night before the test. You may have heard many amazing tales about effective cramming, but don't kid yourself: most of them are false, and the rest are about exceptional people who, by definition, aren't like most of us.

PRAXIS Pointer

Take the practice test under the same conditions you will take the actual test.

- When you take the practice tests, try to make your testing conditions as much like the actual test as possible. Turn off your television, radio, and telephone. Sit down at a quiet table free from distraction.

- As you complete the practice test, score your test and thoroughly review the explanations to the questions you answered incorrectly.

- Take notes on material you will want to go over again or research further.

- Keep track of your scores. By doing so, you will be able to gauge your progress and discover your strengths and weaknesses. You should carefully study the material relevant to your areas of difficulty. This will build your test-taking skills and your confidence!

STUDY SCHEDULE

The following study course schedule allows for thorough preparation to pass the Praxis II ParaPro Assessment (0755 and 1755). This is a suggested seven-week course of study.

However, you can condense this schedule if you are in a time crunch or expand it if you have more time. You may decide to use your weekends for study and preparation and go about your other business during the week. You may even want to record information and listen to it on your MP3 player or CD as you travel in your car. However you decide to study, be sure to adhere to the structured schedule you devise.

WEEK	ACTIVITY
1	After reading the first chapter of this book to understand the format and content of the exam you'll be taking, take the first practice test. Our score chart will indicate your strengths and weaknesses. Make sure you simulate real exam conditions when you take the test. Afterward, score it and review the explanations for questions you answered incorrectly.
2	Review the explanations for the questions you missed, and review the appropriate chapter sections. Useful study techniques include highlighting key terms and information, taking notes as you review each section, and putting new terms and information on note cards to help retain the information.
3 and 4	Reread all your note cards, refresh your understanding of the exam's subareas and related skills, review your textbooks, and read over notes you took in your college classes. This is also the time to consider any other supplementary materials suggested by a counselor or your state education agency.
5	Begin to condense your notes and findings. A structured list of important facts and concepts, based on your note cards, college textbook, course notes, and this book's review chapters, will help you thoroughly review for the test. Review the answers and explanations for any questions you missed on the practice test.
6	Have someone quiz you using the note cards you created. Take the second practice test for your exam, adhering to the time limits and simulated test-day conditions.
7	Review your areas of weakness using all your study materials. This is a good time to retake the practice tests, if time allows.

THE DAY OF THE TEST

Before the Test

- Dress comfortably in layers. You do not want to be distracted by being too hot or too cold while you are taking the test.

- Check your registration ticket to verify your arrival time.

- Plan to arrive at the test center early. This will allow you to collect your thoughts and relax before the test; your early arrival will also spare you the anguish that comes with being late.

- If you are taking the pen and paper test, make sure to bring your admission ticket with you and two forms of identification, one of which must contain a recent photograph, your name, and your signature (e.g., a driver's license). If you are taking the Internet-based test you will not have an admission ticket since there is no pre-registration required. But, you will need to bring the requisite forms of identification discussed above, You will not gain entry to the test center without proper identification.

- Bring several sharpened No. 2 pencils with erasers. You will not want to waste time searching for a replacement pencil or pen if you break a pencil point or run out of ink while taking your test. The proctor will not provide pencils or pens at the test center.

- Wear a watch to the test center so you can apportion your testing time wisely. You may not, however, wear one that makes noise or that will otherwise disturb the other test takers.

- Leave all dictionaries, textbooks, notebooks, calculators, briefcases, and packages at home. You may not take these items into the test center. Please note that examinees **may not** use calculators.

- Do not eat or drink too much before the test. The proctor will not allow you to make up time you miss if you have to take a bathroom break. You will not be allowed to take materials with you, and you must secure permission before leaving the room.

During the Test

- Pace yourself. The Praxis II ParaPro Assessment is administered in one two-and-a-half hour sitting with no breaks. Follow all of the rules and instructions that the test proctor gives you. Proctors will enforce these procedures to maintain test security. If you do not abide by the regulations, the proctor may dismiss you from the test and notify ETS to cancel your score.

- Listen closely as the test instructor provides the directions for completing the test. Follow the directions carefully. Be sure to *mark only one answer* per multiple-choice question, erase all unwanted answers and marks completely, and fill in the answers darkly and neatly. There is no penalty for guessing at an answer, so *do not leave any answer ovals blank*. Remember: a blank oval is just scored as wrong, but a guessed answer has a chance of being right!

- Do your best! Afterward, make notes about the multiple-choice questions you remember. You may not share this information with others, but you may find that the information proves useful on other exams that you take. Relax! Wait for that passing score to arrive.

Reading: Skills and Knowledge

"Reading is to the mind what exercise is to the body."

- Joseph Addison

READING AS A CONTACT SPORT

Imagine that you are on a soccer team ranked second in the state. Tomorrow, you're scheduled to play last year's number one team for the state title. How did you get to this incredible moment? You're vying for the title because you listened to and watched your coaches, and practiced your moves. You evaluated your performance, corrected your mistakes, planned your strategies, and noted your successes. You took your work seriously. This is also what it takes to learn to play an instrument, create art, become a dancer, or drive a car. That's what it takes to be an independent, skilled reader.

Reading is a skill that requires interaction with oneself and others in order to become proficient and maintain a high level of ability. It is not a spectator sport. Reciting (decoding) a stream of words on a page is not reading. Reading requires thinking and puzzling over text. It's often a mystery that needs solving. We make mistakes, we start over, we talk about the words and ideas with others, and we practice, practice, and practice. But, as you no doubt know, it is worth the effort and essential for one to succeed and flourish in the world.

Why Read?

Consider why you read. As a child maybe you were hooked on a particular genre, such as mysteries or biographies, which you continue to enjoy. Maybe you loved to build things, and reading directions was an essential piece in creating your masterpieces. Or your love of dogs led you to check out every book at the library you could find on the subject. Curiosity about unfamiliar people, places, and ideas leads many of us to read.

We read to create meaning from text, be it a newspaper, comic book, textbook, or novel. We read to connect with the world and the myriad characters that inhabit the planet. We read for the pure pleasure reading offers. Reading is an active process that continues throughout our lives as we attempt to make meaning of the print before us. It is a tool that develops our imagination, helps us transform ourselves, and has the power to make change in the world (Santman 2005, 4).

Beliefs About Reading

In school, reading is a requirement. Unfortunately, many students find reading unpleasant. This occurs for a variety of reasons. It may be that reading wasn't a priority or introduced as a pleasurable activity in the home. Children without stable families or homes frequently lose precious time in school and opportunities to read. Some students have undiagnosed learning disabilities and believe they aren't capable of reading. Others haven't received comprehensive reading instruction. And there are an increasing number of English Language Learners (ELLs) who struggle with English. Whatever the reason, too many students find reading a torturous process.

For children to become readers, they must take an active part in the process. For that to occur, reading should have significance for children. They always need to understand the purpose for reading (First Steps 1994). Rather than teaching a text, an educator teaches the skills and strategies to students in the context of the reading. This allows students to extrapolate meaning from the text on their own. Teaching reading does not end in the elementary grades. In middle and high school, students need instruction to understand increasingly complex texts.

We read to make meaning of *text*. Text means all forms of print, including magazines, newspapers, short stories, charts, and more.

As an active process, reading involves:

- an integration of the cueing systems of language.
- readers who bring a range of experiences, background knowledge, and feelings to the text.
- strategies the reader uses for the construction of meaning.

Reading is thinking. Readers use **metacognition** to make meaning of text. Metacognition is an awareness of how one learns, and it leads to students attending to their own learning. It is not **decoding**, the process whereby one sounds out and/or recites words on a page.

In this chapter, you will learn about the skills it takes to master reading for the purpose of supporting your students in this challenging but satisfying endeavor.

The Goal

Various labels, such as *far below basic*, *basic*, and *proficient*, with all their respective attendant characteristics, are used in standardized testing to describe student academic abilities. An expert reader exhibits the following qualities:

- self-motivation
- sees books as a major source of information
- shows confidence and efficiency in using appropriate reading strategies
- understands how to use different strategies for different purposes
- uses reading to explore worlds beyond personal experience
- responds perceptively to literature
- discusses likes and dislikes about authors and justifies opinions
- reflects on and responds to texts critically and provides different interpretations and points of view
- recognizes and describes the purpose and structure of different genres
- finds the main idea and key information in a text
- applies research skills using various texts

These qualities will not be attained in one school year. However, the paraprofessional must be aware of the ultimate goal, and support students in all the incremental stages involved.

To that end, paraprofessionals, like teachers in every content area, must be reading teachers. Every content area has particular text demands. In science, students read tables, diagrams, and formulas. In social studies, students read census data, **primary sources** (texts written by people in a particular time period), diaries, biographical information, and government documents. Textbooks contain tables of contents and indexes. A wide range of textual demands means students must apply different kinds of thinking and strategies in order to comprehend the pages before them.

As an expert reader, you model your own process for making meaning out of text when assisting in the classroom.

NCLB, State Standards, National Standards, and More

The *No Child Left Behind Act* (NCLB), a federal law enacted in 2002, affects K-12 students in public schools. It is based on the theory of *state standards-based* education. Reading received an increased instructional focus through NCLB. Currently, each state is required to set its own measurable academic goals at each grade level in every content area. If a state chooses not to adopt this plan, federal funds are denied. NCLB, while controversial, has highlighted the academic disparity between white children, African-American children, and Latino children. Its aim is to rectify the achievement gap, making states and school districts accountable for every child in public schools. Schools must set achievement goals and meet those goals within a specific time period. State standards vary throughout the nation.

Each state must develop definitions of the knowledge, concepts and skills students should acquire in each content area at every grade level. Assessments test that knowledge and students receive feedback as to where they are on the continuum. Schools are on timetables regarding student improvement. Results from testing have a significant impact on curriculum, budgets, and staffing. Discussion continues regarding the federal government's role in establishing *national standards* while allowing states to work out how they will achieve their goals.

THE ROLE OF THE PARAPROFESSIONAL

Every Teacher Is A Reading Teacher

No matter the classroom content area, paraprofessionals are reading teachers. One of your most important tasks is assessing and monitoring the reading abilities of your students and supporting them as they learn the skills and strategies they need to master various texts.

For you to be a reading teacher, you must reflect on your own process for grappling with text. Some texts will be easy for you, while others will require more effort. When considering your process, you are thinking about how you figured out a new word, what idea an author is trying to convey in a particular chapter, how to keep track of a plot when the author goes back and forth in time, struggling with a sentence that takes up half a page, or making sense of a topic that is new to you.

In the foreword of *Shades of Meaning: Comprehension and Interpretation in Middle School*, Randy Bomer states that author Donna Santman (2005, xi-xii) uses "habits of mind" to watch herself as a reader. She uses what she learns from self-observation when she works with students. Part of her curriculum is teaching students to create their own "habits of mind."

Modeling for Students

Students appreciate the fact that adults struggle at times with reading. One of the most effective ways of teaching reading is to model how you solve any number of challenges when you read. It may be pronouncing or learning the definition of an unfamiliar word, or tracking how an author moves a plot forward and backward in time. Since reading is thinking, sharing your strategies for problem-solving while reading not only helps students figure out their own strategies, but also underlines the message that their brains must be switched on and thinking.

Impact of the Paraprofessional

As a paraprofessional, you've signed on to help your students achieve all the success an education should ideally provide. When students are unable to read at grade level, their chances of dropping out accelerate. Current estimates show that over one million students drop out of high school in the United States each year (Powell 2009). The burdens on students and their families in particular, and on society in general, are devastating. Your role as another observer, assessor, model, and expert reader in the classroom is crucial for student success.

FOUNDATIONS OF READING/WORD STUDY

Before becoming a fluent and expert reader, knowing how words work is essential. While we often assume that students receive this knowledge in early elementary school, that assumption is incorrect. All students, no matter their primary language, must be assessed regarding their knowledge of how letters and words work to create meaning.

Cueing Systems

Cueing systems are clues readers take from their knowledge of how print works. Over time, these cues become more cohesive and reading becomes more fluent. **Fluency** is a reader's ability to read smoothly, accurately, and with appropriate expression (Frey and Fisher 2006). In reading, students must have:

- *Letter knowledge* – The ability to recognize the names and shapes of the letters of the alphabet.
- *Phonemic awareness* – An awareness that sounds make up words. For instance, dividing the sounds in *cat* and changing it into c/a/t. *Phonemes* are the smallest units of sounds in a language.
- *Graphophonic cues* – An awareness of the relationship between symbols or letters and sounds. A grapheme is a single unit in a written language. The word *ship* has four graphemes, but only three *phonemes*: sh/i/p.
- *Syntactic cues* – An awareness of the grammatical rules of the language. The recognition and understanding that words come in a particular order.
- *Semantic cues* – An awareness of the meaning of words. For example, a reader using semantic cues would understand the difference uses of the word *run* in the following sentences: Can you *run* the story? Can you *run* the election? Can you *run* in the race?
- *Pragmatic cues* – The awareness that many words can refer to one thing. For example, the words *Mother, Mama, Ma, Mommy* all refer to the same person. This is particularly challenging for English Language Learners.

Stages of Reading

Children go through several stages on their way to mastering reading. As a paraprofessional, knowing the stages of reading is important for identifying what students already know, and what they need to know to improve their reading abilities. Of course, the stages overlap, and no child will exhibit every indicator in an individual phase. Notice that age or grade level is not a factor when considering the continuum. For various reasons, there are students in the early reading stages in upper grades. These challenging circumstances call for an awareness of the stages and instructional methods that will advance their reading ability. Diana Rees, author of *First Steps Reading Developmental Continuum*, provides a framework for educators to identify where students' reading abilities lie for instructional purposes.

The following are the **primary** characteristics in the continuum. There are numerous studies and books that identify stages of reading. Most approximate the characteristics featured here.

Phase 1: Role Play Reading Characteristics

Making Meaning at Text Level

A child begins reading-like behavior. Look for: holding the book the right way up, turning pages appropriately, looking at words and pictures, and using pictures to construct ideas. The child realizes that print carries a message but when "reading" aloud, the words are different each time. The child can focus on the meaning of a TV program or story. Responses reflect an understanding of what he's seen and heard. The child makes connections to his own experience and what he hears in a story or sees in an illustration. For example, "I have a dog that looks like that."

Making Meaning Using Context

When watching television or listening to a story, a child uses visual and pictorial cues to talk about what they've seen and heard, and relate it to their own knowledge and experience.

Making Meaning at Word Level

At this stage, a child recognizes his or her own name, or a part of it, in print.

Attitude

There is a curiosity about print that plays out with "writing," drawing, and asking, "What does that say?" Additionally, a child wants to look at books, offers to "read," expresses pleasure by joining in orally and responding when listening to familiar stories, and eager anticipation around routine book reading.

Phase 2: Experimental Reading Characteristics

Making Meaning at Text Level

At this stage, a child realizes that print contains a constant message. The words on the page remain the same (hence, the ability of children to parrot a story they've heard repeatedly) but the words of an oral story may change. Children are focused on expressing the meaning of a story instead of getting every word correct.

Making Meaning Using Context

Children use *prior knowledge* of context and personal experience to make meaning. They use memory of a text to match spoken words with written words.

Making Meaning at Word Level

Personally significant words are recognized in context, such as a picture book, a stop sign, or the comics page in a newspaper.

Attitude

The child begins to identify as a reader, and talk about her own reading. The child may ask to be read to, join in, and act out familiar stories. Not only do children select books to be read for pleasure, but they select texts based on interest or familiarity.

Phase 3: Early Reading Characteristics

Making Meaning at Text Level

Beginning confidence is displayed when reading familiar texts. The early reader can retell major content from text, TV, and movies. Children identify and talk about different text forms such as letters, lists, stories, recipes, and TV programs. There's an understanding that no matter the text, authors are expressing their own ideas.

Making Meaning Using Context

When a text is unfamiliar, children may read word-by-word or line-by-line. Fluency is stilted as they focus on decoding rather than reading. Also, they use pictures and knowledge of context to check their understanding of reading.

Making Meaning at Word Level

The reader has a bank of familiar words they recognize in various contexts, such as books, newspapers, and environmental print. Graphophonic strategies (the correspondence of sound and a letter in the alphabet) are being used.

Attitudes

The reader is willing to risk trying unknown words, enjoys listening to stories, reading for a variety of purposes, responding sensitively to stories, and generally talking about books and authors. A critical attitude that must continue and develop across the continuum is selecting one's own reading based on interest, purpose, and difficulty. With the support of an advanced reader, children can reconstruct information gained from their reading.

Phase 4: Transitional Reading Characteristics

Making Meaning at Text Level

The transitional reader shows an ability to make meaning by integrating knowledge of:

- different text structures (letters, poems, reports, etc.)

- text organization (paragraphs, chapters, table of contents, etc.)
- language features (descriptive language connectives: like if, when, because of, therefore)
- subject-specific language (science reports, essays, personal narratives)

Strategies for Making Meaning Using Context

By this stage, a developing reader is trying out and using basic strategies. Briefly, they are:

- making predictions and substantiating them
- self-correcting when reading
- re-reading to clarify meaning
- reading on when encountering a difficult text
- slowing down when encountering a difficult text
- substituting familiar words
- using knowledge of print conventions, such as commas, periods, and speech marks
- replacing one word for another, such as "cool" for "cold"
- increasing knowledge of semantic, syntactic, and graphophonic cueing systems
- the ability to talk about some strategies for making meaning

Making Meaning at Word Level

By this stage, a student's word bank is increasing and includes words that are subject/content specific. For example, words like *experiment*, *government*, and *calculate* are known and used.

The student uses several word identification strategies for making meaning. A reader might use initial letters and sounding out to decode. Or, the student may use the known parts of words, or word segmentation and syllabification, to make sense of a whole word.

Attitude

By the transitional stage, students are self-motivated to read for pleasure. They read for a variety of purposes. They can discuss favorite books and show preferences for genres and authors. Making comparisons with other texts and demonstrating confidence when reading difficult texts are hallmarks of the transitional reader.

Phase 5: Independent Reading (IR) Characteristics

Making Meaning at Text Level

When readers are in the independent reading stage, they've secured a number of strategies, have some knowledge about how words work, can infer deeper meanings in texts, and have the ability to grapple with increasingly difficult text. Key characteristics of an independent reader are:

- the ability to recognize and discuss elements and purposes of different text structures, such as reports, biographies, directions, and narratives
- the ability to read and comprehend abstract text and text that is removed from his or her own experiences
- the ability to make inferences based on implicit information in a text, and to justify those conclusions
- critical comparisons between texts are part of their repertoire
- an understanding that other readers may have a different point of view

Making Meaning Using Context

By this stage, readers are automatically activating their strategies to make meaning from text. Accordingly, they self-correct, re-read, read on, slow down, and sub-vocalize.

Making Meaning at Word Level

Again, strategies are automatic for understanding unknown words. These readers understand graphophonics, word patterns, word derivations, morphographs, syllabification, and affixes.

Attitudes

Independent readers are absorbed in their reading. Often, they lose track of time while reading. They see books as a major source of information, and have strong reading and author preferences. While this may seem like an optimal situation, it can prevent them from independently trying out other genres. IRs also enjoy comparing books and recommending favorites to others.

Phase 6: Advanced Reading Characteristics

Making Meaning at Text Level

Students have hit the mother lode when they become advanced readers. That is not to say their reading abilities have peaked. Reading is often difficult for even skilled readers depending on the text. However, being an advanced reader means one has the knowledge and confidence to face continuous challenges. Since the advanced reader is able to flex a considerable number of reading muscles, the list of characteristics is longer. This is a reader who:

- compares and contrasts different points of view
- critically reflects on and responds to text with different levels of interpretation
- can stand back and reflect on his own reactions to the authors' positions
- recognizes and describes the purpose and structure of different genres
- identifies and integrates layers of facts and concepts
- identifies and discusses different authors' styles
- can recognize texts as "cultural constructs" and analyze the cultural beliefs in the text
- can question texts, articulating problems and formulating relevant questions
- can form and apply research strategies
- can recognize and analyze bias, propaganda and stereotyping in text

Attitudes

For the advanced reader, reading means entering worlds beyond personal experiences. Such readers handle new texts with confidence, respond sensitively and perceptively to literature, and have an emotional investment paired with a reflective detachment when reading.

LITERARY ELEMENTS

Literature has its own lexicon, or vocabulary. These are common terms students must know, and teachers and paraprofessionals must teach. While every content area has its own lexicon, some terms will overlap in content areas (Burke 1999, 343-4 and Frey and Fisher 2006, 467-8). Following is a glossary of these terms:

Action: What happens in a story

Allegory: A story that is used to teach something, usually a moral lesson. Usually the stories are long and require analysis.

Alliteration: When an author uses the same letter or sound to start each word in a sentence or string of words. Alliteration is used frequently with emergent readers.

> *"My style is public negotiations for parity rather than private negotiations for position." Jesse Jackson.*

Allusion: A reference to a well-known person, myth, historical event, etc.

> *The sing-along was a Woodstock for the pre-school set.*

Analogy: An expression that links an unfamiliar idea to a familiar idea to help the reader gain a greater understanding.

> *Organizing 5-year-olds to play soccer is like trying to herd puppies.*

Antagonist: The villain, anti-hero, or most prominent character who acts in opposition to the hero.

Conflict: Conflict is the main source of tension or the major problem in a story. Conflict is often divided into 4 categories:

- the individual versus himself
- the individual versus society
- the individual versus nature
- the individual versus fate/gods

Connotation: Definitions or meanings beyond the meaning stated in the dictionary.

Context: This is helpful as a reading strategy. Use words, phrases, or sentences before and after a passage or word to help make an unknown word or phrase understandable and give it meaning.

Convention: Any established practice authors use in literature. It may be a matter of technique, style, structure, or subject matter.

Denouement: The resolution of the conflict in the story.

Dialect: When necessary, writers give their characters a dialect when they speak. Their speaking denotes regional, cultural, or social class differences. This is also called *vernacular*. Sometimes this is a reading challenge for students.

Dialogue: The speaking that goes on between characters.

Empathy: The ability to put oneself "in the shoes" of another. The reader imagines how the character(s) feels. This is what fiction (and some nonfiction) asks readers to do.

Figure of speech: Rhetorical devices employed for special effect by using words in distinctive ways. Phrases like "racking our brains" or "light as a feather" convey an image in the reader's mind.

Figurative language: Unusual comparisons of unlike things in order to make something clearer or to paint an image in the reader's mind. This is especially common in poetry. In the first two stanzas of "The First Book," by poet Rita Dove, she describes the sensation of opening a book for the first time by using figurative language:

Open it.
Go ahead, it won't bite.
Well…maybe a little.
More like a nip. A tingle.
It's pleasurable, really.

Flashbacks: A pause in the action to portray a scene or incident that took place earlier. This is a challenge for struggling readers.

Foreshadowing: This gives the reader a hint of what's to come. In horror or mysteries, it's usually used to signal something bad is about to happen.

Hyperbole: This is an exaggeration or overstatement of the truth.

Irony: This is used in relaying a message, often saying what something is when the opposite or reverse could be true. Authors use irony to say one thing when they mean another.

Metaphor: Metaphors compare two unlike things in which no word of comparison is used. *The kitchen was a war zone.*

Narrator: The voice or character telling a story.

Onomatopoeia: Words where the meaning is defined by its sound. *Whoosh, plop, grrrr,* and *boing* are examples.

Personification: An author gives human qualities, ideas, and actions to animals. Fairy tales and myths often use personification.

Plot: The plot is the action in a story. Usually there are five elements: exposition, rising action, climax, falling action and resolution (denouement).

Point-of-view: A story is told from a specific point of view. In *first person*, the narrator tells the story and we only know what the narrator tells us. *Second person* narrative means the narrator speaks directly to the reader. In a *third person* narrative, the narrator is *omniscient*, or all-knowing, and conveys different perspectives.

Protagonist: The main character of a story; the hero or heroine.

Setting: If plot is what happens in a story, the setting is where it takes place. There may be many settings in a story. Setting includes not just a room or town, but also a period in time.

Stereotype: A character, setting, or situation is a stereotype when it lacks individuality and is based on broad or exaggerated qualities.

Simile: Compares two unlike things using *as* or *like*.

> *The dog's fur felt like a Brillo pad.*
> *The baby's skin was as smooth as silk.*

Structure: The form or organization that a text takes. Different *genres* (types of writing) have different structures. For example, a poem has a different structure than a textbook. It often affects meaning or action in the story. An understanding of text structure improves reading comprehension.

Style: All writers have a style they bring to text. It's how they use words, images, phrases, and structure to create a feeling or thoughts.

Symbolism: When an object or action means something more than or other than its literal meaning. Some symbols appear frequently in writing, such as crows to signify death or flowers to symbolize love.

Synopsis: A short summary of a piece of text.

Theme: The big idea or ideas in a text. It is of the macro-level meaning of the text's ideas and truths, which are conveyed through the action and exposition of the story. When a reader can say, "This is a story about the impact of family loss on a young woman," rather than, "This is about a girl whose mom left the family, and then her dad died, and then her brothers and sisters all had to live in foster homes," the reader has an understanding of theme.

Tone and mood: The attitude an author takes toward a subject or character. This may include anger, sarcasm, seriousness, and humor. Dialogue, settings, or descriptions help set a tone or mood.

TEACHING READING

Cueing Systems

Cueing systems can be thought of as clues that emergent and early readers use to determine what the lines on a page represent (Frey and Fisher 2006, 80-2). As readers develop, cues become consolidated and reading becomes more fluent. Assessing English Language Learners in their first language regarding their knowledge of cueing systems is necessary to establish an instructional plan. Readers continually use cueing systems to make meaning of text.

Graphophonic cues are those associated with the relationship between symbols (letters) and their sounds. As learners develop this understanding, they recognize the patterns in clusters of letters (*e.g., cat, ran, can*).

Syntactic cues come from the grammatical rules of the language. This does not mean that the reader can name the rule. It means that they recognize that words occur in a particular order. Syntactic cues are connected to the meaning of the words. When a reader uses syntactic cues, they are reading, "The house is large and green," and not "The horse was large and green."

Pragmatic cues are related to the social use of language in a culture. When a reader uses pragmatic cues, they are aware that *Father*, *Dad*, *Daddy*, and *Pa* are all words for the same thing.

Levels of Comprehension

Reading is thinking.

Word calling is not reading. Sounding out words is not reading.

Readers actively engage with whatever text they read and must understand what they read. When readers comprehend text, they are able to identify the main idea or theme, supporting details and facts, distinguish facts from opinions, recognize points of view, make inferences, and grasp the conclusion.

When readers think, they are using **metacognitive** skills. Metacognition is thinking about one's thinking. It is being aware of what one knows and doesn't know.

There are four basic comprehension levels. To help students become sophisticated readers, teachers should emphasize reading for meaning and develop these levels of comprehension.

Literal Comprehension. This is the lowest level of comprehension, which may be found in students of various ages as well as many ELLs. Students at the literal level read line by line and understand only what's on the page. When they respond with facts and details, they often read what is on the page. Some literal readers are unable to paraphrase in their own words.

Interpretive or Inferential Comprehension. This is the second level of understanding. Inferential comprehension means "reading between the lines." Students are able to find the subtleties in the author's work. The text may not give explicit information, or the author may use figurative language students have to figure out. Students have to infer meaning using clues from the writer.

The reader may have to make generalizations, guess, predict, speculate, or anticipate, in order to understand the author's purpose, main idea, or the point of view of the author. Once a student is able to infer, he has taken a big step in reading development.

Critical Comprehension. This is a higher level of understanding. It requires reading and thinking beyond the printed page. These readers are past believing that, "If it's in print, it must be accurate." Readers ask: Is this a fact or an opinion? Is this author biased? Are these sources valid? Are stereotypes being employed? How much of what the writer says are assumptions? Since the internet has become a huge source of information, it is essential that readers develop critical thinking skills and learn to evaluate the credibility of sources.

Creative Comprehension. Readers become involved, often emotionally, with the text. They may identify with the story or a character. They apply their own values and can see other perspectives. Readers have the ability to make individual interpretations of what they are reading.

Reading Strategies

"A strategy is an intentional plan that is flexible and can be adapted to meet the demands of the situation."

-Cris Tovani

All content area teachers are reading teachers and model strategies for navigating text. This includes everything from showing students how to grapple with an unfamiliar word to making sense of a convoluted sentence to establishing the author's purpose for writing. Strategies frequently overlap. Choosing strategies depends on students' understanding of what they're reading, the genre they're reading, the difficulty of the text, and their purpose for reading.

Before Reading

Readers establish a purpose for reading. They use cueing systems, such as thinking about prior knowledge (what they know about the topic, author, setting, text form, context). They begin asking questions about the text. "What is this text about?" "Am I familiar with this genre?" "How is this text organized?" They have a plan for reading.

During Reading

Readers monitor the plan. While reading, they pause and ask themselves if they understand what they're reading. They ask questions of the text. They continue to use cueing systems – employing prior knowledge and asking themselves what makes sense given the context. If they don't understand what they're reading, they ask what they can do to help themselves make meaning of the text.

After Reading

Readers ask themselves questions after reading. "How did I do?" "Did I understand the text?" "Is it necessary to reread any part?"

What's the Point?

There are basic questions a reader asks before, during, and after reading:

- "What is this text about?"
- "What is the author saying about the subject?"
- "What is the 'big idea' or point the author is trying to express?"

Locating the *main idea* depends on several considerations. The length of the text is one. In a paragraph, it could be the opening or last sentence. In longer text, most authors won't state the main idea in the first paragraph. The *main idea* in a text may be found: 1) in the beginning, perhaps in the first sentence; 2) mid-way through a text; 3) at the end; 4) not stated, but implied throughout the work.

When you *preview*, or look over a text, you get a sense of what the story is about. But that is not the main idea, which is different from the subject or topic. The main idea is *why* the author is writing the piece.

When the main idea is *implied*, the reader must use information from the sentences in the text to *infer* the main idea. In the following paragraph from *Volcano: The Eruption and Healing of Mount St. Helens*, author Patricia Lauber (Reader's Handbook 2002, 284) never directly states the main idea.

> *For well over a hundred years the volcano slept. Each spring, as winter snows melted, its slopes seemed to come alive. Wildflowers bloomed in meadows. Bees gathered pollen and nectar. Birds fed, found mates, and built nests. Bears lumbered out of their dens. Herds of elk and deer feasted on fresh green shoots. Thousands of people came to hike, picnic, camp, fish, paint, bird-watch, or just enjoy the scenery. Logging crews felled tall trees and planted seedlings.*

The main idea is inferred from the sentences in the paragraph. The writer wants to contrast the bucolic scene of Mt. St. Helens with what happened when the volcano erupted.

Every day, we make inferences. We do this by looking at and listening to people and making a judgment. Writers *imply* meaning. They don't tell the reader everything. Reading is often a mystery that we figure out by using clues, and so it is with inferring as we read.

For example, you could draw the conclusion (infer) that a person who is frowning, has his arms crossed, and is tapping his foot is either unhappy or angry or both. Students will tell you they can "read" their parents before mom or dad even open their mouth to express what they're feeling. In both cases, no one had to say a word. Based on body language (the evidence) and what they know about such body language, students inferred a feeling or emotion. We can think of making inferences as a math formula.

$$\begin{aligned} & \text{What I Learned (from the text)} \\ + \; & \underline{\text{What I Already Know (from my experience)}} \\ = \; & \text{Inference} \end{aligned}$$

Inferences are not just in descriptions or the dialogue in a text. Book covers, illustrations, diagrams, and photographs all provide clues for inferences.

A writer's main idea has *supporting ideas* or *details*. This is true whether the writing is one paragraph, an essay, or an entire book. Using a graphic organizer helps students locate and "see" supporting ideas in a different way. There are several ways to organize a main idea and supporting details.

- Draw a circle in the middle of a page with the main idea written inside. Lines are then drawn from the center which resemble the spokes of a wheel. Write the details that support the main idea on the lines.
- You can also help students organize their thoughts in configurations like the one below:

Table 2.1 Organization Rubric

Subject: First People in America			
Detail #1	Detail #2	Detail #3	Detail #4
MAIN IDEA:			

As you read, think about the specific evidence that supports the main idea. These are the supporting details, and they describe or explain the main idea. In the following example, the first sentence contains the main idea and subsequent sentences provide supporting details.

Birthday cakes come in many flavors and designs.
Chocolate, vanilla, carrot, and coconut are popular
birthday cake flavors. Sometimes, people order
birthday cakes shaped like footballs, bears, teapots,
or cartoon characters to celebrate someone's birthday.

Organization of Text

To help students find main ideas, supporting ideas, and other specific information, knowing the organization of a text is important. This could be as basic as looking at a *table of contents* in a textbook to see the organizational pattern of information. It also means looking at how a paragraph or a story is structured. How are the different parts of a piece of writing related to each other? Breaking down the text into manageable parts helps determine organization. Organization depends on the author's purpose. Writers may:

- compare and contrast points of view, characters, or settings (how are things the same/different?)
- explain why things occur (cause and effect)
- put forth a theory or hypothesis (an idea based on evidence)
- ask a question and then answer it
- offer an idea and then refute it
- state or imply the main idea and then give supporting details
- place information in chronological order
- state a problem and then give a solution
- state ideas in order of importance
- analyze or criticize something and give evidence

Transitional language clues help readers understand organization. Words and phrases such as *first, second, also, then, finally, for example, however, another, in conclusion, in order to,* or *overall* give clues to the author's intention.

Pay attention to words that are italicized, in boldface, or in large type; headings; numbered lists or outlines; and diagrams and graphics to help figure out how text is organized.

Skimming the text, or moving the eyes quickly over the writing before reading, is another means of determining how an author has organized the text.

In the workshop "Monitoring Comprehension: Teaching Adolescent Readers to Think When They Read," Cris Tovani (2002) offered a comprehensive list of reading strategies.

- **Activate background knowledge** by asking what is already known about the genre, the author, the text form, the topic, and so forth.
- **Make connections** between new and known information. Perhaps students have had a personal experience relating to the text, heard or seen something related to the writing, or read something that connects to the text.
- **Self-question** the text in order to clarify ambiguity and deepen understanding.
- **Draw inferences** from the text using background knowledge and clues from the text. Simply, this is reading between the lines for a deeper interpretation of the text. It's taking what the reader already knows and adding clues the author gives to get at a deeper meaning in the writing.
- **Determine importance** in text in order to separate details from main ideas.
- **Monitor comprehension** in order to make sure meaning is being constructed.
- **Employ fix-up strategies** to repair confusion. Show students right away how to fix what doesn't make sense. For example, slow down, re-read a line, or use a dictionary or thesaurus.
- **Use sensory images** to enhance comprehension and visualize the reading. Telling students to make a movie in their mind of characters, setting, or plot.
- **Synthesize and extend thinking**. This is where we question the author's purpose and meaning. "What's the point?" "What's the big picture?"

Teachers must make sure the texts are not too difficult for students as they begin employing these strategies; have students use text that is somewhat challenging but not incomprehensible. Employing reading strategies takes practice. Paraprofessionals routinely show students how to employ reading strategies until they become second nature to developing readers.

Context Clues

Meaning breaks down for readers when they come across unfamiliar vocabulary words. They can use a dictionary or thesaurus, but when one is not available, students can use *context clues* to unravel the mystery of a word, phrase, or figurative language. Context clues are the words, sentences, or paragraphs around the unknown word(s) that give the reader clues as to its meaning.

Sometimes a familiar word is just before or after the unknown word. At other times, clues may be in another part of the sentence, in another sentence altogether, or in another passage.

A writer may give a synonym or definition of the unknown word, such as, "Most castles have high walls and are surrounded by a water-filled ditch called a moat."

At other times, an author may repeat a difficult word in both familiar and new situations. An example from *Coming to America: The Story of Immigration* by Betsy Maestro illustrates the point (Reader's Handbook 2002, 619)

"America is a nation of *immigrants*. Immigrants are people who come to a new land to make their home. All Americans are related to immigrants or are immigrants themselves."

Also pay attention to context because the definition may change depending on its usage. The meanings of the words *slide*, *wrinkle*, and *bench* differ depending on how they are used. If *slide* is used as a noun, it's an object children play on. If it's used as a verb, it could be something baseball players do when they steal bases.

Remember that figures of speech, expressions common in the English language in which words are not used literally, also affect the definition of a word. "I was so happy that I was over the moon" means one is happy, not that one is literally bouncing into space.

Graphic Organizers

Graphic organizers are used to help students organize, remember, make sense of, and advance their thinking as noted in the examples for identifying main idea and supporting details. They are also used to assess students. There are various graphic organizers. Choosing the graphic organizer that best serves the purpose set by the student and teacher is paramount, as is modeling its use for students. They can be used in all content areas, and are a helpful tool for ELLs, and students who don't speak up in class. Ideally, they are a springboard to writing. Below, in Figure 2.1, you will find an example of an organizer that would help students better comprehend the reading.

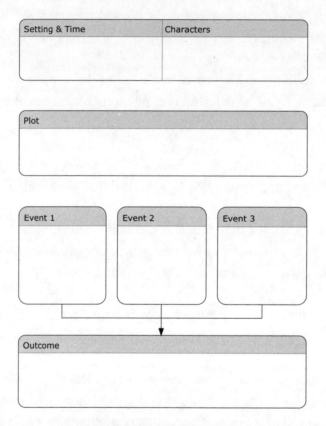

Figure 2.1 Reading Organizer

LITERATURE RESPONSE

Double-Entry Diaries

Have students divide a sheet of paper in half vertically. This can also be done in their writing notebooks. The left side will contain specific information from a text, with page numbers cited. These items may be quotes, facts, or short passages. The right column is for student responses to what's written on the left side of the page. At the top, writing prompts like "I wonder…", "I visualize…", or "This reminds me of…" may help to jumpstart thinking.

As an example, a passage is lifted from a novel the teacher is reading aloud to the class. The teacher then records her thinking for the class. She thinks aloud and models how her background knowledge helps her understand the setting for the novel. At the same time, the teacher emphasizes how important it is to connect personal knowledge to the text.

Writing to Improve Reading Comprehension

Readers must respond to their reading in writing. Their reading ability will improve when they look at specific portions of a text to improve their interpretive or analytical abilities. As previously mentioned, the Double-Entry Diary is one method for students to develop their thinking. In addition, keeping a reading response notebook wherein students write every day about their reading helps them to refine their thinking.

Students may also annotate texts (Jim Burke 1999). Again, you must model this process for students in order for them to be successful. They can mark up their own text, use photocopies, or affix sticky notes to jot down any of the following:

- questions
- quotes
- ideas
- statements
- patterns
- essential information
- textual connections to other texts

Assessing Reading Progress

The purpose of any assessment is to see where a student's abilities lie and then plan instruction around that student's specific needs. By using *rubrics*, formal, written directions that inform students as to what is required in an assignment, students will know what is expected of them and, we hope, perform well on assessments.

State content standards call out what students are expected to know and do in each content area. While these vary from state to state, the National Assessment of Educational Progress (NAEP) is a set of national standards that also measure what students know and can do, but are not mandatory like state standards. Individual districts or schools may have additional requirements regarding student abilities.

Assessments are created by teachers, academic departments, schools, districts, or states. Assessments can come in many forms. Student observations, writing responses, a graphic organizer, a small group presentation, a project, quiz, formal exam, and so on are all means of assessing students in content areas.

There are also numerous assessments for determining a student's reading, writing and speaking or fluency abilities. English Language Learners take state mandated language proficiency tests to determine their abilities in English. Teachers need assessments that measure language comprehension and decoding. If a student has difficulty with understanding spoken language or transforming written words into language, she will have difficulty reading.

INTERPRETING TEXT

Successfully interpreting a text means comprehending one's reading, sharing ideas about the reading with others, and presenting evidence to support assertions. To analyze, interpret and evaluate literature, be aware of gender, historical, cultural, and socioeconomic contexts. Literary criticism defines, classifies, analyzes, interprets, and evaluates works of literature. An awareness of these differences has an influence on the interpretation of a text. There is no single, correct interpretation of a text. However, one must be able to back up one's opinions with solid evidence.

Although background knowledge about historical periods and the cultural context of a story helps interpret text, students (and even more experienced readers) don't always have that information. This is particularly difficult for English Language Learners. If students don't have this knowledge, frontloading information for students before they tackle a particular text is important. Frontloading means providing information such as vocabulary, setting, or the social mores of a time period. A bit of background information that helps familiarize students with what they'll be reading provides support. For example, let's say the assigned reading is *To Kill A Mockingbird* by Harper Lee. Before reading, ask students to jot down what they know (or don't know) about:

- the rural American south in the 1930s
- the use of dialect in a story (how people from different regions speak)

- relations between white and black Americans during that period
- background knowledge they have from other readings, television programs, or movies they've seen

Take what is known and add information that's lacking about historical and cultural contexts before students begin. Background knowledge is one support that aids in comprehension and the ability to form opinions about a text, because you are providing context for the reading.

Another means of supplying background information to students prior to reading the assigned text is to use short picture books and poems that relate to the larger text. For example, prior to reading Sharon Flake's *The Skin I'm In* (1998), a novel about an African-American middle school girl who is teased about her appearance, reading a picture book like *Nappy Hair* by Carolivia Herron (1997) or the poem, *For Brown Skin Girls* by Sharon Harvey Rosenberg may provide a focus for interpreting some of the issues in the novel.

Reading picture books to students of all ages serves many purposes. Picture books are a quick means of offering background information and they lead to new reading topics and interests for students. Multi-cultural picture books are an excellent way to introduce students to writers, characters, topics, and issues that are unfamiliar. Preparing students to read takes some of the mystery and confusion out of the assignment.

Approaches to Interpreting Text

As Jim Burke says in *The English Teacher's Companion* (p.134), "I want my students to walk out of class each day saying they had to think." Burke believes students need:

- time to think and the encouragement to use different strategies
- to be taught to accept the complexity found everywhere in the world
- to have thinking modeled for them in the classroom in order to arrive at a new understanding or thoughtful solution

For students to interpret text—thinking is key. All students, particularly special needs and English Language Learners, require time and different ways to think. There is a repertoire of different modes depending on the task at hand.

- talking

- writing
- drawing
- questioning
- integrating texts

Talk

Talk, "marked by frequent hesitations, rephrasing, false starts, and changes of direction, is important whenever we want a learner to take an active part in learning, and to bring what he learns into interaction with that view of the world on which his actions are based." (Burke 1999, 136) Students enjoy whole-group discussions, but there are other means for student talk that improves their thinking. Working in pairs, small groups, organized debates, or with a paraprofessional, students refine their thinking through talk. Educators must model and train their students to engage in meaningful talk.

Writing

Often we don't know what we think until we write it down. Writing requires thinking. Writing notebooks or journals (again, modeling various aspects of the writing process) used daily as a personal response to reading helps students develop their thinking. This is also an effective tool for students who are uncomfortable speaking in class or for English Language Learners who may be reluctant to share aloud.

Students can write for various purposes. Examples are:

- back and forth to partners
- in response to others ideas
- in response to a particular line or passage in a text
- in response to a focus question by the teacher
- to compare things like characters, plots, settings, texts

Graphic organizers may help some students with organizing their thinking. Always be clear about your purpose and a student's purpose in using graphic organizers.

Drawing

Many students enjoy drawing. Graphic English, using designs and patterns, is an optional medium that can be presented to students to assist with their thinking. Transitioning into writing or increasing the amount of writing while using fewer images and less detail is the goal. Again this is an effective support for English Language Learners. Also, it is particularly effective when introducing new vocabulary words.

Concept Map

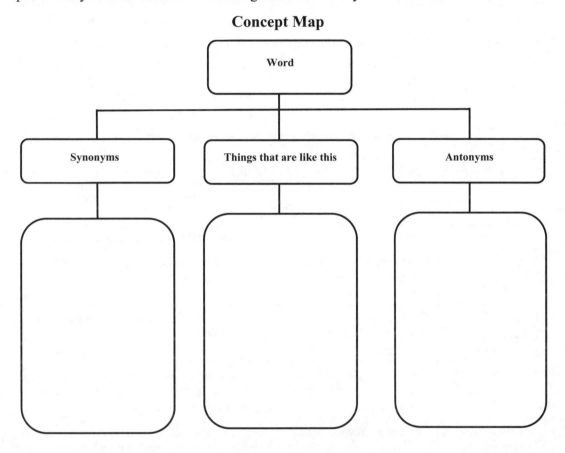

Figure 2.2 Vocabulary Concept of Definition Map

Questioning

Questions invite students to think. Basic questions are important to determine the minimal level of comprehension. But in order to develop deep interpretations of text, we must ask dense questions of students.

Let's return to our previous example, *To Kill A Mockingbird*. Asking, "Why did Jem destroy Mrs. Dubose's camellia bushes?" is a basic comprehension question. In order to dig deeper into the text, students must consider higher-level questions. "Why does Atticus choose to defend Tom Robinson? Do you think you could take Atticus' position? Why? Why not?"

Integrating Texts

Use poems, speeches, and essays containing similar ideas and themes in conjunction with an assigned reading. This not only introduces other literary forms and structures to students, but it also develops deeper thinking about and analysis of a text. These additional readings require students to make connections. Jim Burke calls it "thinking across disciplines," and it is an important way for students to delve deeper into interpreting text (Burke 1999, 152).

Table 2.2 Questions to Make Readers Think

Type of Question	Description	Example
Text	Info found in text	Who is the narrator of the story?
Reader	Reader's experience, values, ideas	Have you ever felt fed up with everything and just wanted to take off, get away on your own?
World, Or Other Literature	Knowledge of history, other cultures, other literature	What other character—in a book or a movie—would you compare the main character to?
Shaded: Text/ Reader	Combine knowledge of text with reader's own experiences, values, ideas	What characteristics do you share with the main character?
Text/World	Combines knowledge of text with knowledge of history and cultures	In what ways are the teenagers in the story similar to teenagers today? In what ways are today's teenagers different?
Text/Other Literature	Combine knowledge of text with knowledge of other pieces of literature	How do relationships in this story compare to relationships in a recent book, essay or story that the student has read?
Reader/World	Combine knowledge of reader's own experiences with knowledge of other cultures, people	In what ways are teenagers in other countries similar to American teens? In what ways are they different?
Reader/Other Literature	Combines knowledge of reader's own experiences with other pieces of literature	In what ways are you similar and/or different from the characters in the writing?
Dense Question Text/Reader/ World Or Text/ Reader/Other Literature	Combines knowledge of all three areas into one DENSE question	Why do the characters feel alienated and how is that related to what many of today's teens feel? Include in your answer a discussion of the extent to which you do or don't share these same feelings and why.

GENRES

Expert readers are able to read and comprehend a broad range of *genres*. A genre is a type or category of writing that can share content, form, or style. Different genres require different reading approaches. Genres are organized differently from one another. It is important to know how different genres are organized, because understanding how text is organized helps identify the author's purpose, and the themes and ideas the writer wishes to convey.

Writing is typically identified as fiction or non-fiction. *Most* genres, whether fiction or non-fiction, are written in *prose* (narrative) style. Prose is typically the everyday way we speak and write but there are exceptions. Let's look at some of the most common genres.

Prose

Realistic Fiction: Realistic fiction is generally presented in the form of a *novel*. It's a *narrative*, which means it tells a story. The narrative in realistic fiction tells a contemporary story that is reality based. It could have or did happen; in fact, many novels are based on true events. Generally, novels are organized in chapters, which are numbered and, often, titled. **Novellas** are frequently realistic fiction. A **novella** is a shorter version of a novel. There are exceptions to the prose form, such as when the story is told in the form of letters or diary entries. Despite the difference in form, the author uses the letters or diary entries to tell a story. There are major and minor characters, a setting or settings, plot line, conflict and denouement. Examples: *The Skin I'm In* by Sharon Flake, *The Jumping Tree* by Rene Saldana, Jr., and *Midwives* by Chris Bohjalian.

Historical Fiction: Historical fiction displays the same characteristics as realistic fiction, however, the setting, characters, and events are from the past. They often take place around real historical events and/or people. There is debate as to how far back in time a story goes before it's considered historical fiction. Generally, we can call a text historical fiction when the narrative takes place at least 30 years in the past. Examples: *To Kill A Mockingbird* by Harper Lee, *Dear Ellen Bee: A Civil War Scrapbook of Two Union Spies* by Mary Lyons and Muriel M. Branch, and *Tom Sawyer* by Mark Twain.

Short Stories: Short stories are fiction. They share the characteristics of narratives in that they have a plot, setting, and characters that tell a complete story, but in relatively few pages. Short stories are generally found in collections by one author or in an *anthol-*

ogy, which means several authors have contributed their stories to the book. They are also published in periodicals (magazines or journals) and online. Examples: *A Burning Decision* by Sarah Thorne, *The Jewelry* by Guy de Maupassant, *Crazy Loco* by David Rice.

Science Fiction: This is fiction that focuses on current or future technology. It may take the form of a novel, novella, or short story. Very often science fiction is about the threat or difficulties of technology. Science fiction contains all the characteristics of a narrative. Examples: *1984* by George Orwell, *Fahrenheit 451* by Ray Bradbury, *Jurassic Park* by Michael Crichton.

Fairy Tale: "Once upon a time…" often introduces fairy tales. Characters such as gnomes, elves, giants, talking animals, and witches often populate a fairy tale. Spells are frequently cast. Despite the modern day references to princesses and the term "fairy tale romance," fairy tales frequently have unhappy endings. Examples: *The Three Little Pigs*, *Little Red Riding Hood*, *Goldilocks and The Three Bears*.

Fantasy: Magic and the supernatural are frequently found in fantasy. Animals are able to talk. Fantastic elements might be set in the real world or an alternative world. The forces of good and evil are pronounced and fight one another. Examples: *Harry Potter* series by J.K. Rowling, *Northlander (Tales of the Borderlands)*, by Meg Burden.

Legend: This is a narrative that takes place within human history. It's told in a conversational way and includes events that are outside the realm of possibility, but may include miracles perceived as really happening. Legends serve as affirmations of commonly held values of a group. Examples: *The Legend of Sleepy Hollow* by Washington Irving, *The Legend of the Indian Paintbrush* by Tomie dePaola, *The Legend of King Arthur and His Knights* by Sir James Knowles.

Myth: Traditional stories concerning a being, hero, or event without fact or natural explanation. Myths often feature a deity or demigod and explain some rite or phenomenon of nature. Examples: *Why the Sun and the Moon Live in the Sky* by Niki Daly, *Keepers of the Night* by Michael J. Caduto and Joseph Bruchac.

Horror: A horror story shocks and frightens the reader by using gore, supernatural forces and/or bloodshed. Example: *The Keeper* by Sarah Langan, *The Tell-Tale Heart* by Edgar Allan Poe.

Mystery: The storyline or *plot* in a mystery involves a crime or other event that isn't solved until the end of the story. Examples: *Nancy Drew* series by Carolyn Keene, *Encyclopedia Brown* series by Donald Sobol, *Blood Shot* by Sara Paretsky.

Parody: Parodies make fun of or ridicule serious literature or other writing. Examples: *Harry Potty and the Pet Rock* by Valerie Estel Frankel, *The Stinky Cheese Man and Other Fairly Stupid Tales* by Jon Scieszka.

Satire: Satire is writing that is sarcastic or ironic in order to put down or expose human stupidity or wrongdoing. Examples: *The People's Doonesbury* by G.B. Trudeau, *Catch-22* by Joseph Heller.

Plays: Plays are published in script form and presented on a stage or in dialogue. However, plays can be seen and heard on television, radio and on the internet as well. Examples: *The Skin of Our Teeth* by Thornton Wilder, *Novio Boy* by Gary Soto.

Poems: Poems are written to create a response to thoughts and feelings from the reader. Poems take many different forms, from free verse to haiku to novel-length verse. Some poems rhyme and most poems contain a particular rhythm. Poems can be fiction or non-fiction. It is good to know the form a poem takes to help your understanding of the author's purpose and the feelings the poet is trying to express.

Poetry has its own vocabulary. Two terms you need to know are **stanza** and **rhyme**. A stanza is a group of lines in a poem. Sometimes they are of a particular length (like a paragraph) or meter or have a rhyme scheme. They divide up a poem. A rhyme is a set of corresponding sounds that occur, especially at the end of a line. Letters are used to show the rhyme scheme. In the following example, note the rhyme of the underlined words.

> Kitchen crickets make a <u>din</u>, (a)
> sending taunts to chilly <u>kin</u>, (a)
> "You're outside, but we got <u>in</u>." (a)
> (Joan Bransfield Graham)

Students frequently think all poems rhyme. As you will see in the following list of poetry forms from *A Kick in the Head* by Paul Janeczko, this is not the case.

Forms of Poetry

Free-verse poems may be one or several stanzas in length. They may also be novels. The rules that exist in other forms of poetry do not apply in free-verse poems.

Closed-form poems are the most common form of poetry. There are specific numbers of lines, rhyme schemes, meter, and/or shape. Here are some examples:

Couplet. A couplet is a two-line poem or stanza that usually rhymes.

Quatrain. A quatrain is a four-line poem or stanza, usually rhymed.

Haiku. A haiku contains three unrhymed lines and includes 17 syllables, arranged in lines of 5, 7, and 5 syllables.

> In the rains of spring,
> An umbrella and raincoat
> Pass by, conversing. ("Spring Rain" Buson 14)

Cinquain (*SING-kane*). A cinquain is as rigorously structured as a haiku. It is composed of a set number of syllables (22) and a per-line syllable count (2-4-6-8-2).

Clerihew. A clerihew is made up of two rhyming couplets that poke gentle fun at a celebrity. The first line is always the celebrity's name.

Limerick. A limerick is a five-line poem with the rhyme scheme *a/a/b/b/a*. It has a bouncy rhythm and is usually humorous.

> There was an Old Lady whose folly
> Induced her to sit in a holly;
> Whereupon, by a thorn
> Her dress being torn,
> She quickly became melancholy (Edward Lear 20).

Sonnet. There are two types of sonnets: Italian and Shakespearean. Both are 14 lines long and usually written in iambic pentameter, which means the lines are ten syllables, with an accent falling on every other syllable. Shakespearean sonnets have a rhyme scheme of *a/b/a/b c/d/c/d e/f/e/f g/g*, which you may recognize as three quatrains followed by a couplet.

Ode. An ode celebrates a person, animal, or object. It's often written without the constraints of formal structure or rhyme.

Acrostic. Acrostic poems are descriptive. The first letter of each line spells out the subject of the poem. Students enjoy writing acrostic poems using their names.

> **C** at lover
> **A** lways on time
> **R** eading maniac
> **O** pposite of quiet
> **L** oves travel

Epic: Epic poems tell long stories that use dramatic, dignified language and celebrate the achievements of a hero. Usually the subject of an epic poem is a legendary or historical figure and the deeds and adventures of his or her life. The theme is often one of human grief, pride and divided loyalties. *The Iliad* by Homer and *Paradise Lost* by John Milton are examples of epic poems.

Ballad. Some ballads are written in couplets, some in six-line stanzas. A ballad tells a story often coming from local history or legend; often, the story involves lost love or tragedy.

Other Forms of Poetry: There are many forms of poetry students will enjoy, such as villanelles, sestinas, epigrams, and aubades, and concrete poems, all with their own organizational structures and characteristics.

Non-Fiction

While many *non-fiction* (writing that is fact-based) texts are prose, there are a number of exceptions. Tables, diagrams, charts, and various other presentations of information are written and read differently than prose. Textbooks, newspapers, magazines, blogs, and internet writing all take forms that present challenges to readers. Students will read more non-fiction than fiction during their lifetimes. A familiarity and understanding of the organization of non-fiction genres is necessary to understand the author's purpose for writing. Let's look at some common examples of non-fiction genres.

Biography: A story about a person's life or particular events in their life written by another person. The majority of information in a biography is fact-based. Examples: *The Story of Walt Disney: The Maker of Magic Kingdoms* by Bernice Selden, *Dare to Dream: 25 Extraordinary Lives* by Sandra McLeod Humphrey.

Autobiography: An individual's life story written by the subject herself. Some people writing autobiographies employ *ghostwriters*, who may or may not receive credit for their writing. Examples: *The Autobiography of Benjamin Franklin* by Benjamin Franklin, *The Autobiography of Martin Luther King, Jr.* by Martin Luther King, Jr., and Clayborne Carson.

Memoirs: Authors write memoirs about their entire lives or about specific incidents. Memoirs are more impressionistic than autobiographies. They usually have the feel that the author is having a conversation with the reader. Examples: *The Glass Castle: A Memoir* by Jeannette Walls, *Bad Boy: A Memoir* by Walter Dean Myers.

More Informational Text: Informational text shares knowledge with the reader about a host of subjects. Animals, physical fitness, medical information, and how things work all fall into the non-fiction category, which is fact-based. Forms of informational text are numerous and include:

- magazines
- historical documents
- books
- textbooks
- newspapers
- the internet
- pamphlets
- diaries
- reports
- charts
- diagrams
- tables
- graphs

Once again, these genres are organized differently, and employ various structures. For example, textbooks normally have predictable patterns. Looking at the table of contents in a textbook illustrates how the information is organized. Reading the index is a quick way to pinpoint a topic in the text.

Tables, diagrams, charts, and graphs are frequently used in non-fiction. All of these appear in textbooks. Teach students to pay attention to them, by **previewing** the graphics before they begin reading the surrounding text. Authors have put them in the text for a purpose: to draw attention to the information they contain.

Interpreting graphics uses some of the same strategies we implement for other genres.

- setting a purpose
- chunking the information helps
- getting an overall impression
- putting the information into your own words
- asking if the information seems reliable
- making a connection with the information

Readers should ask why the graphic is included in the text. For example, perhaps a particular graphic, such as a *bar graph*, is used because it best displays the information the author wishes to convey. Examples of graphics are:

Table of Contents and **Index**. These are commonly found in textbooks. They're used to show how ideas and topics are connected through headings and subheadings. A quick check of either pinpoints if specific information is in the text and where it is located.

Bar graphs. A vertical or horizontal pictorial representation to show quantities and compare amounts of something.

Diagrams. Diagrams show how something works. There's no need to draw conclusions from a diagram. You just need to understand and remember what it shows.

Tables. They're the most common type of graphic. All sorts of data are presented on a table, from population figures to baseball statistics. The data is in columns and rows, and summarizes and simplifies information.

Charts. A circle or pie chart is used to show the parts that make up a whole. The circle is divided into pieces or parts. They emphasize the relative size or importance of different parts of the whole, which is always 100%. The pie chart below represents the pizza preferences of a class of 45 students. The data can displayed as percentages, as it is in the chart below, or it could be displayed in raw numbers totaling 45.

Pizza Preferences of Ms. Stuben's 5th Grade Class

Figure 2.3 Pie Chart

When reading non-fiction, students must learn to be **critical thinkers**. One aspect of critical thinking is discerning between *fact* and *opinion*. Much of non-fiction writing contains both facts and opinions.

A **fact** is a statement that is known to be true and can be proved. An **opinion** is someone's personal belief about a topic that should be supported with facts and details that are verifiable. Not only must readers know the difference, they need to evaluate the two.

You can see examples of both in an excerpt from *The Boys' War* by Jim Murphy (The Reader's Handbook 2002, 281):

> *"An estimated **2,898,304 would serve in the Union army** during the war, while **the Confederate side would see almost 1,500,000 join**.*
>
> *Creating good soldiers began with the officers. Many men had*

> *become officers through political favoritism or because they had been able to sign up enough recruits to make a regiment. **Others were elected by the soldiers themselves, usually because they were popular, easygoing fellows**.*"

In the first paragraph, the text in boldface shows facts. We presume, and can check, that these are accurate statistics. In the second paragraph, the text in boldface is an opinion. We do not know for sure if what the author says is so, as there isn't a way to check this information. Also, the author uses the word *usually*, which shows uncertainty as to whether or not men became officers by a popular vote.

Since there is so much information on the internet, and it is increasingly used in reading, evaluating sources to ascertain fact from opinion is important. *The Reader's Handbook* (2002, 525) suggests the following:

- Check the source of the site. This is often named at the top or bottom of the home page.
- Check the site's credentials. Credentials are educational degrees, job titles, or experience that makes an author an authority on the topic.
- Identify its purpose. Why was the site created? Is it trying to sell a product? Make money? Educate people? Its purpose will help you see its point of view.
- Check the last update on the site. Recent updates will probably have up-to-date information.

ASSESSMENTS

An assessment is not just a weekly vocabulary test, end-of-chapter test, or book critique. It is an individual, small group, or whole group evaluation of skills and knowledge. The purpose of a *formative* assessment is to determine what a student already knows and what they can already do. Determining their abilities forms the basis for instructional decisions regarding what they still must learn. Assessments take many forms. Nancy Frey and Doug Fisher (2006, 364) maintain that assessments are not performed to rank students in comparison to one another.

As was previously discussed, state- and district-mandated testing occurs routinely during the school year. This includes separate testing for English Language Learners at the beginning of the school year. For a full picture of a student, however, implementing a variety of assessments throughout the year is necessary. Formative assessments are implemented during the first week of school and occur on a routine basis throughout the year. *Summative* assessments (testing that determines grades) also occurs throughout the year.

In reading, determining a student's oral language skills, reading comprehension, and reading foundations knowledge is critical. It is only by assessing students that meaningful curriculum is created, which, in turn, moves students forward.

There are numerous reading assessments. For example:

- **Rubrics**. Rubrics explain what students need to do, what they will be graded on, and how they'll be evaluated.
- **Observational checklists**. These can be used as you walk around the classroom and focus on a few students per day.
- **Individual reading conferences**. Talk to students about what they're reading. Make sure you have one or several specific purposes during these conferences.
- **Running records**. This is a simple means of transcribing oral reading behaviors.
- **Reading attitude surveys**. Since motivation and interest is key in developing readers, a survey is helpful to determine how students feel about reading.

REFERENCES

Burke, Jim. 1999. *The English Teacher's Companion: A Complete Guide to Classroom, Curriculum, and the Profession*. Portsmouth, Maine: Boynton/Cook Publishers.

Dove, Rita. Poem. *"The First Book."* personal copy.

Flake, Sharon. 1998. *The Skin I'm In*. New York: Hyperion Books for Children.

Frey, Nancy and Douglas Fisher. 2006. *Language Arts Workshop: Purposeful Reading and Writing Instruction*. Upper Saddle River, New Jersey: Pearson Education.

Harwayne, Shelley. 2000. *Lifetime Guarantees: Toward Ambitious Teaching*. Portsmouth, Maine: Heinemann.

Herron, Carolivia. 1997. *Nappy Hair*. New York: Alfred A. Knopf.

Janeczko, Paul. 2005. *A Kick in the Head: An Everyday Guide to Poetic Forms*. Cambridge: Candlewick Press.

Lee, Harper. 1960. *To Kill A Mockingbird*. New York: Warner Books.

Powell, Colin. www.americasprogress.org. (Accessed April 2009).

Rees, Diana. 1994. *First Steps Reading Developmental Continuum*. Portsmouth: Heinemann.

Rosenberg, Sharon Harvey. Poem. *"For Brown Skin Girls."* personal copy.

Robb, Laura. 2002. *Reader's Handbook: A Student Guide for Reading and Learning*. Wilmington, Maine: Great Source Education Group.

Tovani, Cris. 2000. *Do I Really Have to Teach Reading?: Content Comprehension Grades 6-12*. Portland, Maine: Stenhouse Publishing.

_____. January 26, 2002 Workshop. *"The Comprehension Connection for Grades 5-12 Handout."* San Diego City Schools.

Wilhelm, Jeffrey D., Ph.D. 2001. *Improving Comprehension With Think Aloud Strategies: Modeling What Good Readers Do*. New York: Scholastic.

Reading: Application of Reading Skills and Knowledge to the Classroom

Reading, which includes word study, writing, listening, and speaking, makes up the Language Arts curriculum. This chapter focuses primarily on reading in Language Arts, but is also applicable in other content areas.

WORD STUDY AND LANGUAGE ACQUISITION

"I used to walk to school with my nose buried in a book."

-Coolio

Reading is a pleasurable activity. To convey that to children, reading instruction involves using actual books, learning about children's interests and experiences, and assessing their abilities as you move them along in their instruction. This includes instruction in word study, sometimes referred to as reading foundations or word recognition, and language acquisition. This must be developmentally, instructionally, and age appropriate. It is likely that you will have students who enter the classroom without basic language acquisition skills no matter their age. Assessing students and implementing purposeful, consistent word study is vital to their reading progression.

Research in the early 1970's (Ganske 2000) noted that preschool children matched the names of alphabetic letters they knew to the sounds they tried to write. They relied heavily on where the sounds were formed in the mouth. This invented spelling resulted in consistent letter omissions and substitutions as children tried to understand their word knowledge.

Subsequent research led to a model of developmental spelling that encompassed the preschool years through adulthood. Again, this developmental model is not age specific. All third or eighth graders and so forth will not be at the same developmental stage. This is an important point to consider when working with special needs students and English Language Learners (ELLs) of all ages.

With the rise of immigration in the United States, ELLs, also sometimes called students with Limited English Proficiency (LEP), make up a significant portion of public school enrollment. In the 2005-06 school year, over 5 million ELLs were enrolled in public schools in the United States. Western states have the greatest number of ELLs (Payan). Paraprofessionals will work with students from diverse backgrounds. Depending on their first language, ELLs may encounter sounds in the English language that are not used in their primary language. An awareness of such challenges, as well as adapting word study to serve their language needs, is necessary.

Pre-Reading

Before a child begins to read formally, there are several observations paraprofessionals need to make. Beginning in pre-school and kindergarten, asking a student questions while reading ascertains what he knows about the concept of print. Asking the student to show you how to hold a book, use his finger to indicate the direction of print across and down the page, identify the parts of a book (title, beginning, end), and to recognize the difference between print and pictures gives educators an initial assessment of a student's concept of print. Having the student use a forefinger to track eye movement while reading aloud or silently as you sit next to him shows you how much he is focused on the print. These applications also apply to a child of any age who may enter the classroom pre-literate or in the earliest stages of literacy.

Shared reading (discussed later in the chapter) is one of the most effective ways to help children understand and internalize concepts of print. It is the perfect way to begin introducing all manner of word study, organization of text, and story elements. Adults read aloud from a shared copy of the text for various purposes (including an appreciation of the sheer pleasure of reading), periodically point out what they're focusing on (i.e., examples of short vowel and long vowel sounds), and students can join in at the appropriate times. In any classroom, shared reading is an important part of the curriculum every day.

A print-rich, age-appropriate classroom establishes the goals and purpose for learning. A wide variety of genres at various levels (books, magazines, or other forms of print) must be accessible to students. Large charts reinforcing a particular focus of study, such as lists of common prefixes, antonyms, sight words, or vocabulary for a specific unit of study, should be visible to all students. Clear directions for various procedures, coming events, writing supplies, and reference books at various levels are all part of a print-rich, age appropriate classroom. To maintain order and focus, ask, "Why is this in the classroom and what purpose does it serve?"

Students are confronted daily with *environmental print*. Television, newspapers, signs, advertising, magazines, and public facilities all exhibit environmental print. Make children aware of these opportunities for reading. Point them out at your school site, ask students to bring examples in from their time away from school. Words are everywhere and pointing this out to children helps make them aware of the necessity for reading.

Orthographic Knowledge

An individual's *orthographic knowledge*, or knowledge of the spelling system, is important in both reading and writing words as they attempt to match sounds to letters. Here is a glossary of terms you will find helpful. Students, too, should know basic terms such as consonant, vowel, syllable, and rhyme in order to converse about their work.

Blends - Consonant units made up of two-letter or three-letter sequences.

Consonants – Letters in the alphabet other than vowels.

Digraphs – Pairs of letters that represent a single speech sound. *Th* in *this*, *ph* in *phone*.

Grapheme - A written symbol for speech sounds. When students develop sound/symbol relationships, they recognize the patterns in clusters of letters, *e.g., pan, can, man.*

Morpheme – Any minimal grammatical unit of a language. Each has its own meaning and cannot be divided. *The, write, are, sit.*

Phoneme – Oral speech sounds. The individual sounds in a language. English has 46 phonemes. Phonemic awareness is the ability to manipulate language sounds.

Rhyme – One word agreeing with another in sound, particularly at the end of a line.

Syllable – An uninterrupted segment of speech such as *syll/a/ble*. We normally sound out syllables.

Vowels – The letters *a*, *e*, *i*, *o*, *u*, and sometimes *y* in the alphabet. Vowels have long and short sounds.

An Overview of Spelling Development

Students' orthographic knowledge affects their reading and writing development, so it follows that strengthening students' orthographic knowledge strengthens their reading and writing abilities. Periodically assessing this knowledge and providing instruction in what psychologist and author Lev Vygotsky called the "zone of proximal development" offers instructional support at a student's current stage of development.

The Five Stages of Spelling Development

Emergent Spelling. This is the first stage of spelling development and includes the writing attempts of children who are not yet reading. They scribble, use wave-like lines, attempt actual letter formation, and generally try to "write," *f* but there is no connection between what is on the page and the sounds represented.

Letter Name Spelling. These are beginning readers. Their sight-word knowledge and orthographic knowledge is limited. Use predictable text with rhythm, rhyme, and picture clues to support these novice readers. With instruction, they become competent in initial and final consonants, initial consonant blends, and digraphs.

Within Word Pattern Spelling. These readers have a more fully developed knowledge of sight words, and use this knowledge with success on less predictable text. Generally, they also have greater orthographic knowledge, and are less apt to read letter-by-letter and sound by sound. This leads to greater reading efficiency and the ability to concentrate on constructing meaning in text. Some features are: vowel-consonant-e patterns (V-C-e); R-controlled patterns; common long vowels,\; complex consonant patterns; and abstract vowels.

Syllable Juncture Spelling. Print is processed with considerable efficiency in this stage. Reading and writing to learn assume a greater emphasis. Students understand and explore new genres, and must be given increasing opportunities to do so. Much of a student's writing is in response to what he learns. Some features are: doubling and e-drop with -ed and -ing endings; other doubling at the syllable juncture which depends on pattern knowledge; long vowel patterns in the stressed syllable; R-controlled vowels in the stressed syllable; and vowel patterns in the unstressed syllable.

Derivational Constancy Spelling. This is the last stage of spelling, and one that continues through adulthood. This stage is characterized by knowledge of low-frequency words, many of which have Greek and Latin origins. While some students may achieve this stage early on in elementary school, typically their reading and writing ability is still basic. Vocabulary may be sophisticated but isn't necessarily. Features of this stage are: silent and sounded consonants; consonant alternations; vowel alternations; Latin-derived suffixes; and assimilated prefixes (Ganske 2000, 8-26).

Three excellent resources for assessing student spelling and subsequent word study instruction are: *Word Journeys: Assessment-Guided Phonics, Spelling*, and *Vocabulary Instruction*, by Kathy Ganske (2000), *Guiding Readers and Writers: Grades 3-6* by Irene C. Fountas and Gay Su Pinnell (good for all ages), and *Words Their Way: Word Study for Phonics, Vocabulary, and Spelling Instruction*, by Bear, Invernizzi, Templeton, Johnston (2004).

Phonological Awareness

Phonological awareness is the ability to identify and categorize various speech sounds such as rhyme and alliteration. *Phonics* is the consistent relationship between letters and sounds. Since there are 46 speech sounds and only 26 letters in the English language, it is obvious that English is not a phonetic language. Letters are combined in many different ways to reproduce sounds.

In 1997, the International Reading Association (IRA) and National Council of Teachers of English (NCTE) stated that phonics "...for beginning as well as experienced readers, is only one part of the complex, socially constructed, and cognitively demanding process called reading." (NCTE Position Statement Accessed Online March 2009)

Historically, phonics was the most common method of teaching reading in the United States. Phonics helps students *decode*, or figure out words they do not immediately know. However, since reading is making meaning of text, a variety of other means to teach reading are necessary for creating expert readers. In phonics as well as other methods, rather than using words in isolation, they should be presented in meaningful sentences and passages. Teachers can tell students that this is only one way of learning to pronounce new words and convey to them generalizations about using phonics.

Edward Fry et.al. suggest using phonics for beginning English readers in the following order (Fry, Edward and Jacqueline Kress and Dona Fountoukidis 2000, 9) :

1. Easy consonants with letter, sound, and example:

t	/t/	tap	l	/l/	lap
n	/n/	nap	c	/c/	cat
r	/r/	rat	p	/p/	pat
m	/m/	mat	b	/b/	bat
d	/d/	dog	f	/f/	fat
s	/s/	sat	v	/v/	vet

2. Short Vowels:

aaa sound	mad	*ah* sound	hot
eh sound	let	*uh* sound	cut
ih sound	hit		

3. Long Vowels   final e rule

a_e	/a/	make	o_e	/o/	bone
e_e	/e/	these	u_e	/u/	use
i_e	/i/	nine			

4. Long Vowel (open syllable rule-end of word)

e	/e/	me	o	/o/	go

5. Other single consonants

g	/g/	get	x	/ks/	box
h	/h/	hot	qu	/kw/	quit
k	/k/	kit	z	/z/	zip
w	/w/	wet	y	/y/	yes

j   /j/   jet

It is important to remember that certain consonants have second sounds.

c   /s/   city   g   /j/   gym
s   /z/   his   x   /gs/ exam

Learning Styles

Phonics often works well for *auditory* learners, those who learn best through listening and talking. *Visual* learners, those who need to see and sit close to the teacher and who may think in pictures and require as many visuals as possible to fully absorb their learning, aren't as amenable to phonics instruction. *Tactile* or *kinesthetic* students learn best through a hands-on approach. They need activity and exploration for maximum learning. Many students learn through a combination of learning styles. Whether you are using phonics or other strategies in teaching reading, keep in mind these differences and adapt the curriculum accordingly.

Letters and Sounds

Consonants

Letter name word study begins with initial consonants (Ganske 2000 118-21). Consonants are the letters of the alphabet that aren't vowels or the letter "q." The letter "q" is always pronounced /kw/ and used with the letter "u." At first, it's best to avoid letter combinations that physically resemble each other (*m,n*; *b,d*; *p,q*; *f,t*) as well as those with similar sounds (*g,j*; *c,s,z*; *d,t*; *b,p*; *f,v*; *w,y*).

You can start with easy consonants, those that are high frequency and high contrast. They include: *t, n, r, m, d, s, l, c, p, b, f, v.*

Point out consonant second sounds, which are:

c /s/ city   g /j/ gym   s /z/ his   x /gs/ exam

Children need to work with what they know, so this may dictate other possibilities for instruction. Writing and pronouncing letters, words, and sentences together so that students see, hear, and feel the sounds in their mouth and face is a helpful exercise, and can be done as a whole class.

Tongue twisters are fun and easy for reinforcing student understanding. Have students create their own after you model a few.

> <u>B</u>ored Baby Bobby blew big bubbles.
> <u>Sh</u>e sells seashells by the seashore.

Providing lists of blends that students keep in notebooks, and/or posted in the classroom also reinforce student understanding.

Word sorts, wherein students explore and categorize the sound, pattern, and meaning relationships among words through compare-and-contrast strategies, can be done alone, with buddies, or in small groups. Words are placed on index cards, which students can manipulate to test hypotheses of how words go together. Below is an example: (Ganske 2000, 77-79)

<u>sound sort</u>

got	globe	how
stop	flow	now
fox	bone	down
rob	throw	
	hose	

<u>pattern sort</u>

got	globe	flow
stop	bone	how
fox	hose	now
	throw	
	down	

<u>sound and pattern sort</u>

got	globe	flow	how
stop	bone	throw	now
fox	hose	down	rob

Vowels

Word families and *phonograms* are a good way to introduce students to *short vowels*. Word families are groups of words that share a common rhyme. For example, *cap*, *tap*, *lap* all share the *ap* rhyme. Rhymes (like *ap*) that are found in many words are known as phonograms. This can be introduced after children have a reasonably solid knowledge of initial and final consonants.

What Ganske (2000, 16-20) calls "pattern mastery," particularly the marking of long vowels, is at the heart of instruction for students who have moved from relying on letter-by-letter and sound-by-sound processing. They can chunk parts of words and process them in a more automatic fashion within word pattern spelling. The challenge is in figuring out which pattern and when to use it with long vowel sounds. For example, you can tell students to look for a-consonant-e patterns to pronounce words like *wave*, but that pattern does not apply to words like *train*, *play*, *eight*, *they*, and *great*. Instruction is a matter of introducing various patterns and practicing them.

Break It Down!

When students break words apart, particularly in the context of what they're reading, they can often derive the meaning of a word on their own. A few general pointers before and during word-study instruction are:

- Assess student word study needs.
- Model your method of breaking words apart through shared reading or "noticing" of environmental print in and out of the classroom.
- Maintain a print-rich classroom.
- *Scaffold* instruction. Scaffolding means bridging the gap between what students can do and what they need to do through questions, prompts, and tasks.
- Use various means through whole group, small group, or individual instruction.

Affixes

Affix is the term for *prefixes* and *suffixes*. A prefix is a group of letters with or without its own meaning, in front of a base or root word, such as *re*wind or *over*turn. A suffix is a group of letters with or without its own meaning, at the end of a base or root word that changes its meaning, such as trave*led* or claustro*phobia*. When affixes are added, they frequently change the part of speech of the original word.

Affixes can be taught directly to students. It is also a good idea to explain them and their meanings when students encounter them in their reading or in direct vocabulary instruction. Teachers in content areas can also teach affixes, particularly those used in the lexicon of their content area, such as *bio-* in science, *multi-* in math, or *olig-* in social studies.

There are also opportunities for teaching vocabulary in music, art, and physical education. Depending on their first language, English Language Learners will have some knowledge of affixes and their use. In Spanish, the prefix *mal* means bad. In English, words with the prefix *mal-* also have a negative connotation, such as *malpractice*, *malfunction*, and *malodorous*. Having students keep a running list of known and new affixes in their own language next to unknown English affixes builds their word base. Telling students they actually multiply their vocabulary when they learn, understand, and use affixes is a confidence builder. The following list is from Fry, Kress and Fountoukidis (2000, 85-99).

Common Prefixes

anti	against
dis	not, opposite
ex	former
im, in	not
inter	among, between
mis	wrong, not
multi	many, much
non	not
over	too much
post	after
pre	before
pro	favor, forward
re	again or back
un	not
under	below, less than

Common Suffixes

-able, -ible	is, can be

-ar,-er, -or	one who
-en	to make
-er	more
-ess	one who (female)
-est	most
-ette	small
-ful	full of
-ish	relating to
-less	without
-like, ly	resembling
-ment	action or process
ness	state or quality of
ship	state or quality of

Syllables

As you know, a syllable is an uninterrupted part of a word, such as *ta/ble*, *di/vi/der*, and *ba/na/na*. There are many words that contain only one syllable, such as *once*, *which*, *run*, *dog*. There are rules for dividing words into syllables. However, the most common and the easiest way to break words into syllables is for you to show students how to sound out the word. You can also demonstrate where to find syllable breakdown in a dictionary. When students do this, they can often figure out the meaning or partial meaning of a word. This can be taught as part of phonics, affix, or compound word instruction. Making it a natural part of reading instruction is best and becomes a habit of mind for students.

Root Words

Most modern English words have their roots in other languages. Knowing Greek and Latin roots forms a basis for vocabulary building and understanding unfamiliar words. It's best when roots are taught in families, such as *tele<u>scope</u>*, *micro<u>scope</u>*, *peri<u>scope</u>*.

Students whose first language is a romance language such as Spanish, French, or Italian frequently don't know they have an advantage when it comes to root words. There are many *cognates*, words derived from the same language that are similar to English. Linking these words, particularly for Spanish speakers, offers excellent support.

Just as with affixes, there are common and less common root words (Fry, Kress and Foutoukidis 2000, 108-111). A few common root words (using (L) for Latin and (G) for Greek) are:

anti	against
dis	not, opposite
ex	former
im, in	not
inter	among, between
mis	wrong, not
multi	many, much
non	not
over	too much
post	after
pre	before
pro	favor, forward
re	again or back
un	not
under	below, less than

Compound Words

When two whole words are joined, they form a compound word. This is one of the easiest ways students can figure out unfamiliar words. The joined words can be two nouns (*doghouse*, *bookstore*, *stepmother*) two non-nouns (*checkup*, *takeoff*, *worthwhile*), or a noun and a non-noun (*bluebird*, *shortchange*, *flashback*). When they form a compound word, the meaning changes. Some words are compound but separated by a hyphen (*trade-off*, *knock-knee*, *one-way*), or have a blank space between them (*time clock*, *pinch hitter*).

Using a common base word (a word family) is one way for students to practice and build their understanding and vocabulary. For example, using the word *house* is a start for building compound words.

schoolhouse
farmhouse
firehouse
warehouse
doghouse
birdhouse
clubhouse

Students can keep lists, spot compound words in their assigned and independent reading, the paraprofessional can point out compound words while reading aloud or doing shared reading, and examples can be posted on poster paper in the classroom.

Homophone

We use homophones, also called *homonyms*, every day. They're words that sound the same but have different meanings and usually different spellings. You can understand why this is confusing and a challenge for students. Students rely heavily on computer spell-check programs, but these do not correct for homophones.

Using the same strategies for identifying compound words above, you can include games, jokes and riddles (Fry, Kress, and Fountoukidis 2000). It's also helpful for students to keep their own reading and writing notebooks with personal lists of spelling nemeses, which may include homophones.

Some of the most commonly confused homophones are everyday words that dramatically change meaning such as:

Confused Homophones
already/all ready
by/bye/buy
its/it's
no/know
one/won
our/hour
so/sew
their/they're/there
through/threw
where/wear
which/witch
whole/hole
would/wood
your/you're

Honing Homophone Skills:

- Develop homophone-based riddles and jokes. "What is a large animal without its fur?" (A bare bear.) "An insect relative?" (An ant aunt.)
- Make flashcards. Put one of a homophone pair on each side. Student sees one side and tries to spell the other. Discuss meaning of both and use in sentence.
- Have an old-fashioned spelling bee with homophones (Fry, Kress, and Fountoukidis 2000, 258-9).

Antonyms and Synonyms

Like homonyms, understanding what antonyms and synonyms are and how they're used in language helps us understand unfamiliar words, text meaning, and expands our vocabulary.

An antonym is a word that means the opposite or nearly the opposite of another word. Antonyms are often used in tests and language drills. An antonym may be for only one meaning of a word with several meanings. When students have a fuller understanding of a word, they can usually offer an antonym for the word. If you tell students to remember the definition by using the "ant" and think "anti" or against/opposite, it helps them fix the meaning in their brains. Some common antonyms are:

above	below
bad	good
cold	hot
dull	sharp
gain	lose

Conversely, a synonym is a word that is similar to another word. These, too, are used in tests and students can usually think of a synonym for a word when they know the word well. Telling students that *similar* or *almost the same* is the definition of synonym helps them recall the meaning. Some common synonyms are:

gift	present	donation
leave	depart	go away
say	state	remark
take	grab	seize
walk	stroll	saunter

Alphabetizing Words

Alphabetizing is an essential skill that helps students perform tasks such as research and locating books in the library.

The website All About Spelling (www.all-about-spelling.com) says that for younger students, the Alphabet Song is a good beginning. Older students can recite the song. Any student can practice using letter tiles similar to those in a Scrabble game. They can be laid out randomly and you can model placing them in alphabetical order. Say the letters as you place them.

Show students how to begin the song or recitation using different letters such as those found in the middle of the alphabet. Or hand them random tiles and have them use the song to continue through the alphabet. Ask questions such as, "What letter comes after q?" or "Is 'h' in the first half or the second half of the alphabet?"

Once students have mastered putting the letters in alphabetical order, explain that words are also alphabetized, and that we look at the first letter of a word to alphabetize it.

Write several words on index cards, each word beginning with a different letter. It is best to begin with one-syllable words. Students can line up the cards in alphabetical order. This can be done by individual students, with partners, or in small groups.

The next step is to teach that when we have several words that begin with the same letter, we must look to the second or third letter in order to alphabetize them correctly. Write the following words on index cards:

care chose cool cent

Since all the words start with *c*, we have to alphabetize by the second letter. Have the student identify the second letter and alphabetize the words above. Now add two more index cards with these words:

cat can

Point out to students that all six words begin with a *c*, but there are now two words with the same second letter. Explain that in this case, we must look at the *third* letter to alphabetize those words.

Students can then practice alphabetizing whole words by using cards with single words that begin with various letters of the alphabet.

Practical Applications:

- Take students to the library to locate fiction books, which are alphabetized by author.
- Have them alphabetize the last names in the class.
- Look up names in the phone book.
- Call out words for students to look up in the dictionary.

Context Clues

When students are confronted with an unfamiliar word or phrase, possessing a number of strategies for grappling with words builds student confidence and ability.

As students progress, they can use context clues (the signals writers give their readers to explain a word's meaning) for decoding unknown words or phrases. Picture clues or reading the words around the unknown word may help. Sometimes students need to isolate a letter, letters, or a word in order to figure out the meaning. Blocking the text with a cardboard rectangle with a hole cut in the middle enables students to implement word attack strategies.

Nancy Frey and Doug Fisher (2006, 273) list five types of context clues with examples. The vocabulary word is in bold and the contextual clue is italicized:

Definition: **Philosophy** was important to the ancient Greeks. Philosophy means the *beliefs, ideas, and values of the arts and sciences*.

Synonym: Socrates was accused of teaching his students to **rebel** against the government. Officials said Socrates encouraged students to *fight against the rulers* of Athens.

Antonym: Aristotle came from an **impoverished** background, unlike the *rich* philosopher Plato.

Example: The government of **city-states** such as *Athens* and *Sparta* did not always welcome philosophers, especially if their ideas might threaten the government.

General: Aristotle studied **politics** to explain *how people were governed*, and *how rulers were chosen*.

Read Alouds and Shared Reading

We practice **Read Alouds** in myriad settings. We read parts of a story, text from the internet, newspaper, report or magazine to a friend, partner, child, or colleague. We read picture books to children. In the classroom, a Read Aloud serves multiple purposes for students of all ages. They are read by the teacher or paraprofessional for a specific purpose. That purpose may be to share a story and, within that context, demonstrate the structure and organization of a story; or it may be to have a student hear fluent reading and thereby have fluency modeled for them (Frey and Fisher 2006, 312-3).

A Read Aloud in the classroom may be an entire book, part of a book, a poem, or another text choice.

Effective Read Alouds contain several elements:

- readings are appropriate to content, students' emotional and social development, and interests
- practice the selection
- model fluent oral reading
- engage students and hook them into listening to the text
- stop periodically to comment, clarify and/or ask questions. Plan questions for critical thinking, write them on a post-it and place them in the text.
- engage students in book discussions
- typically no more than 15 minutes in length
- make explicit connections to students' independent reading and writing (Frey and Fisher 2006)

Shared reading is different from a Read Aloud in that copies of the text are accessible to students. This can be done with a big book, textbooks, photocopied materials, or document cameras that project text onto a large screen, an invaluable technological tool in classrooms. Again, there is always a purpose for shared reading. And because students have a copy of the text, it can be used for many purposes, such as word study, vocabulary study, exposure to literary elements, or characterization. The students follow the print silently as the teacher reads. A shared reading can be above a student's independent reading level due to the support it offers.

Some characteristics of a shared reading are:

- Short and lively.
- Large print in the K-2 big books.
- Brief, engaging lessons that encourage student participation.
- Repeated readings to reinforce concepts.
- Emphasis on skills at the letter, word, sentence, and text levels.

Shared reading is an excellent tool for word study, whether you are examining vowel sounds, affixes, compound words, homonyms, new vocabulary, rhymes, or other foundations of literacy (Frey and Fisher 2006, 35-6).

Literacy Links for Word Study

Short picture books are useful for illustrating specific word study elements for *all* students. For example:

Word Families
> Gregorich, B. (1996). *Jog, Frog, jog*. Grand Haven, MI: School Zone.
> Wildsmith, B. (1982). *Cat on the mat*. New York: Oxford University Press.

Short Vowels
> Coxe, M. (1996). *Cat traps*. NY: Random House.
> Foster, K. & Erickson, G. (1993). *What a day for flying*. Hauppauge, NY: Barron's.

Blends
> Cutting, B., & Cutting, J. (1996) *Are you a ladybug*? Bothell, WA: Wright.
> Cowley, J. (1998). *The scrubbing machine*. Bothell, WA: Wright.

A Word About Students Reading Aloud

Generally, there is no useful purpose for students in the classroom reading aloud during whole-group instruction. An exception is reading their own writing with the use of the document camera or photocopies of their writing as they share their work. Another exception is reading parts in a play or other dramatic reading. In that case, they should practice prior to reading. Teachers and paraprofessionals are the expert readers in the room, and should model that accordingly.

Pre-Reading Strategies

Frequently, students begin reading a book, magazine, newspaper, or online content without thinking about the task at hand. Tell students that smart drivers don't put their foot on the gas and go; they think about the task at hand. First, they know where they're going. They make sure the car is in park, and that the brake is on before they turn on the ignition. Then, they check the gas gauge; look out for other drivers, bicyclists, and pedestrians; take off the brake; put the car in gear; and, finally, ease into traffic. Once they're in traffic, there's more thinking to be done. So it is with pre-reading. Pre-reading takes a small amount of time, but being prepared is the first step in making meaning of a text.

- **Set a purpose**. Students are reading for a reason. What is it? What do they expect to know when they're done?
- **Preview** the text. Check it out. What does the student already know about the topic or the type of text they're reading? Is there a title? Illustrations? Headings? Sub-headings? A table of contents? How long is the text? Are there chapters? How long are they?
- **Plan**. What reading strategies are needed for this particular text? Have students think about the genre (biography, magazine feature article, and memoir) and the best strategies for understanding that particular text. Students should consider, "How long will it take me to read this text?" When they read outside of class, students should ask themselves, "Where's the best place for me to read so I can focus on the text?" This is all part of students knowing their own particular needs around reading.

Reading Strategies

Focused instruction plays a key role in facilitating reading comprehension in the classroom. Modeling strategies for students teaches them how to approach reading as a purposeful and active process. As Frey and Fisher report (2006 8), our understanding of reading has grown considerably in the last few decades. Research reports that *effective instruction* includes:

Comprehension monitoring that encourages readers to be aware of when they do and do not understand.

Cooperative learning opportunities so students can work on strategies together.

Graphic organizers and story maps to create a visual representation of text. These must be used judiciously. Students must know the teacher's and their own purpose for using GOs.

Question answering and question generation to answer the teacher's questions and create their own.

Story structure instruction to aid in retelling and recall.

Summarization instruction to describe themes and main ideas.

The following is a summarization of reading strategies by Cris Tovani (2000 51).

Activate prior knowledge: Relating to the text through personal experience or background knowledge aids comprehension. Have students questions themselves. "What do I already know about this topic?" or "Who does this character remind me of?" gets them thinking about what they already know.

Predicting or asking questions: Questioning is the strategy that keeps readers engaged. When they ask questions even before they read, they begin to clarify understanding. Encourage students to wonder about the topic, the vocabulary the author has chosen, dialogue, characters, or the validity of information presented in the text. Tell students to use *who, what, when, where, why,* and *how* to ask questions about the text.

Visualizing: Engaged readers visualize all sorts of things in text, such as settings, characters, and plot details. Telling students to make a movie or video in their head about what they're reading helps them stay connected to the text. They can also connect prior knowledge. "I can feel the cold just like that time it snowed and I forgot my boots."

Drawing inferences: Inferring is a bit like a math formula; readers take what they know and add clues from the text, which results in a judgment about something in the text or a prediction about what may occur next in the story. We also say it's reading between the lines. The writer doesn't tell something directly; instead, the author gives the reader hints. Have students look at book covers, titles, pictures, or illustrations, vocabulary, or when and where a story takes place when you begin to model making inferences.

Determining important ideas. Inexperienced and struggling readers often find it difficult to separate out main ideas and details. Using graphic organizers with a short text and gradually advancing to longer or more complicated text helps these readers distinguish the 'big' ideas from the details.

Synthesizing information. Synthesizing means to take new information and combine it with existing knowledge to form an original idea or interpretation. One way to help students synthesize is to have them draw comparisons between what they know about a topic and what the author says about the topic. This is fairly sophisticated thinking that requires students to understand that it is possible to re-learn something and relinquish old ways of thinking.

Repairing understanding: Confusion while reading comes from many problems while reading, such as long sentences, unknown words, a style of writing that is unfamiliar, or a student's inability to understand or use punctuation while reading. Students must have a metaphorical 'tool kit' for fix-up strategies. First, they must understand that it's normal to be confused at times, and that it's smart thinking to stop and say, "I don't get it," and then figure out what to do.

Chunk the text: This is a term used for reading text in pieces. When students chunk the text, they take a section (several lines, a paragraph, a page) to make sure they're 'getting it.' It's also wise for students to look at photos, pictures, tables, diagrams, the table of contents, or charts and ask themselves how they connect back to the text.

Reflecting: Students think about what they've just read, whether it is a paragraph, a chapter, or the end of a text. They should ask themselves questions about the text. Talking with a partner, the paraprofessional, or in a small group helps them reflect. Writing about their thoughts, ideas, and questions is another way for students to reflect on their reading.

The Role of Talk in Teaching Comprehension

Focused talk about reading is an excellent way for students to develop their comprehension at increasingly sophisticated levels. Have them prepare for talk by jotting down questions, ideas, comments, and confusions either in their journals or on sticky notes. Or questions can be teacher-directed. Students can:

- turn and talk with the person to their left or right
- talk in small groups.
- 'talk' through writing that's passed back and forth with another student.
- talk in text groups – over a poem, short passage, essay, feature article, or books.

You will always need to model preparing for talk and how to talk with others about their reading.

TEACHING THE STRATEGIES

- Teachers and paraprofessionals model strategies.
- Students use text they can read.
- Students practice with assigned and independent reading.
- Educators scaffold strategies. Give students feedback about their use of strategies.
- Teach students to pick and choose strategies as necessary to comprehend their reading.

We know reading is thinking and that comprehension means understanding the text. Comprehension skills include:

- The ability to identify supporting details and facts.
- The ability to identify the main idea or big idea.
- The ability to identify the author's purpose.
- The ability to identify and know the difference between fact and opinion.
- The ability to identify point of view, make inferences, and draw conclusions.
- The ability to analyze, summarize, and synthesize.

There are different levels of comprehension. **Literal comprehension** is the most basic level of comprehension. This is an understanding of basic knowledge. *Who, what, when, where, why*, and *how* often begin basic knowledge questions. It means reading and understanding what is on the page. Facts and details are part of literal comprehension. Questions in this category comprise about 80 percent to 90 percent of the questions educators ask students (*www.officeport.com/edu/bloomq.htm*). For example, in the novel *The Skin I'm In* (Flake 1998), checking for literal comprehension could mean asking:

> What happened to Maleeka's father? (**A factual question**)

> What happened when the girls broke into the school? (**Sequence of events**)

Application questions apply information to produce some result. It's the use of facts, rules and principles to problem solve. An example in *The Skin I'm In* is:

> Why is Char a significant character in the story?

Analysis questions identify motives, separate a whole into component parts, find the underlying structure of a communication, or subdivide something to show how it's put together. Another example from Flake's novel:

> How does Maleeka's attitude about Ms. Saunders change from the beginning of the story to the end of the novel? (**compare**)

> What are the plot elements that lead to the climax? (**subdividing something to show how it comes together**)

Interpretive or synthesis questions ask students to read between the lines, or *infer*. When they make an interpretation, they must back up their interpretations with evidence from the text and their own prior knowledge. Some examples of interpretive questions used for *The Skin I'm In* are:

> What do you think the title of the book means? (**deriving meaning**)

> Why do you think Sharon Flake decided to make Maleeka the daughter of a single parent? (**purpose**)

> Why do you think the author had Maleeka break into the school after she was beginning to do well at school? (**interpretation**)

Critical, creative, evaluative levels of comprehension describe the ultimate goal for students. They make judgments about what they read and give evidence to support their statements. Students must read *beyond* the lines. They speculate based on evidence. Is the text true or false, fact or opinion, propagandistic or stereotypical? Is the writer qualified to expound on the topic? Could one action be better than another? What are some alternatives? Using Sharon Flake's novel, a few examples are:

What's the most important event that changes Maleeka's behavior? (**value decisions**)

Do you think the author 'got it right' with her characterization of Char, Raina and Raise in the novel? Why? Why not? Aren't they just stereotypes of young, poor African-American girls? (**emotional response and alternative ways of thinking**)

What does the title *The Skin I'm In* mean? (**development of opinions**)

The goal is creating an independent reader who knows what personal strategies they need to understand a text. Offer students a variety of ways to work on word study and reading comprehension. In addition to reading strategies, Read Alouds, and shared reading, students can keep word study notebooks with personal vocabulary lists, orthographic supports they need, and self reflections on their learning. Hang sight word lists and vocabulary words germane to current class study on easel paper in the classroom. Keep reference books (dictionaries, thesaurus, and basic grammar books) at various skill levels available.

Observing Students

Some students are quite proficient at "fake reading." Seemingly, they attend to the page, but their eyes are drifting, and their minds are elsewhere. Cris Tovani (2000) suggests that when meaning breaks down, a student:

- Recites only the words and doesn't converse with the author.
- Can't visualize a picture of what she's reading.
- Can't make connections or analogies to known information.
- Doesn't have enough meaning to ask questions other than word meanings.

- Doesn't remember what she's read and can't paraphrase.
- Is unable to rephrase the reading in another fashion.
- Rereads the same line or word over and over again.
- Is hindered by too many unknown words.
- Notices her mind wandering.

Your observations will help you and the student create a reading plan so that she can practice using text she can and wants to read.

Checking for Understanding

Teach students that they can check their own understanding of text by:

- Using sticky notes to mark text with questions or thoughts or ideas. This is a way for students to hold on to their thinking.
- Talking with a partner, the teacher, the paraprofessional, or a small group about what they understand or don't understand.
- Noticing, and then stopping, when they aren't paying attention to a text.
- Looking at words or phrases before and after the word or portion they don't understand.
- Using word attack strategies to figure out unfamiliar words or phrases.
- Rereading what's confusing.
- Questioning the text or author. It comes as a shock to some readers that not everything they read is true.
- Thinking critically about a text and being willing to disagree. Have the evidence to do so.
- Determine the best strategies to deal with the problem. Be selective with strategies.

Questioning for Understanding

There are numerous questions readers ask before, during, and after reading to check their understanding. Sharing how you ask questions of yourself and the text while reading engages students and supports their practice. Modeling questioning and posting questions through collaboration on large sheets of poster or easel paper supports their practice. Active readers ask questions. Remind students about using *who, what, when, where, why,* and *how* as a beginning. A few examples are:

- Why is the author talking about this?

- Why did the author use that word or phrase?
- Who says this is true?
- What does that (word, phrase, idea) mean?
- Who does this character remind me of?
- Have I been to a place like this before?
- When did I have a similar experience?
- Does the author support his point?
- Is there another side to the story?
- What structure is the author using in this text?
- I'm stuck. How can I figure out…?

Shari Frost (2009) cautions against teachers overusing reading strategies and makes a case for teachers being selective while modeling and guiding students in their use. Her advice includes:

- "Walking the walk" by forming educator study groups to examine how they process and comprehend their own reading.
- Long-term professional development so educators truly know how to teach comprehension well.
- The careful use of children's literature, so that students practice on texts they **can** read, have texts they **enjoy** reading, and **limit** the amount of reading done with one book since students need a variety of genres for effective instruction.

Graphic Organizers

Graphic organizers provide support for student comprehension if they are used purposefully. A graphic organizer is a scaffold and shouldn't take the place of writing or become a mindless fill-in-the-blank exercise. It is a bridge to writing and thinking, a support for talk, a quick assessment for a teacher, or the means for students to organize literary elements. ELLs and special needs students should find them especially helpful.

Double Entry Journals

The purpose of a Double Entry Journal or diary is to clarify individual thinking, wonder, or ask questions of a text.

Table 3.1 Double Entry Journal

The left-hand column of the journal is the place for the student to document a brief plot summary of what they have read.	***The right-hand column*** is where the student reflects on what she has read. *This section should be in 1st person.*
Possibly Includes: • Notes • Quotations • Summary paragraphs/Main ideas • Facts/Concepts/Evidence • Key terms • Illustrations (pictures, graphs, drawings, concept webs) • Questions • Responses to specific questions • Descriptions of events	**Possibly Includes:** • Immediate reactions • Reactions after learning new information about the topic (e.g., through discussions, further reading) • Answers to questions • What more would you like to learn? • Agree? Disagree? Why? • What you understand/don't understand • Compare/Contrast • Connections to other sources/to what you already know • Your interpretation of what you experienced • Why is your question important? • Perspective/Bias

Literature Responses

Another form to get students thinking about their reading is this Literature Response form:

Literature Response

Student's Name:

_____

Directions: After reading your selection, choose one of the following sentence stems to write a response to what you read. Write your response on a separate sheet of writing paper.

After reading _____,
(the book, chapter, story, or poem)

I noticed…	I know the feeling…
A question I have is…	I loved the way…
I wonder why…	I realized…
I began to think of…	I was surprised…
It seems like…	If I were…
I can't really understand…	I discovered…
I'm not sure…	

Figure 3.1 Literature Response Form

Story Map

A story map helps delineate literary elements such as theme, main idea, major and minor characters. Usually the concept or title is written in a circle in the center of a paper. Arrows or lines are used to make connections or consolidate information. It's a visual representation of the story or reading selection. Story maps take many forms, such as a tree with branches, a sun, or a free form diagram. A class reading Wilson Rawls's *Where the Red Fern Grows* created the story map below.

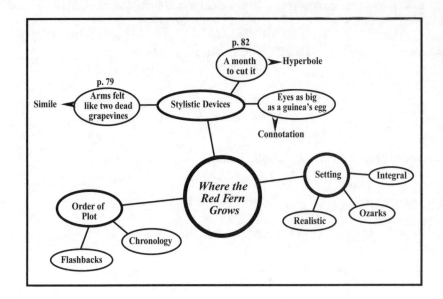

Figure 3.2 Story Map

Fish Bone Map

The fish bone map (on the next page) can be used for cause and effect, the cause of an action and its consequence. This can be used as an outline for subsequent writing.

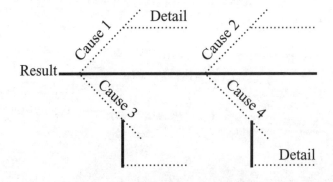

Figure 3.3 Fish Bone Map

Student's Hand

Students can either outline their hands on the page or use a preprinted hand graphic organizer. Some possible uses are writing the main idea in the palm of the hand, with supporting details written on the fingers. Students can also write a character's name in the palm with character traits written on the fingers.

Dictionary Use

When students are unable to determine a word in a text through word attack strategies, using a dictionary will help them find the meaning. A dictionary is an indispensable tool for readers. Students should know the basic parts of speech such as nouns, verbs, adjectives, and adverbs. Depending on the context, word meanings change and dictionaries define a word according to its part of speech.

It's advisable to have several levels of dictionaries for students. Simple paperbacks, student or junior dictionaries, and collegiate dictionaries should all be available, as well as several levels of thesaurus. A thesaurus will provide synonyms for the unknown word, which may offer additional support.

Depending on the skill level of the student, you may want to begin with a basic or junior dictionary. Teach the parts of a dictionary to students (Reader's Handbook 2002, 626-29).

Guide Words: These are the words at the top of the page that tell the first and last word on that dictionary page. They help you locate the word you want.

Entry Word: Entry words are listed in alphabetical order and are in bold face type. Entry words show how a word is spelled and whether or not it should be capitalized. They also show how the word is divided into syllables.

Definitions: With more than one definition, the dictionary will number each. Tell students to read every definition and choose the one that works best for their purpose. The first definition is not always the best or main one, *and* it may just restate the word as another part of speech.

Word History: Some entries tell the origin of the word, or from what language the word was derived.

Pronunciation: Right after the entry word, the pronunciation is shown in parentheses. It looks unusual because the respelling shows how to say the word and where the accented syllable is.

Part of Speech: This is in italics right after the respelling. It's usually abbreviated.

Inflected Forms: At the end of an entry are other forms of the word.

Illustrative Example: Sometimes there is a phrase or sentence illustrating the definition. In some junior dictionaries or dictionaries for second language learners, drawings are added to some entries.

Interpreting Written Directions

Ignoring written directions is a common problem with many students, no matter their age. Tell students that failing to follow directions can mean a recipe doesn't turn out right, or that medical complications arise. In fact, using a cell phone and learning to drive are both contingent on following directions. They can probably come up with many of their own examples.

For students to do well academically, following directions is essential. Here are a few tips on helping students interpret written directions:

- Have students ask, "Who, What, When, Where, Why, and How" of the directions.
- Students can use some reading strategies such as chunking the text.
- Teach students to look for key words such as: *first, second, then, next, finally, due.*
- Tell students to repeat back the directions in their own words to you or another student.
- Teach students that reading directions slowly and carefully is key. Skimming and scanning is not a strategy to employ when reading directions.
- Make sure students know that it is acceptable to ask for help when they're stuck.

Assessing Comprehension

Students receive mandated testing throughout the year. English Language Learners and students with special needs receive additional assessments. Your district may provide specific reading assessments during the school year. These are known as *summative assessments*. Summative assessments also include end-of-unit or chapter tests and end-of-term semester tests. Think of summative assessments as a way to gauge student learning in relation to content standards at a particular point in time.

A much different assessment is the *formative assessment*. This helps educators adjust teaching and learning while they're occurring. It lets both teachers and students know how they're progressing. Formative assessment is thought of as "practice." Students aren't held accountable for these assessments in the way they are for Adequate Yearly Progress (AYP) or report card grades. Students should be involved with formative assessment. That way they know what's expected of them and where they are on the continuum of learning.

While mandated testing is not flexible, there are all manner of summative and formative reading assessments teachers and paraprofessionals can administer. These can be oral or written questions that demand only one answer, or questions that allow for synthesis, evaluation, and critical thinking. Think about the levels of understanding discussed earlier in the chapter when assessing students for understanding of their reading.

Assessments are:

1. tied to instruction.
2. driven by learning goals.
3. systematic.
4. take the learner's needs into account.
5. integrated into a manageable system.

A small sampling of common reading assessments are:

Cloze tests. Cloze procedures omit every fifth word from a passage. The reader fills in the missing words using context clues and syntactic strategies to complete the passage accurately. These are easy for the teacher or paraprofessional to prepare. At least 250 words with 50 words omitted in a passage are best. The first and last sentences are kept intact.

Observational tests. These are best used in real learning situations. You can obtain and analyze the information immediately and adjust instruction. Observational assessments may be kept in a teacher's daily log.

IRI. The *informal reading inventory* is a popular assessment which uses several grade-level passages to measure a student's accuracy as well as his ability to answer literal and inferential questions. These are usually commercially prepared narrative and expository passages that also have a student Read Aloud component used for miscue analysis. IRI's take time to administer individually, but supply comprehensive information.

Conferences. Talking informally with students about their reading, using literal questioning as well as higher level questions, is an excellent way to plan future instruction.

Self-assessments. Meta-cognition is key here. Self-assessment helps develop meta-cognitive awareness. This helps students create their own plans, reflect on their strengths and weaknesses, and take on the learning process as their own.

Spelling Inventory. This is an excellent way to determine students' awareness and application of the foundations of reading per their development stages. It assesses their awareness and understanding of phonemes, letter patterns, syllables, vowels, and consonants. Again, it gives valuable information about instructional needs (Frey and Fisher 2006).

Vocabulary Study

Word-study and reading strategies will help students expand their vocabulary. Every content area has its own lexicon and students should learn this lexicon through direct instruction.

When the class reads the same text, teachers must frontload significant vocabulary they believe will help students make meaning of the text. These are not necessarily obscure words only found in a particular writing. Since you cannot provide direct instruction for each word a student might encounter, you can use the following chart to help choose vocabulary (Frey and Fisher 2006, 275).

Table 3.2 Selecting Vocabulary

Considerations For Selecting Vocabulary to Teach	Questions to Ask
Representative	Is the concept represented by the word critical to understanding the piece?
Repeatability	Will the word be used again during the school year?
Transportable	Will the word be used in other subject areas?
Contextual Analysis	Can students use context clues to determine meaning?
Structural Analysis	Can students use structural analysis to determine meaning?
Cognitive Load	Have I identified too many words?

Since students have varying word knowledge, assess students before the reading. Not only will you know what they know, they will have an understanding of where they are on the continuum and where they need to be. For students to "own" a word, they must use it repeatedly and in a variety of contexts. Vocabulary instruction is done as a whole class for frequently used words with an organizer. They can make their own organizer by defining the word, denoting the part of speech, presenting synonym and antonyms. Using the word in a sentence and representing the word by drawing or magazine cut-outs will help the students to remember their word. In addtion, students can keep a personal vocabulary list for words they're curious about, overhear, or encounter in their reading.

Children's Literature

Children's literature is often associated with the term, "children's classics." This is defined as writing of high quality, with popular appeal, which has stood the test of time and is still in print. American and English authors, such as Louisa May Alcott, Charles Dickens, Frank Baum, Mark Twain, Dr. Seuss, and Laura Ingalls Wilder are all considered authors of classic literature.

The term "literature" has had a rather high-minded connotation. However, at *www.dictionary.reference.com* the simple definition is "any kind of printed material" or "the entire body of writings of a specific language, period, people, etc."

Since we want to develop students who are motivated to read, love to read, talk about their reading, and advance their reading skills, we can think of children's literature in the following way: children's literature is what a student can read, finds pleasurable or interesting, and is suitable and appropriate for his age. This opens the door to all manner of writing, including comic books; graphic novels; newspapers; magazines; chapter books; series like *Captain Underpants*, *The Magic Tree House* and *Harry Potter*; picture books such as *The Stinky Cheese Man*; or even cereal boxes.

Meeting a child's present reading abilities and desires, with an eye toward consistently developing and expanding her reading skills and choices is the goal.

Enlisting parents to read to and with students of all ages at home is vital to improving reading skills and interest. Also, parents' talking with their students about their own reading and the student's reading increases the potential for student success.

REFERENCES

Bear, Donald M., Marcia Invernizzi, Shane Templeton and Francine Johnston. 2004. *Words Their Way: Word Study for Phonics, Vocabulary and Spelling Instruction*. Upper Saddle River, New Jersey: Pearson.

Blau, Sheridan. 2003. *The Literature Workshop: Teaching Texts and Their Readers*. Portsmouth, New Hampshire: Heinemann.

Booth, David. 1998. *Guiding the Reading Process: Techniques and Strategies for Successful Instruction in K-8 Classrooms*. Portland, Maine: Stenhouse.

Frost, Shari. 2009. *"Towards Thoughtful Strategy Instruction."* www.choiceliteracy.com. Accessed April 2009.

Frey, Nancy and Douglas B. Fisher. 2006. *Language Arts Workshop: Purposeful Reading and Writing Instruction*. Upper Saddle River, New Jersey: Pearson.

Fry, Edward Bernard, Ph.D., Jacqueline Kress, Ed.D. and Dona Lee Fountoukidis, Ed.D. 2002. *The Reading Teacher's Book of Lists*. New Jersey: Prentice Hall.

Ganske, Kathy. 2000. *Word Journeys: Assessment Guided Phonics, Spelling, and Vocabulary Instruction*. New York: Guilford Press.

Payan, Rose M. and Michael T. Nettles. *"Current State of English-Language Learners K-12 Student Population."* www.ets.org/Media/Conferences_ and_Events/pdf/ELLsympsium/ELL_factsheet.pdf Accessed April 2009.

Rawlings, Wilson. 1961/1976. *Where the Red Fern Grows*. New York: Bantam.

"Resolution on Phonics as a Part of Reading Instruction." 1997 NCTE Position Statement. http://ncte.org/positions/statement/phonicsinreadinginst.htm Accessed March 2009.

Robb, Laura. 2002. *Readers Handbook: A Student Guide for Reading and Learning*. Wilmington, Maine: Great Source Education Group.

Tovani, Cris. 2000. *I Read It But I Don't Get It: Comprehension Strategies for Adolescent Readers*. Portland, Maine: Stenhouse.

Mathematics: Skills and Knowledge

Number Sense and Basic Algebra

All real numbers can be placed on a **number line**. A **number line** is a line that allows you to see the relationship that numbers have to each other. By placing numbers where they belong on a number line, you can compare them to each other. The farther to the right a number is, the larger it is. The farther to the left a number is, the smaller it is. Number lines continue infinitely; however, we can only examine a finite portion of the number line.

The first set of numbers we are exposed to as children are the **counting numbers**. **Counting numbers** begin with 1 and continue infinitely: {1, 2, 3...}.

The set of **whole numbers** is the same as the set of **counting numbers** with one more member in the set, 0. The set of **whole numbers** begins with 0 and continues infinitely: {0, 1, 2, 3...}.

Integers include all of the **whole numbers** and their **opposites**. The **opposite** of a number is the same distance from 0 as the number itself. Opposites have opposite signs—one is positive and the other is negative. Sometimes a positive number will have a positive sign in front of it; if there is no sign in front of a number, it is assumed to be positive. In the number line below, 8 and –8 are opposites, –4 and 4 are opposites. Every number has an opposite except for 0, which is its own opposite. You can also think of 0 as having no opposite, since it is the number that separates the negative and the positive numbers on a number line. As you can see, **counting numbers**, **whole numbers**, and **integers** do not have any fractional or decimal parts. Therefore, $3\frac{1}{2}$, 17.2, and $-\frac{19}{4}$ are not counting numbers, whole numbers, or integers.

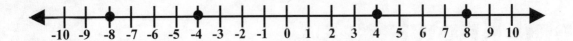

Figure 4.1 Number Line

When working with **integers**, you must know the rules for each of the four operations. Every integer has an **absolute value**, defined as a number's distance from 0 on the number line. The absolute value of 11 is 11. The absolute value of –11 is also 11. The reason both 11 and –11 have the same absolute value is that both numbers are 11 units from 0. An alternate way to explain this is to say that the absolute value of a number is the number without a sign.

When adding two positive integers, the answer is positive: $8 + 2 = 10$. When adding two negative integers, the answer is negative. To add two negative numbers, add the absolute values of the numbers: $(8 + 2 = 10)$, then, add the negative sign: $(-8 + -2 = -10)$. When adding one positive and one negative number, there are two steps to follow.

Let's look at the following problem as an illustration:

$$-7 + 2 = ?$$

1. The first step is to subtract the number whose absolute value is smaller from the number whose absolute value is larger, ignoring the signs of the numbers. In this example, subtract 2 from 7 to get 5.
2. The second step is to take the sign of the number with the larger absolute value and attach it to your answer. In this example, –7 has the larger absolute value because it is farther from 0 than 2, so put a negative sign in front of the 5. So,

$$-7 + 2 = -5$$

Let's look at another example:

$$10 + -3 = ?$$

Subtract 3 from 10 to get 7.

1. Take the sign of the 10, which is positive. Your answer is 7.

Subtracting integers is best accomplished by rewriting the subtraction problem as an equivalent addition problem. Rewriting a subtraction problem as an addition problem requires leaving the first integer alone, changing the subtraction to addition, and then changing the second integer to its opposite. Once the problem is an addition one, you can follow the rules of adding integers described above.

For example:

$-4 - -3 = ?$
Rewrite as $-4 + 3$.
The answer is -1.

Another example:

$2 - 6 = ?$
Rewrite as $2 + -6$
The answer is -4.

Both multiplying and dividing integers follow the same rules. If both numbers have the same sign, the answer is positive.

$$4 \times 5 = 20$$
$$-4 \times -5 = 20$$
$$16 \div 8 = 2$$
$$-90 \div -9 = 10$$

If the numbers have different signs, then the answer is negative. It does not matter whether the first or second integer is negative; *the answer is negative*. For example, $-3 \times 7 = -21$ and $18 \div -9 = -2$.

Divisibility Rules

How can you tell if a number is divisible by another? Here are some divisibility rules you can follow:

- Divisible by 1: All whole numbers are divisible by 1.
- Divisible by 2 (also called even): If a number ends in 0, 2, 4, 6, or 8, it is an even number. So, 560, 28, and 1236 *are* divisible by 2. However, 465, 9803, and 37 are *not* divisible by 2.
- Divisible by 3: Add up the digits of the number; if that sum is divisible by 3, then the number is divisible by 3.

  - Look at the number 451: Add the digits: $4 + 5 + 1 = 10$. 10 is *not* divisible by 3, so 451 is *not* divisible by 3.
  - Look at this one: 7035: Add the digits: $7 + 0 + 3 + 5 = 15$. 15 *is* divisible by 3, so 7035 *is* divisible by 3.

- Divisible by 5: A number is divisible by 5 if it ends in 5 or 0. So, 80, 385, and 110 *are* divisible by 5. However, 753 and 92 are *not* divisible by 5.
- Divisible by 9: A number is divisible by 9 if the sum of its digits is divisible by 9. So, 441 and 8163 *are* both divisible by 9, but 238 and 4004 are *not* divisible by 9.
- Divisible by 10: If a number ends in 0 it is divisible by 10. So while 330 and 2640 *are* divisible by 10, numbers like 609 and 305 are *not* divisible by 10.

Every whole number is divisible by 1 and itself. If a number is only divisible by 1 and itself and has no other factors (therefore having only 2 factors), it is a **prime number**. The **prime** numbers less than 20 are 2, 3, 7, 11, 13, 17, and 19. Going beyond 20, there are an infinite number of prime numbers. If a number has more than two factors, it is a **composite** number; there are more composite numbers than there are prime numbers. The number 1 is neither prime nor composite since it does not fit into either category: 1 has only one factor, the number 1.

Mathematical Operations

In mathematics, there are four **operations—addition (+)**, **subtraction (−)**, **multiplication (×)**, and **division (÷)**. When adding two **whole numbers** together, you arrive at a **sum** (the answer to an addition problem) that is greater than either number. When you add, you are increasing the amount, so $4 + 5 = 9$ because you are *adding* 5 to 4. You can also think of the problem as adding 4 to 5.

The value of a digit depends on where it shows up in the number, called its **place value**. That is, the 3 in 73 is equal to 3, while the 3 in 38 is equal to 30. One way to see the value of each digit in a number is to look at the number in **expanded form**. For example, the number 1,234,567 in expanded form would be:

$$(1 \times 1{,}000{,}000) + (2 \times 100{,}000) + (3 \times 10{,}000) + (4 \times 1{,}000) + (5 \times 100) + (6 \times 10) + (7 \times 1)$$

By looking at a number in expanded form, you can see that each digit's value comes from the place that it is in. The most important thing to remember when adding (and subtracting) multi-digit whole numbers is to line up the correct place values underneath each other when calculating. For example, when adding 23 and 145, you must line up the 2 with the 4 (because both are in the tens place) and the 3 with the 5 (because both are in the ones place) as shown below. You add like place values together.

```
    1   4   5
+       2   3
―――――――――――――
    1   6   8
```

In this example, you get 168 as your answer. That is, the **sum** of 145 and 23 is 168.

There are addition problems you may encounter that require you to **regroup** in order to come up with the correct answer. The problem below is an example of one in which you would need to apply this concept.

```
      1   1
          7   5
+     1   4   8
―――――――――――――――
      2   2   3
```

You begin, of course, by adding the ones place first. As you can see, $5 + 8$ is 13, which is a two-digit number. Looking ahead to the tens place, $7 + 4$ results in 11, which is also a double-digit number. It is not possible to write two digits in one space in your answer. However, there is a way to solve this problem. When adding multi-digit numbers, it is customary to add from the right to the left, starting with the ones place.

In this example, $5 + 8 = 13$: you can **regroup** 13 as $10 + 3$. Put the 3 in the ones place in your answer and write the 1 above the tens column in your problem; this 1 represents 1 ten. Now you can add the numbers in the tens column. You have $1 + 7 + 4$, which equals 12. Since you're adding in the tens column, you've got 12 tens, which is 120. You can regroup 120 as $100 + 20$. The 2 of the number 20 goes in the tens column of your answer and you write the 1 above the hundreds column; this 1 represents 1 group of 100. Now add $1 + 1$ to get 2 (which is really 200), and write 2 in the hundreds column in your answer.

Subtracting means taking one amount from another. When working with whole numbers, the **difference** (the answer to a subtraction problem) is less than the first number you start with. For instance, if you have $20 and spend $8, how much money would you have left? This is an example of subtraction. Because $20 - 8 = 12$; you would have $12 left. Just as in addition, when you subtract multi-digit numbers, you must line up the correct place values underneath each other. See the example below:

$$
\begin{array}{ccc}
3 & 5 & 9 \\
- & 2 & 3 \\
\hline
3 & 3 & 6
\end{array}
$$

By subtracting like place values from each other, you arrive at the answer of 336. By starting at the ones place, you can see how this answer was found. $9 - 3 = 6$; $5 - 2 = 3$; there is nothing in the hundreds place of the number we are subtracting, so we are subtracting nothing (or 0) from 3, resulting in 3.

Multiplication is an operation that is a shortcut to adding the same number many times; multiplication is a more efficient way to complete repeated addition. If you wanted to know the total number of tires on five cars, for example, you could certainly add $4 + 4 + 4 + 4 + 4$, which would show you that there are 20 tires all together. However, when you have a problem that asks you to add the same number many times, as in this example, you can also use multiplication. The answer to a multiplication problem is called the **product**. In the example above, instead of the addition problem presented, you could do the corresponding multiplication problem, 5×4, which can be translated as 5 groups of 4. Facility with the multiplication facts (commonly refered to as *multiplication tables*) from

1-12 is important; math is far less tedious when you know the number facts in all four operations.

Let's try another example. If Paula runs six miles a day, how many miles would she run in a week? This problem is well suited for multiplication because you want to find the total number of miles in seven days. The problem 7×6 makes sense here; the answer is 42 miles. The **product** of 7 and 6 is 42.

Dividing means putting a number into groups of the same size. For instance, if a child gets an allowance of $35 a week, and he wants to spend the same amount each day, how much would that be? This problem requires dividing 35 into 7 groups—one for each day of the week. $35 \div 7 = 5$. That means that the child should spend $5 each day.

Just as multiplication is a shortcut way to do repeated addition, division is a shortcut way to do repeated subtraction. If you baked 36 cookies and plan to put four cookies in each bag to give as gifts, how many bags will you need? You could certainly solve this problem with subtraction. That is, put four cookies in the first bag, and you have 32 left, because $36 - 4 = 32$. Put another four in the next bag, and you have 28 cookies left, because $32 - 4 = 28$. If you continue in this way, you will discover that you need exactly nine bags for your cookies. Although you will arrive at the correct answer, it is more efficient to solve this problem, and ones like it, using division; the corresponding division problem for the example above would be $36 \div 4 = 9$.

Let's try another. If you want to know how many weeks there are in 56 days, you could solve the problem $56 \div 7$. What this problem is asking is, how many groups of 7 are there in 56? The answer is 8. There are 8 weeks in 56 days. Each number in a division problem has a name. The number you are dividing *by* is called the **divisor**. The number you are dividing *into* is called the **dividend**, and the answer to a **division** problem is called the **quotient**. Therefore, the quotient of 56 and 7 is 8.

Fractions

A **simple action** has a **numerator**, a **denominator**, and a **division** symbol. In the fraction $\frac{3}{4}$, 3 is the **numerator** and 4 is the **denominator**. The line between the numerator and denominator indicates **division**. A trick for remembering *numerator* is to recognize that it is the number that is "north" in the fraction. *Numerator* and *north* both begin with the letter *n*. *Denominator* and *down* both start with the letter *d*, so you can remember that the *denominator* is the number that is "down" in the fraction. A fraction represents a division problem. Therefore, $\frac{3}{4}$ is the same as the problem, $3 \div 4$.

A **mixed number** includes both a whole number and a fraction. The fraction $7\frac{1}{2}$ is an example of a **mixed number**.

If a fraction's numerator is the same or greater than its denominator, then the fraction is said to be **improper**. Two examples of **improper fractions** are $\frac{6}{6}$ and $\frac{18}{5}$. There may be occasions when you need to rewrite mixed numbers as improper fractions or vice versa, so it is important that you know how to make these conversions. To explain how to rewrite a mixed number as an improper fraction, it is helpful to look at an example. If you have the mixed number $5\frac{3}{8}$, multiply the denominator by the whole number, then add that answer to the numerator. That answer is the numerator in your improper fraction. The denominator remains the same. In this example, you do $8 \times 5 + 3$ to get the numerator 43, which you put over 8 to get $\frac{43}{8}$ therefore, $5\frac{3}{8} = \frac{43}{8}$.

Similarly, there is a process to rewrite an improper fraction as a mixed number. Let's look at $\frac{27}{4}$: Divide the denominator into the numerator; see how many times it divides into the numerator without going over. In this case, 4 goes into 27 six times because $4 \times 6 = 24$. So, 6 is the whole number of the mixed number; as you can see, 27 is 3 more than 24. Therefore, 3 is the numerator of the fraction. The denominator remains the same—it is 4. So, $\frac{27}{4} = 6\frac{3}{4}$:

It is customary to write simple fractions in **lowest terms**. A fraction is in **lowest terms** if the only whole number factor that the numerator and denominator have in common is 1. Some examples of fractions in lowest terms are $\frac{4}{7}$; $\frac{15}{19}$; and $\frac{35}{51}$:

To rewrite a fraction so that it is in lowest terms, you must find the **greatest common factor (GCF)** of both the numerator and the denominator. The **GCF** is the largest whole number that divides evenly into both the numerator and denominator. For example, let's look at the fraction $\frac{18}{24}$. The factors that both numbers have in common are 1, 2, 3, and 6, so the *greatest* common factor is 6. To simplify the fraction so that it is in lowest terms, divide both 18 and 24 by 6, the **GCF**; this gives you $\frac{3}{4}$. Therefore, $\frac{18}{24}$ is equivalent to $\frac{3}{4}$; and $\frac{3}{4}$ is in lowest terms.

Adding and subtracting fractions with the same denominator requires only examining the numerators because the denominator remains the same when you add or subtract fractions with the same denominators.

If you have $\frac{3}{8} + \frac{2}{8}$, add the numerators $3 + 2$ to get 5 and keep the denominator the same. In this way $\frac{3}{8} + \frac{2}{8} = \frac{5}{8}$.

If you have $\frac{9}{10} - \frac{1}{10}$, subtract 1 from 9 which is 8, and keep the denominator as 10. $\frac{9}{10} - \frac{1}{10} = \frac{8}{10}$. In this example, you need to rewrite $\frac{8}{10}$ so it is in lowest terms. The GCF of 8 and 10 is 2 so divide both 8 and 10 by 2. This gives you $\frac{4}{5}$. Unless instructed otherwise, always remember to rewrite a fraction in **lowest terms**.

Adding and subtracting fractions with unlike denominators requires that you find a **common denominator** before you can add or subtract the fractions. The number in the denominator of a fraction tells how many parts there are in a whole. If 6 is the denominator, there are 6 pieces in a whole. If 3 is the denominator, then there are 3 pieces in a whole. Therefore, if you are trying to combine fractions with different denominators, you are working with different-sized pieces, which is why it is necessary to rewrite the fractions so that they both have the same denominators.

Let's look at some examples. If you want to add $\frac{3}{5}$ and $\frac{1}{10}$, you need to find a common denominator. It is most efficient to find the **least common multiple (LCM)** of both denominators. The **LCM** is the smallest number of which both 5 and 10 are factors. In this case, 5 is a factor of 10, so 10 is the LCM for 5 and 10. You can leave $\frac{1}{10}$ alone since it already has the denominator of 10, but you will have to rewrite $\frac{3}{5}$ as an **equivalent fraction** with 10 as its denominator.

Equivalent fractions are two fractions that are equal to each other, but have different denominators; **equivalent fractions** both simplify to the same fraction when they are written in **lowest terms**. Some examples of **equivalent fractions** are: $\frac{1}{8}$ and $\frac{2}{16}$; $\frac{4}{12}$ and $\frac{12}{36}$; and $\frac{11}{22}$ and $\frac{1}{2}$.

It is helpful to find the **equivalent fraction** with the following setup:

$$\frac{3}{5} \times \frac{?}{?} = \frac{?}{10}$$

You are looking for the number that multiplies by 5 to get 10. That number is 2. So, you also multiply the **numerator**, which is 3, by 2 to get 6. Since $\frac{2}{2} = 1$, you are multiplying $\frac{3}{5}$ by 1. This does not change the value of $\frac{3}{5}$, because $\frac{6}{10}$ is equivalent to $\frac{3}{5}$. Now that you have the same **denominators**, you can add $\frac{1}{10}$ and $\frac{6}{10}$, which is $\frac{7}{10}$.

Let's look at another example: $\frac{11}{12} - \frac{3}{8}$. In this example, 8 is not a factor of 12, so we cannot use 12 as our **LCM**. In cases like this where the smaller denominator is not a factor of the larger one, it is a good idea to list the **multiples** of each denominator until you find one that they share. **Multiples** of a number are found by multiplying that number by the counting numbers, starting with 1. The first four multiples of 12 are 12, 24, 36, 48. The first four multiples of 8 are 8, 16, 24, 32. As you can see, both numbers share the multiple 24, so that is the **LCM**.

$$\frac{11}{12} \times \frac{?}{?} = \frac{?}{24} \text{ and } \frac{3}{8} \times \frac{?}{?} = \frac{?}{24}$$

Use the set-up described above to find an equivalent fraction for $\frac{11}{12}$ with a denominator of 24. You will need to multiply the first fraction by $\frac{2}{2}$, because this will result in a denominator of 24. Then multiply 11 by 2 to get 22 for the **numerator**. In the second fraction, to get 24, you must multiply 8 by 3. Multiply 3 by 3 to get 9 in the **numerator**. So, $\frac{9}{24}$ is equivalent to $\frac{3}{8}$. Now that we have rewritten both fractions with a common denominator, we can do the subtraction. $\frac{22}{24} - \frac{9}{24} = \frac{13}{24}$.

When adding mixed numbers with like or unlike denominators, you may find that your answer contains a whole number along with an improper fraction. When you get such an answer, there is an extra step needed to complete the problem. Let's look at the example of adding $3\frac{3}{5}$ and $4\frac{4}{5}$.

$$3\frac{3}{5} + 4\frac{4}{5} = 7\frac{7}{5}$$

As you can see, your answer has a whole number and an improper fraction. You cannot leave the answer in that form. You need to rewrite $\frac{7}{5}$ as a mixed number $(1\frac{2}{5})$, and then combine that mixed number with the whole number (7). You will get $7 + 1\frac{2}{5}$, which equals $8\frac{2}{5}$. If the two mixed numbers you are adding have different denominators, the process is the same, although you must first find a common denominator before combining the mixed numbers.

When subtracting mixed numbers with like or unlike denominators, you may find that you need to borrow from the whole number in order to do the subtraction. Let's look at the example $7\frac{1}{8} - 3\frac{7}{8}$.

$$
\begin{array}{r}
7\frac{1}{8} \\
- 3\frac{7}{8} \\
\hline
\end{array}
$$

As you can see, you cannot subtract $\frac{7}{8}$ from $\frac{1}{8}$ because $\frac{1}{8}$ is smaller than $\frac{7}{8}$. What you need to do is borrow from the whole number—in this case, it's a 7. If you take 1 away from the 7, it becomes a 6. Now you need to add that 1 you've borrowed to $\frac{1}{8}$. Since you are working in eighths, 1 whole equals $\frac{8}{8}$. Therefore, add $\frac{8}{8}$ to $\frac{1}{8}$, which gives you $\frac{9}{8}$. See the rewritten (and equivalent) problem below.

$$
\begin{array}{r}
6\frac{9}{8} \\
- 3\frac{7}{8} \\
\hline
\end{array}
$$

Now do the subtraction. The answer is $3\frac{2}{8}$, which in lowest terms is $3\frac{1}{4}$.

To **multiply** simple fractions, just multiply the **numerators** together and multiply the **denominators** together as in the example: $\frac{3}{4} \times \frac{2}{5} = \frac{3 \times 2}{4 \times 5} = \frac{6}{20}$. Remember to simplify the fraction $\frac{6}{20}$ by dividing both the numerator and denominator by the **GCF** of 2. This will give you $\frac{3}{10}$. If one or both of the fractions that you are multiplying is a **mixed number**, rewrite them as **improper fractions**, then multiply the **numerators** together and **multiply** the **denominators** together.

Let's look at $3\frac{1}{4} \times \frac{2}{7}$. Rewrite $3\frac{1}{4}$ as $\frac{13}{4}$, then follow the procedure described above. $\frac{13}{4} \times \frac{2}{7} = \frac{26}{28}$. Simplify the fraction by dividing both numerator and denominator by their **GCF**, which is 2. This gets you $\frac{13}{14}$.

When you are multiplying fractions, you can simplify before you **multiply**, if you would like. This is sometimes helpful because you avoid having to multiply large numbers. Simplifying before multiplying is similar to simplifying fractions. However, not only can you simplify within one fraction, but you can also simplify using the **numerator** of one fraction and the **denominator** of the other fraction. Let's use the following problem to illustrate how to simplify before multiplying: $\frac{8}{9} \times \frac{3}{16}$

As you can see, 8 and 16 have a **GCF** of 8. Divide 8 by 8 to get 1 and divide 16 by 8 to get 2. Put a slash through the 8 and replace it with the 1. Also, put a slash through the 16 and replace it with the 2. Now look at the 3 and 9. They have a **GCF** of 3. Divide the 9 by 3 to get 3. Divide 3 by 3 to get 1. Put a slash through the 9 and replace it with the 3. Put a slash through the 3 and replace it with the 1. Now the simplified (and, it's important to remember, *equivalent*) problem is: $\frac{1}{3} \times \frac{1}{2}$. The answer is $\frac{1}{6}$. Simplifying first is easier because the numbers we have to multiply are smaller. If we had multiplied first and simplified later, we would have had to multiply 8 by 3 and then 9 by 16, which would have been more work.

In order to divide fractions, you must rewrite the division problem as an equivalent multiplication one, and then follow the procedure for multiplying fractions. Let's look at the example $\frac{7}{8} \div \frac{1}{3}$. When you rewrite a division problem as a multiplication one, leave the first fraction as it is. In this case, $\frac{7}{8}$ stays as $\frac{7}{8}$. Rewrite the division as multiplication. Rewrite the second fraction as its **reciprocal**. The **product** of a number and its **reciprocal** is 1. A quick way to find the **reciprocal** of a number is to switch the numerator and denominator with each other. Hence $\frac{7}{9}$ and $\frac{9}{7}$ are reciprocals. $\frac{4}{5}$ and $\frac{5}{4}$ are reciprocals. So in the problem $\frac{7}{8} \div \frac{1}{3}$, the reciprocal of the second fraction, $\frac{1}{3}$, is $\frac{3}{1}$. Therefore, the equivalent multiplication problem is $\frac{7}{8} \times \frac{3}{1}$. The answer is $\frac{21}{8}$. This improper fraction can be rewritten as a mixed number as $2\frac{5}{8}$. When dividing fractions, rewrite any mixed numbers as improper fractions before rewriting the problem as an equivalent multiplication problem. Remember, too, that you can simplify before multiplying, and you should write your final answer as a simple or mixed number in lowest terms.

Decimals

All of the real numbers are **decimal numbers**. Not all decimal numbers have decimal points in them. A decimal point is only used when there is a number less than 1 or a part less than 1 added to an integer. If there is a part less than 1, it comes after the decimal point. The following are all decimal numbers: 189, –4.3, 2.498, and –10.

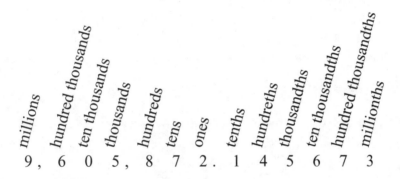

Figure 4.2 Place Values

The first six place values that come after the decimal point are tenths, hundredths, thousandths, ten thousandths, hundred thousandths, and millionths. For describing operations with numbers with decimal points, when we say "decimal number" we mean a number that has a decimal point in it.

Just as you line up the same place values when adding or subtracting whole numbers, you must do the same when adding or subtracting decimal numbers. Line up the same place values below one another. Bring the decimal point straight down in the answer as in the example below:

$$15.443$$
$$\underline{-9.121}$$
$$6.322$$

When **multiplying decimal numbers**, it is not necessary to line up the decimal points. What makes most sense is to line up the digits, not necessarily those with the same place value. If you are multiplying 4.3 × 8.56, you would set up the problem as shown below: As you can see, the place values are not lined up under each other. You would still get the right answer if you did line up the place values, but it is unnecessary and may result in extra work. Perform the multiplication as if the numbers were whole numbers. Placement of the decimal point comes at the end, after you have completed the multiplication.

$$
\begin{array}{r}
8.\ 5\ 6 \\
4.\ 3 \\
\hline
3\ 6\ 8\ 0\ 8
\end{array}
$$

Once you have the digits in the answer, then you have to put the decimal point where it belongs. Look at the two numbers you are multiplying. The number 8.56 has 2 numbers *after* the decimal point. The number 4.3 has 1 number *after* the decimal point. So add 2 + 1 to get 3—that means there will be 3 places after the decimal point in the answer; so the answer is 36.808.

When dividing a decimal number by a whole number **divisor**, just follow the procedure for dividing whole numbers and put the decimal point in your answer directly above where it is in the **dividend**.

Dividing a decimal or whole number by a decimal divisor requires a little more work. Since it would be very difficult to figure out how many times a portion of a number such as .4 or .25 goes into a number, it is customary to rewrite the problem so that the **divisor** is a **whole number**. It makes sense that if you are going to change the divisor, you will also have to change the dividend; otherwise, you will be solving a different problem than the one that was presented to you. What you want is to solve an equivalent problem. In the division problem $\frac{3.78}{.2}$, you can see that the **divisor** is a **decimal** number. We are going to multiply both the divisor and the dividend by a power of 10 that will result in the divisor becoming a whole number. In this example, we use 10 because multiplying a number by 10 moves the decimal point one place to the right. If you multiply a number by 100, the decimal point moves two places to the right, and so on. Multiplying both 3.78 and .2 by 10 gives us the problem. Since we have multiplied both numbers by 10, we have multiplied the fraction by 1 because $\frac{10}{10}$ is 1. Therefore, $\frac{37.8}{2}$ is equivalent to the original problem $\frac{3.78}{.2}$ and the answer is 18.9.

Math Symbols

Mathematical symbols allow you to compare numerical expressions. Common symbols are:

$=$ **equals**
$>$ **greater than**
$\geq$ **greater than or equal to**
$<$ **less than**
$\leq$ **less than or equal to**.

The **equals** symbol states that two expressions or terms are equal to each other. $\frac{15}{5} = 3$ and $9 + 1 = 10$ are two examples of how an **equal sign** can be used.

The **greater than** symbol shows that the expression on the left side of the symbol is **greater than** the expression on the right side. $12 > 4$ and $19 + 7 > 50 - 43$ are two examples of using the **greater than** sign correctly.

When using the **greater than or equal to** sign, the expression on the left may be **equal** to the expression on the right or it **may be greater**. Therefore, $8 \geq 8$ is true as is $8 \geq 7.5$.

The **less than** symbol shows that the expression on the left side of the symbol is **less than** the expression on the right side $-5 < 0$ and $\frac{34}{7} < \frac{19}{5}$.

The **less than or equal to** sign may indicate that the expression on the left is **equal** to or **less than** the expression on the right $4 \leq 6.3$ and $18 \div 3 \leq 6$.

Making sense of the "greater than or equal to" and "less than or equal to" signs is best illustrated when examining real-life situations. If you want to represent the ages of senior citizens who can receive a discount on the price of a movie ticket, you could use the $\geq$ symbol. Let A = the age you must be to receive a discount. In this example, we will say that the age for a senior is 55 years old. Then $A \geq 55$ shows all of the various ages people could be to receive a discount—those who are equal to 55 as well as those who are over 55.

Let's look at an example for "less than or equal to." You are going shopping and are planning to spend only the cash that you bring with you, which is $100. Let M = the money you can spend. Then $M \leq 100$ represents the different possible amounts you could spend. You could spend any amount less than $100, but you could also spend exactly $100.

Numbers in Different Forms

Quantities may be presented in a variety of ways—as decimals, percents, or as fractions. Depending on the situation, it may be appropriate to use one form over another. Therefore, it is beneficial to be able to convert among the three forms with ease.

Writing a fraction as a decimal is simple if the denominator of the fraction is a power of 10, such as 10, 100, or 1000. For example:

$$\frac{2}{10} = .2, \frac{17}{100} = :17 \text{ and, } \frac{45}{1000} = .045$$

All you have to do is put the digits in their correct places. If the denominator is not a power of 10, then you can divide the numerator by the denominator as shown below.

What is $\frac{4}{5}$ as a decimal? When you divide 4 by 5, you need to add a decimal point and a 0 after the 4, so you are dividing 4.0 by 5. Completing this division gives you 0.8. So, $\frac{4}{5} = 0.8$.

To write a decimal as a fraction, write the numbers in the decimal number in the numerator of a fraction (do not include the decimal point). Find the digit that is the farthest to the right in the number and write its place value as the denominator. If the fraction needs to be simplified, then simplify it.

Let's look at some examples: Write .55 as a fraction.

Write 55 in the numerator and 100 in the denominator $\frac{55}{100}$. Simplify the fraction to $\frac{11}{20}$.

How about 4.2? Write 42 in the numerator and 10 in the denominator: $\frac{42}{10}$, then simplify the fraction to $4\frac{1}{5}$.

There are two steps to write a decimal as a percent. First move the decimal point two places to the right (this may result in the decimal point being at the end of the number; in that case, you can leave it off). The next step is to add the percent sign. For example, to write .09 as a percent, first move the decimal point two places to the right, and then add the percent sign to get 9%. Notice how the decimal point at the end of the number is not included because it is not necessary.

There are also two steps to write a percent as a decimal. First, move the decimal point in the number two places to the left. If there is no decimal point, it means that the number in front of the percent sign is a whole number. The decimal point in a whole number is actually at the end of the number. In the number 19, for example, the decimal point (not written) would be at the end of the number: 19. is the same as 19 without the decimal point. After moving the decimal point two places to the left, take away the percent sign.

Let's try an example. Write 14% as a decimal. Since we do not see the decimal point, it is after the 14, so we can write 14%. Move the decimal point two places to the left and drop the percent sign. You get 0.14, so 0.14 is equivalent to 14%.

To write a percent as a fraction, write the number in front of the percent sign in the numerator of a fraction. Since we are working with percents, which are parts of 100, we always put 100 in the denominator. Remember to simplify the fraction, if necessary. Let's try a few examples. To write 91% as a fraction, simply place 91 over 100 to get $\frac{91}{100}$. To express 8% as a fraction, we first arrive at $\frac{8}{100}$, which simplifies to $\frac{2}{25}$.

To write a fraction as a percent, follow the steps for writing a fraction as a decimal. Then follow the steps for writing a decimal as a percent. For example, to write $\frac{1}{8}$ as a percent, first $\frac{1}{8} = 0.125$. Then, $0.125 = 12.5\%$.

If you are asked to compare numbers to each other and they are presented in a variety of forms, it is helpful to put them all in the same form—whichever is easiest for you, or whichever form makes most sense in the problem. For instance, let's say you have to put the following numbers in order from least to greatest: 0.18, $\frac{1}{8}$, 15%, and 10%. You could rewrite $\frac{1}{8}$, 15%, and 10% as decimals. Then it would be easy to see how to order them. $\frac{1}{8} = .125$; 15% = .15; and 10% = .10, giving us 0.18, 0.125, 0.15, and 0.10. So, the numbers in ascending order are 10%, .125, 15%, and .18.

Percentages

If you want to find the percent of a number, such as in the example, what is 25% of 800, the easiest way is to rewrite the percent as its decimal equivalent and then multiply. So here you would multiply .25 × 800 to get 200.

If you need to know what percent one number is of another, you need to set up and solve a proportion with one of the ratios having 100 as a denominator. A proportion is an equation stating that two ratios are equal. A ratio is a comparison of two numbers. To illustrate, $\frac{3}{5} = \frac{9}{15}$ is a proportion because $\frac{3}{5}$ and $\frac{9}{15}$ are equal ratios. For example, if you are asked what percent of 50 is 10, you are solving $\frac{10}{50} = \frac{y}{100}$. To solve a proportion, first cross-multiply. In this example, that means multiplying 50 by y and then 100 by 10. That gives you $50y = 1000$. Then, divide by the number in front of the variable. In this case, divide both sides by 50, which gives you $y = 20$. So, $\frac{10}{50} = 20\%$.

If you are asked to find the whole when given the part and the percent, you can also write a proportion. An example might be: 20% of what number is 12? The proportion would look like this: $\frac{20}{100} = \frac{12}{Z}$. Cross multiply which gives you $20Z = 1200$, then divide both sides by the number in front of the variable, 20, to get $Z = 1200 \div 20$; so $Z = 60$.

Exponents

If you find that you need to multiply a number by itself a number of times, you may need to use **exponents** as a more efficient way to write the problem. If, for example, you would like to write 10 × 10 × 10 × 10, you can do that in a shorthand way by writing 10^4. 10 is the **base** and 4 is the **exponent**. The exponent tells you how many times you must multiply the base as a factor. When computing the value of an expression presented in exponential form (a base number with an exponent), it is often a good idea to write the expression out in expanded form (3^4 in expanded form is 3 × 3 × 3 × 3) to make sure that you arrive at the correct answer. If you have 2^5, a common error is to multiply 2 by 5 and get 10. This is incorrect. Writing the expression out in expanded form ensures that you will not make this mistake. In this case, 2^5 is the same as 2 × 2 × 2 × 2 × 2, which is 2^5 written in expanded form. 2^5 is the same as 32. *Exponential form* means a base number written with an exponent and *expanded form* means written out using multiplication symbols.

Order of Operations

Mathematics follows rules and procedures. If you encounter a problem with different operations or one that also has parentheses and exponents in it, you must know in what order to simplify the problem. Without being given any instruction on this topic, you might think that you would simplify from left to right; however, this is not always correct. There is a specific **order of operations** that must be followed in multi-operational problems. Let's start by looking at problems that only contain the four operations of addition, subtraction, multiplication, and division. By following the rules of the **order of operations**, you must do multiplication and division (from left to right) before you do addition and subtraction (which you also do from left to right). Therefore, in the problem $4 + 7 \times 2$, you would multiply 7 by 2 first, and then add that answer to 4. The answer is 18.

Let's look at this problem: $12 \div 3 \times 5$. This problem has both multiplication and division. Neither multiplication nor division comes before the other; they are to be done as they occur from left to right. In this problem, do 12 divided by 3 and then multiply that answer by 5—you get 4×5, which is 20.

If, in addition to any of the four operations, a problem has parentheses or exponents, you must do them first, with what's in parentheses considered before exponents. Here is the complete **order of operations**:

1) Simplify expressions inside parentheses
2) Simplify exponents
3) Complete multiplication and division from left to right
4) Complete addition and subtraction from left to right

Let's look at a problem that has parentheses, exponents, and several operations. $6 \times (8 + 2) \div 5 - 3^2$

Following the order of operations, you will complete the problem in the following order:

1) Add 8 and 2 (10)
2) Simplify 3^2 (9)
3) Multiply 6 by 10 (60)
4) Divide 60 by 5 (12)
5) Subtract 9 from 12

6) The answer is 3.

Estimation

Sometimes it is not necessary to get an exact answer to a problem—only an **estimate** is required. When that happens, it is important to be able to round numbers so that they are easier to work with. If you need an **estimate** of how much money you would need to buy 12 packages of crackers when each package costs $2.89, you could round $2.89 up to $3 and then multiply by 12, which would give you $36. You would need *about* $36 to buy the crackers.

If you needed to estimate the area of a field that was 190 meters by 217 meters, you could round 190 meters up to 200 meters, and you could round 217 meters down to 200 meters. Therefore, the approximate or estimated area would be 200 × 200, which is 40,000 square meters.

Algebra

An algebraic equation may contain one or more **variables**. A **variable** is a letter that takes the place of a number. Equations with one operation can often be solved by mental math. Sometimes it is easy to figure out what number the **variable** represents without much effort. Let's look at some equations that are easy to solve with mental math.

In the equation x + 5 = 12, if you "plug in" 7 for *x*, you will get 12.

For *y* − 2 = 9, you can see that if you start with 11 and decrease it by 2, you will get 9.

In 8*p* = 16, if you multiply 8 by 2, you will get 16; therefore *p* = 2.

For $\frac{m}{4} = 5$, you should think what number when divided by 4 gives 5? The answer is 20, so *m* = 20.

It is not always possible to solve an algebraic equation using mental math; therefore, it is valuable to know a procedure that will work in all cases. To solve an equation involving one operation, you must apply the **inverse operation** to the problem in order to solve it. The **inverse operation** means the opposite operation. The opposite of addition is subtraction and vice versa. The opposite of multiplication is division and vice versa.

Let's look at one example where we can apply the use of inverse operations.

$$.5x = 11.3$$

Because the problem is a multiplication one, we will divide in order to solve it. We divide by the number that is being multiplied by the variable. In this case, we do $11.3 \div .5$; so $x = 22.6$.

If you have to solve $y - 9 = -3$, you will use addition because the equation contains subtraction. So, add -3 and 9 and you get $y = 6$.

Sequences

A **sequence** of numbers is an ordered set of numbers. Sometimes a sequence is **arithmetic**, which means that in order to find the next number in the sequence, you have to add (or subtract) the same number. For example, the sequence 2, 5, 8, 11…starts with the number 2, and each subsequent number is found by adding 3 to the previous number. That is, $2 + 3 = 5$; $5 + 3 = 8$, and so on. If you want to find the next number in an **arithmetic sequence**, then you need to find the **difference** between each two numbers of the sequence. Once you have discovered this **difference**, you can continue the sequence infinitely.

Here's another example: 45, 40, 35, 30…. Starting with 45, each subsequent number is found by subtracting 5. You can see that $45 - 5 = 40$; $40 - 5 = 35$, and so on. The next number in the **sequence** after 30 is 25 because $30 - 5 = 25$. Sequences of numbers can also be **geometric**, which means that you multiply (or divide) by the same number to find each subsequent number. An example of a **geometric sequence** is 1, 2, 4, 8… Examine the numbers and see what you need to multiply (or divide) each number by to get the next number. In this case, it is times 2 because $1 \times 2 = 2$, $2 \times 2 = 4$, and $4 \times 2 = 8$. So the next number in the sequence is found by multiplying 8 by 2, which is 16. It may not always be easily apparent whether a sequence is arithmetic or geometric; sometimes it is neither. To check if it is an arithmetic sequence, see if there is a common difference between each number and the one that follows it. If there is, then you know it is an arithmetic sequence. If not, then you can see if it is geometric by dividing each term by the one before it. If you get the same **quotient** each time, then it is **geometric**. Once you have determined the kind of **sequence** you have, it is easy to find the next number.

Measurement

When working with time it is important to know how to convert among different measures of it. A day has 24 hours, each hour has 60 minutes, and each minute has 60 seconds. You should know how to describe time in different ways. For example, you might tell a friend that you are running $\frac{1}{2}$ hour late; since an hour has 60 minutes, $\frac{1}{2}$ of 60 is 30, so you are running 30 minutes late. The same time can sometimes be expressed in two different ways. For example, 6:45 could also be described as a quarter to 7:00, because 15 minutes out of 60 minutes ($\frac{15}{60}$) simplifies to $\frac{1}{4}$, which is a quarter of an hour.

You must also know that we have a 12-hour clock—there are 12 hours between noon and midnight and another 12 hours between midnight and noon.

Here's a typical question that requires your facility with time. It is 3:30 PM. Sal has to get to his piano lesson at 5:45 PM. How much time does he have? To figure this out, break up the time from 3:30 until 5:45 into easy chunks of time. There is one hour from 3:30 to 4:30 and another hour from 4:30 to 5:30. There are 15 minutes from 5:30 to 5:45. Therefore, Sal has 2 hours and 15 minutes until his lesson. You can also say that Sal has $2\frac{1}{4}$ hours until his lesson because $\frac{15}{60}$ is equivalent to $\frac{1}{4}$.

A dollar bill is equal to 100 cents, which is 100 pennies. A nickel is worth 5 cents; a dime, 10 cents; and a quarter, 25 cents. A penny is $\frac{1}{100}$ of a dollar; a nickel $\frac{5}{100}$ or $\frac{1}{20}$ of a dollar; a dime $\frac{10}{100}$ or $\frac{1}{10}$ of a dollar; and a quarter is $\frac{25}{100}$ or $\frac{1}{4}$ of a dollar.

The standard unit of measurement in the United States is the foot, which has 12 inches in it. Three feet make up a yard. If you need to convert inches to feet, you need to divide by 12 since there are 12 inches in each foot.

For example, if you have 42 inches, how many feet do you have? When you divide 42 by 12, you get 3 with a remainder of 6. Since your divisor is 12, $\frac{6}{12} = \frac{1}{2}$; therefore, you have $3\frac{1}{2}$ feet.

Here's another example: If you have 16 inches, how many feet do you have? When you divide 16 by 12, you get 1 with a remainder of 4. Since your divisor is 12, $\frac{4}{12} = \frac{1}{3}$;

therefore, you have $1\frac{1}{3}$ feet. Similarly, if you have 8 inches, which is less than a foot, you would divide $\frac{8}{12}$ and put the fraction in lowest terms to arrive at $\frac{2}{3}$ of a foot.

If you want to find out how many feet you have in a given number of yards, multiply by 3 because every yard has 3 feet. Let's look at an example. How many feet do you have in 8 yards? Since $8 \times 3 = 24$, you have 24 feet. If you wanted to know how many inches that was, multiply 24 by 12, since each foot has 12 inches. Because $12 \times 24 = 288$, there are 288 inches in 24 feet (and in 8 yards).

The metric system is another system of measurement, which for some is simpler to work with because all its measurements are in base 10. For example, a **meter** (m) has 100 **centimeters** (cm) and a **centimeter** has 10 **millimeters** (mm). Therefore, a **meter** has 1000 mm. If something is 4 m long, it is 400 cm long because $4 \times 100 = 400$ cm. If an object is 8.4 m long, then it would be 840 cm because $8.4 \times 100 = 840$ cm.

How many **meters** are in 735 cm? Since there are 100 cm in one meter, you must divide 735 by 100, which gives you 7.35. Therefore 735 cm = 7.35 m.

If you wanted to know how many mm there are in a number of meters, multiply by 1000 because there are 1000 mm in one meter. How many mm are in 5.8 meters? Since $5.8 \times 1000 = 5800$, there are 5800 mm in 5.8 meters.

Geometry

Geometry is a branch of mathematics that examines various shapes. A **polygon** is a closed shape whose sides are line segments. The smallest polygon you can make has 3 sides and is called a **triangle**. A 4-sided figure is a **quadrilateral**. A 5-sided figure is a **pentagon**.

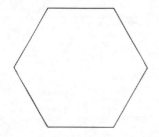 A 6-sided figure is a **hexagon**.

A 7-sided figure is called either a **heptagon** or a **septagon**. An 8-sided figure is an **octagon**. A 9-sided figure is a **nonagon**.

The 10-sided figure to the right is a **decagon**.

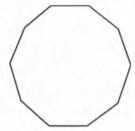

A **regular polygon** is one whose sides are all the same lengths and whose angle measures are all the same. Hence, a **square** is a regular **quadrilateral**.

Triangles are three-sided shapes that lie on one plane and can be classified according to their angle measures or according to the lengths of their sides. The sum of all angles in any triangle is 180 degrees. The classification of triangles by the degree of the angles follows: An angle whose measure is less than 90 degrees is an acute angle. A triangle that has three **acute** angles is called an **acute triangle**. The triangle below, which has a **right** angle and two **acute** angles, is called a **right triangle**.

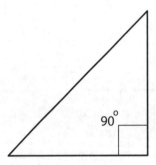

An angle which is greater than 90 degrees but less than 180 degrees is **obtuse**. A triangle with an **obtuse** angle and two **acute** angles is called an **obtuse triangle**. In the obtuse triangle below *a* is the obtuse angle.

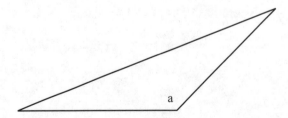

The classifications of triangles by lengths of sides are as follows: If all sides are the same length, the triangle is **equilateral**. The angles of an equilateral triangle are also equal, hence the name—equilateral.

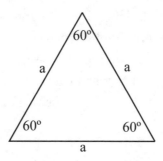

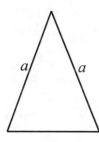

An **isosceles** triangle has two sides of equal length. An isosceles triangle can have three sides of equal length, as illustrated by the triangle above. A **triangle** with all three sides the same length is by definition both **isosceles** and **equilateral**.

A **triangle** whose sides are all different lengths is **scalene**.

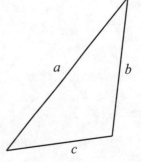

There are also different names for special **quadrilaterals**, or four-sided polygons. In order to classify the different quadrilaterals, it is important to understand what parallel means. Two lines are **parallel** if they never touch, no matter how far they are extended. A **quadrilateral** with only one pair of parallel sides is a **trapezoid**. A quadrilateral with two pairs of **parallel** sides and whose opposite sides are of equal length is a **parallelogram**. A **quadrilateral** with two pairs of **parallel** sides and all four sides of equal length is a **rhom-**

bus. A **quadrilateral** with two pairs of **parallel** sides, opposite sides equal, and four **right angles** is a **rectangle**. A **quadrilateral** with two pairs of **parallel** sides, all sides of equal length, and four **right angles** is a **square**.

A polygon can accurately be classified by different names. For example, a **rectangle** is also a **parallelogram** and a **quadrilateral**. However, it is customary to select the "best" name for a **quadrilateral**; that is, you should choose the name that labels the shape most specifically. For example, there could be a shape that is a quadrilateral, parallelogram, and rhombus; the "best" name for this shape would be a rhombus because that describes the shape most precisely.

The **perimeter** of a shape is the distance around it. A perimeter is like making a fence around the shape. In order to find the **perimeter** of a shape, add up the lengths of all of the sides. Sometimes the **perimeter** can be found by using a formula, and this may be a more efficient approach.

For example, if you need to find the **perimeter** of a **regular octagon** whose sides are each 7.3 cm long, it would make more sense to multiply 7.3 by 8 than it would be to add 7.3 eight times. The **perimeter** comes out to be 58.4 cm no matter whether you multiply or add.

In order to find the perimeter of the **obtuse scalene triangle** below, add the three sides:

$$14.3 + 9.7 + 7.2 = 31.2$$

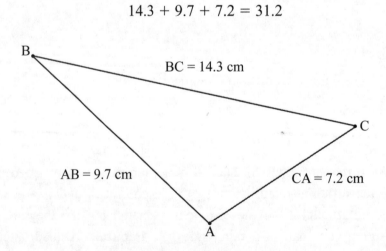

Figure 4.3 Obtuse Scalene Triangle

Since a **square's** four sides are all the same length, in order to find its **perimeter**, all you need is the length of one side, which you can multiply by 4. The perimeter could be written using the formula: P = 4s where s = the length of one side. To find the **perimeter** of a **square** whose side length is 12 cm, plug 12 into the formula P = 4s.

$$P = 4 \times 12$$
$$P = 48$$

Opposite sides of a **rectangle** are equal. That is, a **rectangle** has two lengths that are the same measure and two widths that are the same measure. In order to find the **perimeter** of a **rectangle**, you could use the formula P = 2L + 2W, where L = length and W = width, or you could double the length and add it to double the width. We can find the **perimeter** of a **rectangle** with a length of $5\frac{1}{4}$" and a width of $3\frac{1}{2}$" using the formula P = 2L + 2W.

$$P = 2(5\frac{1}{4}) + 2(3\frac{1}{2})$$
$$P = 10\frac{1}{2} + 7$$
$$P = 17\frac{1}{2}$$

Area is the size of the region that a shape covers. **Area** is a two-dimensional surface, like a piece of paper, and is measured in square units. In order to find the area of a specific geometric shape, you have to apply the formula for finding the area of that shape.

To find the **area** of a **triangle**, use the formula A = $\frac{1}{2}bh$, which is sometimes written as A = $\frac{bh}{2}$, where b is the length of the **base** of the **triangle** and h is the **height** of the triangle. Any side of the triangle can be considered the base or bottom. However, the height of a triangle depends on the base that you select. The height of a triangle is found by measuring a **perpendicular** (drawn at a right angle) segment from the **base** to the **vertex** (a point where two segments meet) above it.

In the obtuse triangle below, the **base** is the distance from A to B. The **height** is found by measuring the segment that is **perpendicular** to the **base** and connects to the **vertex** above it; in this example, the distance from D to C is the height. A, B, and C are the vertices of the triangle (vertices is the plural of vertex). If the length of AB is 8 cm and the distance from D to C is 3 cm, what is the area of triangle ABC?

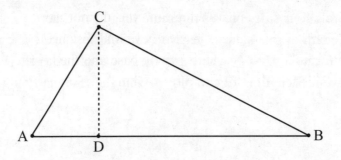

Figure 4.4 Obtuse Triangle

Use the formula: $A = \frac{1}{2}bh$ and substitute 8 for **b** and 3 for **h** to get $\frac{1}{2} \times 8 \times 3$ which equals 12. Therefore, the area of triangle ABC is 12 cm².

To find the area of a **rectangle**, you need to multiply the **length** by the **width**; this can be written as **LW**. It does not matter whether you name the shorter side the **width** or the longer side the **width** since you will to be multiplying **length** by **width** anyway, and the order in which you multiply does not affect the answer (e.g., 3 × 5 = 15 and 5 × 3 = 15).

A **square** is also a **rectangle**, but one whose length and width are the same measure. Sometimes you will see the formula for the area of a square written as A = s × s or A = s². To find the **area** of a **square** with side lengths of 6.5 cm, use the formula:

$$A = s^2$$
$$A = (6.5)^2$$
$$A = 42.25 \text{ cm}^2$$

The formula for finding the area of a **parallelogram** is **A = bh**, where **b** is the **base** and **h** is the **height**. Remember that the **height** is the perpendicular distance from the **base** to the **vertex** above it. See the diagram below:

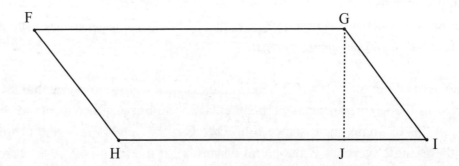

Figure 4.5 Parallelogram

When finding the area of a parallelogram, you do not need to know the length of the side that is not the base. In the example above, the distance FH and GI (which is the same) is not needed. You only need to know the base and the height. Find the area of the parallelogram above if HI = 18 cm and GJ = 10 cm.

Using the formula:

$$A = bh$$
$$A = 18 \times 10$$
$$A = 180 \text{ cm}^2$$

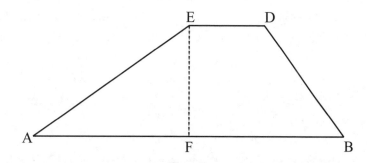

Figure 4.6 Trapezoid

The formula for the area of a **trapezoid** $A = h\dfrac{b_1 + b_2}{2}$ where $h =$ the **height** and b_1 and b_2 are the **bases**. A **trapezoid** has two **bases**. One is labeled $b1$ and the other is $b2$. It doesn't matter which one you label b_1 and which one you label b_2 since you are finding the average of both **bases** and then multiplying that by the **height**. As mentioned during the discussion of parallelograms, when finding the area of a trapezoid, you do not need to know the length of all of the sides. All you need are the lengths of the two bases and the height. Find the area of the trapezoid above if ED = 4 cm, AB = 12 cm, and EF = 6 cm.

$$A = h\frac{b_1 + b_2}{2}$$
$$A = 6\frac{12 + 4}{2}$$
$$A = 6 \times \frac{16}{2}$$
$$A = 6 \times 8$$
$$A = 48 \text{ cm}^2$$

A **circle** is a geometric shape that is not considered a polygon because it does not have straight edges. The distance around a circle is called the **circumference**; the term *perimeter* is used for polygons. Measuring around a circle in order to find its circumference would be very difficult because the shape is curved. It is more accurate and simpler to use the formula for finding the circumference because it involves measuring a segment that is straight and therefore easier to measure than the curved circumference itself. There are two different straight measures you can use. First is the distance from the center of the circle to a point on the circumference, which is called the **radius**. Or, you can measure all the way across the circle from one point on the circumference to another, through the center of the circle; this is called the **diameter**. The diameter is twice the length of the radius. There are two different formulas to find the **circumference** of a circle, and either can be used depending on the information provided in the problem. These formulas are: $C = 2\pi r$ and $C = \pi d$ where r = radius, d = diameter, and π represents the mathematical constant which is approximately equal to 3.14. In math, π is the ratio of the **circumference** to the **diameter** of any and every circle.

Let's try some examples. Find the **circumference** of a circle whose radius is 6 cm. Write your answer in terms of π, which means leave π in your answer; do not plug in 3.14.

$$C = 2\pi r$$
$$C = 2\pi \times 6$$
$$C = 12\pi \text{ cm}$$

Find the circumference of a circle whose diameter is 20 cm. Use 3.14 for π.

$$C = \pi d$$
$$C = 3.14 \times 20$$
$$C = 62.8 \text{ cm}$$

To find the **area** of a circle, use the formula $A = \pi r^2$. You may be asked to write the area in terms of π or asked to substitute in a numerical value for π, typically 3.14.

Find the **area** of circle G to the right if GH = 8 cm. Use 3.14 for π.

$$A = \pi r^2$$
$$A = 3.14 \times 8^2$$
$$A = 3.14 \times 64$$

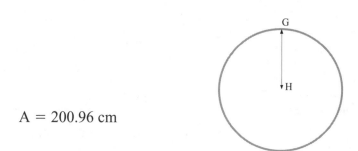

A = 200.96 cm

Three-dimensional geometric shapes are not flat like triangles, parallelograms, and circles. They have **volume**, which is defined as the amount of space occupied by a three-dimensional object. An object can have volume if you can imagine filling it up with water or even air. Common three-dimensional objects are cubes (think of a die), rectangular prisms (think of a cereal box), and spheres (think of a tennis ball). The volume of a rectangular prism is found by multiplying: width × length × height. This is the same formula for finding the volume of a cube, except since all of the sides of a cube are the same length, you can write the formula for finding the volume of a cube as $V = s^3$ where $s =$ the length of a side. Therefore, the volume of a cube whose side length is 9 inches would be 729 in^3 (read as 729 cubic inches) because $9 \times 9 \times 9 = 729$.

To find the volume of a rectangular prism with a height of 8 inches, a width of 4 inches, and a length of 7 inches, use the formula V = L W H

$$V = L\,W\,H$$
$$V = 7 \times 4 \times 8$$
$$V = 224$$

The formula for finding the volume of a **sphere** is $V = \dfrac{4}{3}\pi r^3$, so if you wanted to find the volume of a sphere whose diameter is 18 cm, you would use the formula above (leave your answer in terms of π). However, since you are given the diameter, which is 18, and you need the radius, you must divide 18 by 2 to get the radius. Remember that the radius of a circle is half of its diameter. In this example, the radius is 9 cm.

$$V = \frac{4}{3}\pi r^3$$
$$V = \frac{4}{3}\pi \times 9^3$$

$$V = \frac{4}{3}\pi \times 729$$
$$V = 972\,\pi$$

Plotting Coordinates

A coordinate grid is made up of two **axes**, one **horizontal** and one **vertical**. Both axes are number lines. The **x-axis**, which is horizontal, continues indefinitely in both directions with negative numbers to the left of 0 and positive numbers to the right. The **y-axis**, which is vertical, also continues indefinitely in both directions with negative numbers falling below zero and positive numbers above 0. The two axes break up the coordinate grid into four separate quadrants as shown below. The quadrants are numbered using Roman numerals. Quadrant I is in the upper right corner and quadrants II, III, and IV are found by going counterclockwise from quadrant I. The point where the *x*- and *y*-axes intersect has the coordinates (0,0) and is called the **origin**.

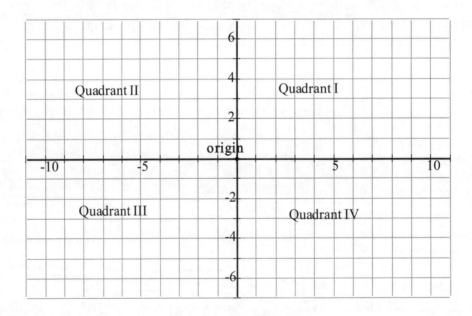

Figure 4.7 Coordinate Grid

Plotting points on a coordinate grid requires both an *x*-coordinate and a *y*-coordinate. The *x*-coordinate (which is the first coordinate in an ordered pair) tells you how many units to move left or right from the origin. The *y*-coordinate (which is the second coordinate in an ordered pair) tells you how many units to move up or down.

If you want to plot the point (4, 3) you will start at the origin. Move four spaces to the right, then move three spaces up. To plot the point (–2, 5) start at the origin, move two spaces to the left, then move five spaces up. To plot (1, –8), start at the origin. Move one space to the right and then eight spaces down. To plot (0, –3), start at the origin. Do not move any spaces left or right, then move three spaces down. See these points plotted below.

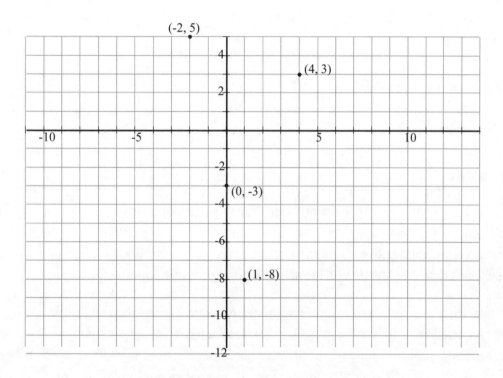

Figure 4.8 Plotted Coordinate Grid

To figure out the coordinates of points that are plotted, start at the origin. Move left or right on the *x*-axis until you are directly above or below the point. Count the spaces you moved. Moving right is positive and moving left is negative. Then, to determine the *y*-coordinate, move up or down until you get to the point. Moving up is positive and moving down is negative.

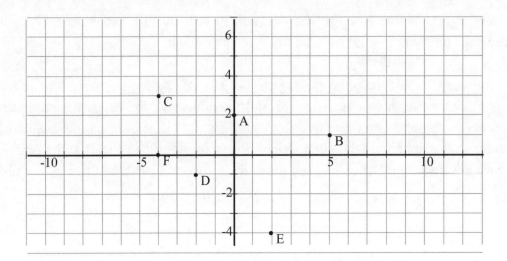

Figure 4.9 Coordinated Grid

Can you figure out the coordinates of the points graphed on the grid above? The coordinates for the points above are as follows: A (0, 2), B (5, 1), C (–4, 3), D (–2, –1), E (2, –4), and F (–4, 0).

Data Analysis

Collecting data is only part of statistics. The more important part of statistics is *analyzing* the data you collect so that you can see what it indicates. There are two kinds of data: **quantitative** and **qualitative**. Qualitative data deals with descriptions like colors or styles, while quantitative data deals with numbers like heights or amounts of money.

It is common to be asked to find the **mean, median, mode,** and **range** of a set of data. The **mean, median,** and **mode** are also called **measures of central tendency**. If you have numerical data, it is advisable to put the numbers in order from least to greatest. When the numbers are in ascending order, it allows you to find the **range, mode,** and **median**.

If you are collecting **qualitative** data, which deals with descriptions, it can be helpful to create a table to organize the data as you are collecting it. For example, if you asked a class of 25 first grade students to name their favorite color, you could make a **frequency table** to organize their responses. A **frequency table** is a special table that allows you to see the frequency of each data item. We can make a frequency table for the above example of favorite colors of first graders. The first column would be titled *colors* and will list the various colors the children may choose. (You should leave several blanks for any unexpected choices.) The second column is labeled **tally marks**, where you will make one tally for each response. It is common to group the tallies in groups of five by slashing the fifth tally across the first four, making what looks like a small bundle. The third column is titled *frequency*, which is the number of tally marks written as a numeral. Below is an example of what a frequency table for this data would look like.

Favorite Colors

Color	Tally Marks	Frequency
Red	~~////~~ //	7
Blue	///	3
Green	~~////~~	5
Orange	//	2
Pink	////	4
Purple	///	3
Yellow	/	1

With **qualitative data**, you cannot find all of the measures of central tendency, but you can find the **mode**, if there is one. The **mode** is the data item (or items) that occurs the most in a set of data. One trick to remember what mode means is to note that both *mode* and *most* start with the letters *mo*. As mentioned previously, it always makes sense to organize your data before trying to analyze it. In this example, red was the favorite color of the first graders—7 students chose red. It is possible to have more than one mode. If two or three colors were tied for the most popular, then those colors would all be considered to be the modes.

Quantitative data is numerical data. Quantitative data need not be collected in a frequency table. Because you are dealing with numbers, it is easy to put them in ascending order after you have collected the data in order to analyze it.

Let's say that you would like to take a closer look at the heights of a small class of seventh graders. The students are put into groups and asked to measure their heights to the nearest centimeter.

Here are the measurements collected:

145 cm	160 cm	155 cm	175 cm	162 cm
168 cm	170 cm	164 cm	170 cm	
148 cm	163 cm	67 cm	159 cm	

First, put the numbers in order from least to greatest. It's always a good idea to cross out the numbers as you reorder them, so that you don't miss any.

Here are the numbers in order:

145, 148, 155, 159, 160, 162, 163, 164, 167, 168, 170, 170, 175

A quick glance at the ordered data allows you to pick out the smallest and largest numbers. The largest number is 175 and the smallest is 145. The *difference* between those two numbers is the **range**. The range tells you how spread out the data items are. In this example, the range is 30.

Is there a **mode**? That is, is there a data item that occurs more frequently than any other? Each of the heights occurs once, except for 170 cm, which occurs twice. Therefore, the **mode** is 170. Remember, the **mode** is the *number of the item* that occurs most frequently, not the *number of times* that it occurs. It is a common error to think that the **mode** is 2 because 170 appeared twice; however, this is not correct.

The most common measure of central tendency, often referred to as "the average," is the **arithmetic mean**—usually called the **mean**. There are two steps you must follow in order to find the **mean**. First, you must find the sum of all of the numbers. Second, divide that sum by the number of numbers there are. In this example, when you add up all of the heights you get 2106. Divide that total by 13, because there are 13 heights recorded in the data set. The division in this example results in a whole number; the **mean** of these seventh graders' heights is 162 cm. If, however, the quotient does not turn out to be a whole number, feel free to round the answer. It makes sense to round your answer to the precision that your data represents. In this situation, since the heights are given to the units place, rounding to the units place is logical. Finding the mean requires the most work. You have to add all the numbers and then do long division, which is sometimes quite time-consuming. A strategy for remembering which is the mean and which is the median (commonly confused terms) is to remember that doing all that work is *mean*. The **mean** is the measure that requires the most mathematical computation.

Another measure of central tendency is called the **median**. Just as with the **mean**, finding the **median** requires two steps. First, put the data in order from least to greatest (we have already done that); second, find the number right in the middle. A great way to remember that the **median** is the middle number is to think of the median strip on a highway, which is found in the *middle* of the highway. In the example we are looking at, there are 13 numbers. How do you find the middle number? There are two ways that it can be done, and both work equally well. One way is to slash out the first and last number in your list. Then slash out the second number and the second to last number. In such a way, you will find that you have only one number left, which is the middle number, the median. Here the middle number is 163, so the median height is 163 cm.

Another way to find the middle number is to add 1 to the total number of items and divide that by 2. With 13 items, add 1 to get 14; 14 divided by 2 is 7. Therefore, the seventh number in the ordered list is the median.

What happens, however, if you do not have an odd number of data items? There will not be one middle number; there will be two middle numbers. When this happens, all you have to do is find the middle of those two middle numbers. Sometimes this is easy to do and can be done using mental math. For example, if the two middle numbers are 9 and 11, the number in the middle, or median, is 10. If the two middle numbers are 40 and 50, then the middle number, or median, is 45. But what if it is not so obvious? It is helpful to have a mathematical procedure to follow. Let's say the two middle numbers are 18 and 21. It is not so clear what number is halfway between them. You need to add the two numbers up and then divide by 2. This will give you the number right smack in the middle of the two numbers. First, $18 + 21 = 39$, then, $39 \div 2 = 19.5$. Therefore, 19.5 is the median. This process works with any two numbers you are confronted with—even ones that you can do in your head as shown above. Using the process above with the two numbers 40 and 50, you would add 40 and 50, which results in 90. Then, divide by 2 to get 45. If following a procedure is more comfortable for you, then you can always follow the one described above to find the **median** when you have an even number of data items.

Sometimes a set of numerical data can have a number that is much higher or lower than the rest of the numbers. When you have one of these numbers that seems to stand apart from most of the data items, it is called an **outlier**, because it lies outside the group of data. When there is an outlier (or two), the mean will be affected. Outliers may occur due to an error or may actually be accurate; even so, a number that is much larger or smaller than most of the data items will bring the mean up or down, sometimes significantly.

A simple graph, called a **line plot**, is suitable for presenting a small amount of data. Because line plots are easy to construct and read, they can be used with young children. Below is an example of a line plot detailing of a group of children's favorite animals.

Favorite Animal

```
  X
  X                                      X
  X          X                           X
  X          X          X          X     X
─────────────────────────────────────────────
 dog        cat       monkey      bear   hamster
```

Questions about line plots may be of a comparative nature, such as asking how many more children chose hamster over monkey. That answer would require subtraction, and we would need to compute that $3 - 1 = 2$. Or, you might be asked how many total children chose monkey, cat, or dog. In this case, you would have to add $1 + 2 + 4 = 7$. The visual aspect of a line plot makes it easy to see the results of the data without having to do any work.

When you are asked questions about information presented in a table, chart, or graph, you must make sure that you understand what information you are looking at, how it is being presented, and how it has been organized before you attempt to answer any questions posed. It is well worth the time to review the table, chart, or graph fully. In addition to making sure you have full comprehension of the data presented to you, you must also reread the questions asked about the data carefully. A quick reading of a question may result in a misunderstanding.

One kind of graph that is used to display data is a **pie graph**, which is also called a **circle graph**. A pie graph is used to show the relationship of parts to a whole, such as how a family spends its monthly budget. How a child spent one day is depicted in the pie graph below.

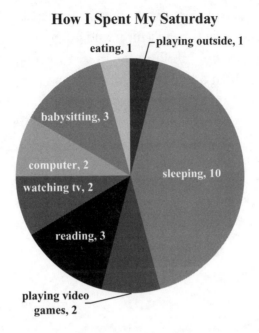

Figure 4.10 Pie Chart

The numerical value written next to each pie piece is the number of hours the child spent on each activity. ParaPro test questions may ask you to compare pieces of the graph to each other or may ask you to find the percent of the total. In this graph, there are eight pieces to the pie graph. You can see that the largest amount of the child's time was spent sleeping. The sum of all of the values is 24, the number of hours in one day. Sometimes this total number is not given, and you must find it by adding up all the values in the graph. Below are some questions that might be asked about the pie graph.

What percent of the day did the child spend babysitting?
Set up and solve the following proportion to answer the question.

$$\frac{3}{24} = \frac{x}{100}$$
$$x = 12.5$$

Therefore, the child spent 12.5% of his day babysitting.

How much more time did the child spend sleeping than reading?

$$10 - 3 = 7$$

The child spent 7 more hours sleeping than reading.

Another common graph is a **line graph**, which is used to show change over time. Some examples of data that is well-suited for a line graph are the amount of money in a bank account, a child's height from birth to the present, temperature of water over time, and population. Questions about a line graph may ask about a particular time period, but more often than not will ask you to compare the amount at one time to another time or to identify trends, such as during what time period there was the most change.

The line graph example below shows the depreciation of an automobile over a seven-year period. Notice that the x-axis shows the number of years from 0 to 7. The y-axis shows the amounts from 0 to $14,000 in $2,000 increments. Some questions about the line graph follow:

Automobile Depreciation

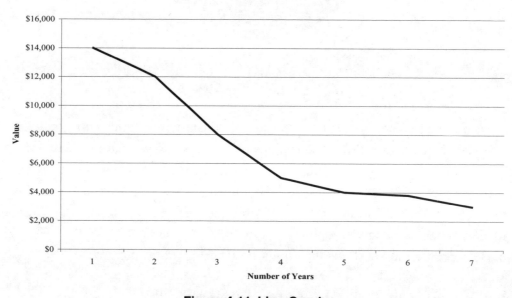

Figure 4.11 Line Graph

How many years after purchasing a new automobile does its value decrease $10,000?

> *Since the starting value of the car is $14,000, $10,000 less than $4,000. By looking at the graph, you can see that after 4 years, the car is worth $4,000.*

Between which two years does the automobile's value decrease most?

> *By examining the graph, you can see that between the first and second years after purchase the value of the car decreases $4,000. This is the highest decrease in one year. The next highest amount is between years two and three, where the value of the car decreases about $3,000.*

Line graphs are used to display a certain type of data, and bar graphs are used to display another type of data. Information about discreet quantities that can be compared to one another may be displayed in a bar graph. When interpreting the information from a bar graph, pay attention to the scale. Do not assume that each line is one unit; it may be 2, 5, or 500. The bars in a bar graph may be horizontal or vertical. The bar graph below shows the different hair colors of a class of students. Some questions about the graph follow:

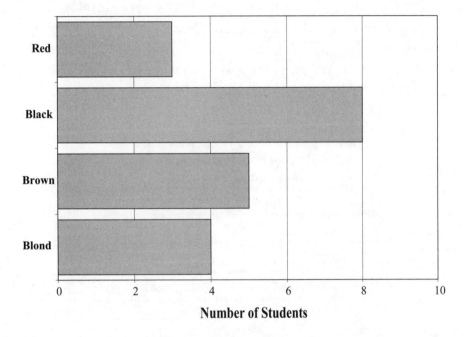

Number of Students

Figure 4.12 Bar Graph: Students' Hair Color

How many students in the class have red hair?

3 students have red hair.

How many more students have black hair than blond hair?

8 students have black hair and 4 students have blond hair, so subtract 4 from 9 to get 5. There are 5 more students who have black hair than blond hair.

What percent of the children in the class have brown hair?

Write the proportion below and solve it to answer the question.

$$\frac{6}{20} = \frac{x}{100}$$
$$x = 30$$

30% of the students in the class have brown hair.

Another common way for information to be presented is in a **table** or **chart**. Below is a table that shows the departure and arrival times for some trains traveling from Cold Spring, New York to Grand Central Terminal in New York City. You need to be able to read such a table in order to plan a trip or get to an appointment in time. Refer to the table below when answering the following questions:

**Travel Time on Metro North Railroad from
Cold Spring, New York, to
Grand Central Terminal**

Departure time	Arrival time
7:52 AM	9:10 AM
8:25 AM	9:37 AM
9:14 AM	10:26 AM
9:58 AM	11:14 AM
10:58 AM	12:18 PM
11:58 AM	1:18 PM

Which train will get you to the city before noon in the shortest amount of time?

In order to answer this question, you must figure out how long the trips are for the first four trains listed (the last two get in after noon). The first train is 78 minutes. The second and third are 72 minutes, and the fourth train is 76 minutes. Therefore, the two trains that you could take would be the one departing at 8:25 a.m. and the one departing at 9:14 a.m.

How many more minutes is the trip on the 10:58 a.m. train compared with the trip on the 7:52 a.m. train?

The 10:58 a.m. train takes 80 minutes, while the 7:52 a.m. train takes 78 minutes. Therefore it takes 2 more minutes on the 10:58 a.m. train.

Mathematics: Application of Math Skills and Knowledge to the Classroom

When assisting students who are working on math problems, especially word problems or those that have several steps, it is critical that you make sure the student reads the problem carefully; this usually involves reading it at least two times. It is not possible to arrive at the correct answer to a problem if you do not know what the question is. When a student asks for help, a good first step might be to ask him to read the problem aloud to you. It is tempting to tell a student what to do when he is confused or struggling. In fact, many students are hoping that you will do exactly that. However, don't explicitly direct the student. The student will not strengthen his mathematical or problem-solving skills if you step in and solve the problem for him. You want the student to learn how to get "unstuck" by herself. The best thing you can do when students are asking for help with challenging math problems, whether they are at the beginning of the problem or in the middle of it, is to ask the right questions that allow them to move forward.

Some good questions to ask the student:

- What are you trying to find?
- What is the problem asking?
- What information do you know?
- Is there any unnecessary information that you can disregard?
- Have you seen a problem like this before?
- Would it be helpful to draw a picture or a diagram?
- Do you understand all of the vocabulary in the problem?
- Should you organize the information in a table or chart?

- What might be a good first step?
- What do you need to know in order to answer the question?
- Should you organize the information in the problem in a different way?
- Is there more than one way to approach the problem?
- Is there a formula that you need to use?

Coordinate Geometry, Geometry, Ratios

Alisa plotted a rectangle with the following coordinates: A (5, –1), B (8, –1), C (8, –5), D (5, –5). She wanted to create another rectangle that would have twice the area of the first rectangle, and she plotted E (4, 1), F (10, 1), and G (10, 5). What would be the coordinates of the fourth point H, which would create a rectangle with twice the area of the first rectangle? What is the length of segment EH?

When given a problem that refers to points on a coordinate grid, it makes sense to ask the student if plotting the points might help her to answer the question. Many times students will not realize that they are expected to plot the points or draw a diagram if the problem does not specifically instruct them to do so. After plotting the points A, B, C, and D, the student will see that the area of that rectangle is 12 square units. After plotting the points E, F, and G, the student will see that point H must be located at (4, 5). Also, the student can then see the length of segment EH is 4 units. Encourage the student to check that the area of rectangle EFGH is, in fact, twice that of rectangle ABCD. Rectangle EFGH's area is 24 square units, which is twice that of rectangle ABCD's area. Attempting to approach this problem without a diagram would not be a good choice.

Time, Fractions, Working Backward

Hortence was planning to take the 8:45 AM train into the city. She wants to jog for $\frac{1}{2}$ hour, take a shower (15 minutes), stop and get coffee (10 minutes), and eat breakfast ($\frac{1}{3}$ hour). What time should she set her alarm for? It takes her 20 minutes to drive to the train station.

This problem requires that the student work backwards from the departure time of 8:45 AM. Notice that two of the times are written as a fraction of an hour ($\frac{1}{2}$ and $\frac{1}{3}$) rather than as a number of minutes. Asking the student if he needs to know how many minutes there are in $\frac{1}{2}$ an hour and $\frac{1}{3}$ of an hour will help focus him in on the fact that all of the times should be in minutes rather than fractional parts of an hour; this will make the problem easier to solve. There are 60 minutes in an hour, so divide 60 by 2 to find there are 30 minutes in a $\frac{1}{2}$ an hour. $\frac{1}{3}$ of an hour is found by dividing 60 by 3, which is 20.

Now that all the times listed are in minutes, ask the student how much time Hortence needs before getting on the 8:45 AM train? You will need to add the following: 30 + 15 + 10 + 20 + 20. The sum is 95 minutes. Hortence must set her alarm for 95 minutes before 8:45 a.m. At this point, ask the student how he can break up 95 minutes into easier to work with chunks. A logical way would be 60 minutes + 35 minutes = 95 minutes, because 60 minutes equals one hour. If you go back in time one hour before 8:45, you arrive at 7:45. Then you need to go back another 35 minutes, which brings you to 7:10. Therefore, Hortence needs to set her alarm for 7:10 AM. To check that the answer is correct, the student can start at 7:10 and then add the various amounts of time to see if he arrives at 8:45.

Divisibility

Carla's teacher asked the class to find all the numbers that are less than 100 and are divisible by 2, 3, 5, 9, and 10.

This problem requires that you have a thorough understanding of divisibility rules. A simple way to approach this challenge is to list all of the numbers that are divisible by 10 (that are less than 100). In such a way, you can drastically pare down the number of numbers you are dealing with. The multiples of 10 that are less than 100 are 10, 20, 30, 40, 50, 60 70, 80, and 90. Notice that all of these numbers are also divisible by 2 and 5. Now we have to check which of the above numbers are divisible by 3 and 9. Notice that 3 is a factor of 9, so any number that is divisible by 9 is also divisible by 3. So which numbers are divisible by 9? The only number in the group that is divisible by 9 is 90. Therefore, there is only one number that is less than 100 and is divisible by 2, 3, 5, 9, and 10; that number is 90.

Working With Time

Angel mows lawns during the summer. He charges $30 to cut each lawn and $10 if he weedwacks as well. During the months of July and August Angel mowed 48 lawns. He was only asked to weedwack one-third of those lawns. Angel rented the lawnmower for $50 for the summer. How much profit did he make?

There is a lot of information in this problem. Therefore, you must read it carefully so that you get all of the necessary details. In order to find Angel's profit, you need to know the total amount of money that he made and then subtract his expenses. Sometimes it's helpful to write out the information that you know in a list form.

How many lawns did Angel mow? 48

How many lawns did Angel weedwack? 16 ($\frac{1}{3}$ of 48 is 16 because 48 ÷ 3 = 16)

How much did he earn for mowing lawns? $1440 (48 × $30)

How much did he earn for weedwacking? $160 (16 × $10)

How much money did he spend on expenses? $50

Now that we have the information clearly presented, we can easily find the answer to the question with the following equation: (1440 + 160) – 50. Angel's profit was $1550.

Divisibility and Geometry

A parallelogram has an area of 80 cm². What are the possible measures of its height and base if both measures must be whole numbers?

This problem requires you to know the formula for the area of a parallelogram, which is base times height. However, this is really a divisibility problem because you are looking for all the whole number pairs that multiply to get 80. Remember the divisibility rules to find the factors of 80, and remember that factors come in pairs. Your list of factors should be 1, 2, 4, 5, 8, 10, 16, 20, 40, 80. However, this does not answer the question which asks for the possible bases and heights for the given parallelogram. One way to organize your answer is to make a chart of the different measures possible:

Base	Height
1	80
2	40
4	20
5	16
8	10
80	1
40	2
20	4

16	5
10	8

Statistics, Data Analysis

Mr. Singh earned \$400 a week for 8 weeks, then he earned \$600 a week for 4 weeks, then he earned \$350 for one week, then he earned \$675 for 3 weeks. What is greater: the *mean* or *median* amount of money that Mr. Singh earned during that time period?

The question asks you to determine whether the mean or median amount is greater. The data for this problem has not been presented in a list form; therefore, it is advisable to write out each weekly amount, so that no numbers are forgotten (For example, there were 8 weeks when Mr. Singh earned \$400, not just one.). Ask the student how many weeks Mr. Singh worked? By drawing his attention to this question, the student will notice that Mr. Singh worked for 16 weeks. The amounts that Mr. Singh earned are as follows:

400, 400, 400, 400, 400, 400, 400, 400
600, 600, 600, 600
350
675, 675, 675

Now that Mr. Singh's earnings are written out as one number for each week he worked, ask the student if it is necessary to organize the data in order to find the mean or the median. It will be necessary to put the numbers in order from least to greatest to find the median.

The numbers in order are:

350, 400, 400, 400, 400, 400, 400, 400, 400, 600, 600, 600, 600, 675, 675, 675

In order to determine the *median*, the student must select the middle number. However, this problem has 16 numbers. Ask the student how to find the median when there is an even number of numbers. The student should know he must find the average of the two middle numbers, which in this case are both 400; therefore, the median is \$400.

Ask the student how to find the mean of a group of numbers. This requires adding up all of the numbers and dividing by the number of numbers there are. Since there are 16 numbers (because Mr. Singh worked for 16 weeks), the sum must be divided by 16. The sum of all 16 numbers is 7975, and 7975 divided by 16 equals 498.4375. Since this problem is about money, the answer could be rounded to the nearest cent; therefore the mean is $498.44. It would also make sense to round to the nearest dollar, since the weekly amounts were presented in whole dollar amounts; therefore, you could round the answer to $498. After figuring out both the median and the mean, the student should be redirected to the question in the problem, which asks him to determine whether the mean or median is greater. The mean is greater than the median.

Statistics

Carlos has one more math test to take. His scores on the first five tests were 85, 92, 77, 80, and 100. What score must he get on his sixth test to have a mean of 87?

This problem requires a deep understanding of how to find the mean, because the student is not being asked to find the mean from a group of numbers, which is what he is usually asked to do. Instead, he is given the mean and some of the numbers. He must supply the missing number that would give a mean of 87. This problem can be approached by employing a guess-and-check method, trying different scores for the sixth test until a mean of 87 is found.

This method can be set up as follows:

$(85 + 92 + 77 + 80 + 100 + x) \div 6 = 87$
Plug in values for x, adjusting as you go along, until you get to a mean of 87.
Let's try $x = 95$
$(85 + 92 + 77 + 80 + 100 + 95) \div 6$
When $x = 95$, the mean would be 88.2, which is too high.
Let's try $x = 85$
$(85 + 92 + 77 + 80 + 100 + 85) \div 6$
When $x = 85$, the mean would be 86.5, which is too low.
Let's try $x = 90$
$(85 + 92 + 77 + 80 + 100 + 90) \div 6$
When $x = 90$, the mean would be 87.3, which is a little too high.
Let's try $x = 88$

$(85 + 92 + 77 + 80 + 100 + 88) \div 6$

When $x = 88$, the mean would be 87.

Therefore, Carlos must earn 88 on his final test to have a mean of 87.

A more mathematical method can also be used, which is more efficient. If the mean of the six tests must be 87, then the sum of all of the test scores must be 522, which is found by multiplying 87 by 6. The sum of all 6 tests must be 522, but Carlos has only taken five tests. The sum of the first five tests is 434. So, to find out what Carlos needs to score on the sixth test to have a mean of 87, subtract 434 from 522. This gives 88, which is what Carlos must earn on the sixth test.

Writing Skills and Knowledge

GRAMMAR (SYNTAX)

Grammar is the study and the formulation of how words relate to one another in a sentence. Consider the non–native attempting to speak English:

"Please…fish…little…cost…good…thank you."

The foreigner doesn't know English grammar. He or she has learned some words but not how to put them together. When the speaker develops his/her language skills, he learns to make connections. He doesn't have to cover his heart with folded hands, drop to his knees, and look longingly with his eyes only. He can say: "*I love you.*" To a native speaker, this sentence seems so "natural," what else could it be? Well, if you were a Roman, the verb would come last, and there would be no separate *I*. In some languages, the three words would be one word alone. In short, there are more than six thousand human languages that we know of, and all of these have different ways of relating words to each other; all have different grammars.

Remarkably, by the time children are three years old they have "learned" the grammar of their native languages. However, like the fish who takes the water it swims in for granted, unless we study our language, we may be unaware that the connections we make are not natural, nor are they given. Rather, we have absorbed a human-made system.

We speak and write our language following rules about how the words and phrases can be strung together. Grammar or syntax is the collection of rules that describe how to connect words, what goes next to what, in which order. To communicate what's inside our heads or hearts to another, we need to know what does, what can, and what words and phases can't go together.

Functions: In addition to rules of relationship, grammar also identifies what the different parts do, or their function. Let's examine the sentence:

> *Jack looked at Jill lovingly.*

Jack is the subject. That is, the function of the word *Jack* is as doer of an action. *Looked* is the action that *Jack* did. We call such action words *verbs*. *Jill,* unlike Jack, is "the done to." Jill's function is as *object,* not *subject*. Then, take the word *lovingly*. This word functions to describe the verb/action (how did *Jack* look?). *Lovingly* is functioning as an adverb, a part of speech we will soon discuss.

The words and groups of words in any sentence are identified, then, by their function, the way the players in a baseball game are identified. Ted Williams may be the batter at one time, and at another, an outfielder. It depends on what function he is performing. So, too, a word can play various functions depending upon how it relates to other words in a sentence. In the example above, *look* is an action verb, what *Jack* did. However, consider the difference: *The look of love is in your eyes*. In this case, *look* is a noun and subject of the sentence.

EIGHT PARTS OF SPEECH: DESCRIBING THEIR FUNCTIONS

English grammar is built upon the interrelationships of eight functions, or parts of speech: *nouns, pronouns, verbs, adjectives, adverbs, voice, prepositions, and conjunctions*. These are described and studied in this section. We will also identify the grammar and punctuation problems that often occur with parts of speech. Some of these problems are discussed again in other sections.

Nouns

Nouns name people, things, places, animals, items that have shape and form, things we can touch. Things, however, can be less tangible and refer to abstractions such as ideas of freedom, independence, or concepts such as number and shape, or disciplines such as the sciences, the arts. Some nouns name groups of persons or things.

Number: nouns change in number–they can be one (singular), or more than one (plural.) Most nouns show this change in number by adding an *s*. One boat becomes two boats. However, some nouns show number change differently. One woman doesn't become two womans, rather, she becomes two women.

Collective nouns often cause difficulties because of number. They can be confusing because they refer to something made up of more than one.

Jury (of citizens)   flock (of geese)   team (of players)
Band (of musicians)   collection (of coins)   committee (of members)

But grammatically they are treated as singulars, as *its* rather than *theys*. For instance, *"the team played their last game"* is grammatically incorrect and should be *"the team played its last game."*

Table 6.1 Types of Nouns

Common Nouns		Proper Nouns	
book, bicycle, cat, ice cream cars, house, skyscraper		Tom Cruise, Macy's, General Lee, Madonna	
Concrete	**Abstract**		**Collective**
stone, hand, skunk, picture	democracy, free speech, freedom, independence		club, army, squadron, team, committee, group

Noun Case: What do nouns do? First, the subject of a sentence is always a noun, as was *Jack*. But nouns can also be objects, as was *Jill* (the receiver of the verb's action). Or, in their Possessive Case form, nouns are expressing belonging to, or a quality of. Case, then, means the function a noun plays in relationship to other words. There are three cases, and we will see the same when we examine pronouns.

Table 6.2 Types of Noun Case

Subjective Case a noun that is the subject	Objective Case a noun that is an object	Possessive Case a noun that owns or belongs to something
The cat chased the mouse. Cat is a noun in subjective case.	*The cat chased the mouse.* Mouse is a noun in objective case.	*I lost Jack's ticket.* Jack's is a noun in possessive case

Note, however, we can rearrange these nouns – depending on what we want to say – changing their function and their case, like moving Ted Williams from the outfield to first base:

> *The mouse escaped from the cat.*

Now, our rodent is the subject, and our *cat* is the object of the preposition *from*. And we mean something different from our first sentence.

Note, too, the noun in the **Possessive Case** indicates ownership by use of apostrophe (') and the letter *s*: *The cat's prey instinct made him constantly hunt for mice.* (whose instinct? The cat's). Or, *The girls' dates were all waiting for them outside in the schoolyard.* (Whose dates? The girls'.)

Pronouns

Pronouns stand–in for a noun and give us ways to substitute for nouns, and thus we can speak with fewer and shorter words and phrases, and with greater variety! Consider what we would face without pronouns:

> *Jimi Hendrix is well-established in the history of music. Hendrix is the King of Rock, and Hendrix's guitar playing is legendary. Jimi Hedrix's death by an overdose made Hendrix an icon of the 1960s. Like Janis Joplin, Jimi Hendrix was the image of overindulgent youth.*

Now, with pronouns:

> *Jimi Hendrix is well-established in the history of music. He is the King of Rock, and his guitar playing is legendary. Jimi Hendrix's death by an overdose made him an icon of the 1960s.Like Janis Joplin, he is the image of overindulgent youth.*

Antecedents: Because a pronoun substitutes for a noun, when one is used, the noun for which it is substituting has to be clear. For example, the pronoun "*he*" only communicates if we know the noun for which "*he*" is substituting. An example would be: *He died by assassination*. This sentence without a reference to which the pronoun is referring, makes little sense. However, the following sentence clears up any confusion:

> *Abraham Lincoln is a symbol as much as he is a former President. He died by assassination.*

Now, the pronoun *he* is comprehensible because we have the antecedent noun for which it is substituting: Abraham Lincoln is *he*.

Antecedent is a term you will see in several important language situations. It means that which comes before. In the case of a pronoun's antecedent, it is the noun to which the pronoun refers. Every pronoun has its Abraham Lincoln, if it is being used clearly! A clear and consistent relationship between the pronouns and to what or to whom it refers (antecedents) is a major grammar concern called **Pronoun Agreement** (A^2 = Antecedent + Agreement).

Pronoun Types & Cases: In the examples above, we have used different forms of pronouns (he, him, I, and me), so let's give these differences a name and description. The most frequently used are the *Personal Pronouns*. But glance at the left column in the table below to view the eight various types of pronouns.

Table 6.3 Pronouns: Their Number and Function

Pronoun Types	Singular/Plural	Plural	Function
Personal	*I, me*	*we, us*	Refer to specific persons or things, always to a noun: *The ship is lost. It was last in contact 2 days ago.*
	you, you	*you, you*	
	he, it, she, him, her	*they, them*	
Possessive	*my, mine*	*our, ours*	Indicate possession: *my dog; your cat; his car; our home; their luggage*
	your, yours	*your, yours*	
	his, her, hers, its	*their, theirs*	

(continued on next page)

Table 6.3 Pronouns: Their Number and Function
(continued from previous page)

Pronoun Types	Singular/Plural	Plural	Function
Reflexive (intensive)	*myself*	*ourselves*	Emphasize a noun or pronoun: *Myself was shocked.* *You can get your candy yourselves.*
	yourself	*yourselves*	
	him, her, itself	*themselves*	
Relative	*that, which, who, whom, whose*		Introduce a relative clause that describes/modifies a subject: *The book that caused great controversy.*
Interrogative	*that, which, who, whom, whose*		Introduce a question: *Who said that?*
Demonstrative	*this, that, these, those*		Point to a specific noun, and may also serve as the subject. *That book is controversial.* *That solves the problem.*
Indefinite	*Every, each, everyone, nothing, something, everything no one, nobody, neither, everything, anybody, one* (Number=Singular)		Refer to nonspecific things; mostly function as nouns. But also can work as adjectives. *Something must be done.* *Each day is better than the last.*
	Few, both, many, several (Number=Plural)		Number agreement *Many are called but few are chosen.*
	All, any, more, most, some (can be singular or plural)		*Some of the mail has arrived.* *Some of the letters have arrived.*
Reciprocal	Same as reflexive above		*I gave myself a haircut.*

In addition to the eight types, **pronouns**—like nouns—have three cases. Recall, case refers to function in relations with other words. For instance, the personal pronoun *I* is the **Subjective Case** since its meaning (the doer, the subject) also puts it in a specific relation to another word, a verb:

> *I gave my ticket away.*

I, however, has different meanings and relations with verbs and these differences are expressed by case. Thus, when *I* is not the doer/subject of the verb, it may be the *done to* and object of the verb. When this occurs, the pronoun *I* changes its case to the **Objective Case** and becomes *me*.

> *John gave me his ticket.*

Table 6.4 Personal and Relative Pronouns

Pronoun Type	Subjective (Nominative) Case		Objective Case		Possessive Case	
	Singular	**Plural**	**Singular**	**Plural**	**Singular**	**Plural**
Personal Pronoun	I	we	me	us	my, mine	our, ours
	you	you	you	you	your	yours
	he, she,	they	him, her	them	his, hers	their, theirs
	it		it		its	
Relative Pronouns	who	whoever	whom	whomever	whose	whosever

Notice, too, *his* which expresses belonging is in the **Possessive Case**. Only two of the eight pronoun types have the case form or aspect. Unlike nouns that show possession by adding an apostrophe *s*, or by changing their ending (e.g., *woman* to *women*) pronouns in the possessive case remain unchanged. The **relative pronouns** bring up an important topic. That is, how we speak is sometimes different from how we write. In speech, we are allowed to be ungrammatical. For instance, many, perhaps most of us, would ask: *Who did you go to the movies with*? But this is not correct. *Who* is not the subject, *you* is the subject. It is the object of the preposition *with*; hence, the question needs the objective case: *Whom did you go to the movies with*? Again, like nouns, pronouns are either singular or plural.

Verbs

Verbs are where the action is! *The cannibals ate their victims*. The **action verb** is *eating*. Another kind of verb doesn't so much describe an action, but rather it connects, and is called a ***linking verb***. For example: *Jack seems excited to have gotten that telephone call. Seems* is a linking verb; it doesn't describe an action such as eating, or travelling, or snoring. It does connect *Jack* to *excited*, and in making this link, it tells us something about *Jack*.

A third kind of verb is called a ***helping verb***. These help another verb – which is the major one – to express a nuance, often a time aspect of the main verb. For instance: *I am going to the movies. Going* is the real action, the main verb; *am* is helping by giving *going* the sense of in process. Or, consider this sentence: *I had seen her before she saw me*. Seen is the main verb (act of seeing); *had* is its helping verb. It expresses that the seeing was done earlier, before she saw me. In fact, *to be* and *to have* are the most common, frequently used helping verbs, and they are used primarily to indicate verb tense as you will see below.

However, there are other, less common helping verbs, and there are a few more things to be said about active verbs, so let's examine this table below before moving on to verb tenses.

Table 6.5 Types of Verbs

Action Verbs Two forms	Linking Verbs Connect the Subject to a complement, usually an adjective or a subject complement (see below)	Helping or Auxiliary Verbs Two forms
Transitive Verb is one that can have an object: *Lincoln gave his famous speech.*	Major linking verbs: *be, feel, become, seem, smell, remain, look, taste, keep, appear, stay, grow, act*	*Auxiliary: to be, to have; to do*. The verbs *to be* and *to have* are so frequently used that you should be familiar with their various forms
Intransitive Verb: does not have an object, usually followed by an adverb: *The Dow fell sharply today.*	*I feel good*. Good is an adjective. *Dr. Jekyll became Mr. Hyde*. Mr. Hyde is the subject complement. *The speaker of the house is Nancy Pelosi.* Nancy Pelosi is the subject complement.	*Modal Auxiliaries* express special meanings such as *obligation, doubt, possibility, can, must, may, should, could, ought to* *He should see a doctor.* *You can travel now.* *She must be on time.*

Grammar Highlight: Action verbs usually are followed by adverbs; but linking verbs are followed by adjectives. Because of how they sound in speech, modals with *have* are often incorrectly written as *of*: *The car must of run out of gas.* Which should read: *The car must have run out of gas.*

Verbs have various forms. Identifying these helps us understand the various ways a verb is used. Right from the start, we need to know how to distinguish between the two forms. Regular verbs that follow the same general pattern: add *–s* on to the verb base to form the 3rd person, singular in present tense. Past tense adds *–ed* to the base verb. Irregular verbs are stubborn individuals who follow their own patterns (**irregular verbs**). Consequentially, since the irregulars are individuals who dance to their own tune, we cannot apply rules to them, but have to learn them as individuals. Irregular verbs change either the 3rd person singular, or the past tense, or both, and some verbs like to be make unique changes in other persons and tenses (see lie, lay, rise below).

Look at the tables above where both to be and to have, irregular verbs, can be studied and contrasted with regular verbs. All regular verbs follow the same pattern in 3rd person singular and in past tense.

Table 6.6 Verb Person

Person	Present Tense Singular (add s for 3rd, person singular)		Plural		Past Tense (base+*ed*)	
1st person, singular or plural	I	I act	we	we act	I acted	we acted
2nd person, singular or plural	you	you act	you	you act	you acted	you acted
3rd person, singular or plural	he/she/it	she acts	they	they act	he/she/it acted	they acted
1st person, singular or plural	I want		we want		I wanted	we wanted
2nd person, singular or plural	you want		you want		you wanted	you wanted
3rd person, singular or plural	she wants		they want		they wanted	they wanted

Verb Person: which of the 3 available is doing the action or linking? Is it the 1st, 2nd, or the 3rd?

Number: as with pronouns, how many? One, or more than one? Singular or plural?

Table 6.7 Verb Tense

Present Tense		Past Tense		Past Perfect		Verb Tense
Singular	**Plural**	**Singular**	**Plural**	**Singular**	**Plural**	**Verb Number**
I am you are he/she/it is	you are we are they are	I was you were he/she/it was	we were you were they were	I have been you have been he, she, it has been	we have been you have been they have been	The underlined verbs identify where agreement problems occur. Note that the verb to be uses the verb to have as its helping verb to express a past tense.
I have, you have he/she it has	we have you have they have	I had you had he, she, it had	we had you had they had	I have had you have had he, she, it has had	we have had you have had they have had	Note that to have uses itself as a helping verb to express the past perfect time.

Table 6.8 Regular and Irregular Verbs

Verb form	Regular	Regular	Irregular	Irregular	Irregular	
Base	want	talk	be	have	get	Problems with verb agreement in 3rd person, singular of present tense. Problems with irregular verbs in 3rd person, singular of present tense, and also with past tense
Infinitive	to want	to talk	to be	to have	to get	Infinitive phrase as subject of sentence: *To talk too much is rude.*
Past	wanted	talked	was/were	had	got	
Past Participle	wanted	talked	been	had	gotten	Past participle–*to be*–forms passive voice *Jesse James was wanted for robbery.*
Present Participle	wanting	talking	being	having	getting	Present in process: *I am talking to her right now.*
Gerund	wanting	talking	being	having	getting	Gerund phrase as subject: *Getting a job has proven to be difficult.*

Verb Tenses: Verbs also change according to the time of their action or linking. These time changes are called **tenses**. Consider how tense adds to our ability to communicate with one another. Imagine, for instance, arriving at someone's house who, being a generous host, offers you lunch. We take for granted that it's a simple matter to decline without offense by explaining: *No, thank you, I ate lunch but an hour ago.* If we had no past tense, we would be forced to act out and hope to be understood, perhaps by: "I eat..." and then indicating past by gesturing behind our shoulder with our hand.

In writing, we dramatically alter the meaning of what we say by our use of tense:

I was studying when the lights went out and threw the dorm into darkness for the rest of the evening.

I had already studied when the lights went out and threw the dorm into darkness for the rest of the evening.

Present Tense: actions occurring now, actions occurring regularly, or general truths:

I see you sitting there; every day.

I speak to the homeless man.

Love is stronger than hate.

Past Tense: Actions that happened before now and are over and done with:

I ate dinner an hour ago.

Future Tense: Action that will happen in the future:

I will eat dinner within the hour.

Finally, there are a few verbs that give people trouble such as the differences between the verbs *to lay* and *to lie*, or those between *raise* and *rise*.

Table 6.9 Irregular Verbs–To Lay, To Lie or to Rise

Infinitive	Present Participle	Present Tense	Past Tense	Past Participle
To lie—recline, be prostrate	lying	lie: *he lies in be*d	lay	lain
To lay—to place	laying	lay	laid	laid
To rise	rising	rise	rose	risen
To raise	raising	raise	raise	raised
To lie—express a falsehood	lying	lie	lied	lied

Subject Verb Agreement (agr): Speaking trains native speakers to follow this rule quite 'naturally'; however, there are some grammatical structures that give many writers problems. First, let's look at the typical sentence and how the law of agreement works:

Yesterday the children ate their lunches at their desks.

The verb must agree with the subject's person and number. The subject is *children*; its number is plural and its person is the 3rd (see chart above). Now it's true that the writer also had to know the correct past form of the verb *eat* which is *ate* and not *eated*, and also the correct tense.

Most agreement problems have to do with number, which means determining if the subject is singular or plural. Indeed, verb agreement with subject is very similar to pronoun agreement with antecedents, and the chart below will help this.

Table 6.10 Verb Agreement

Problem or Issue	Verb must agree with number of subject	Pronoun must agree with number of antecedent
Compound subject: two subjects connected by *and* (N=P)	*Susan B. Anthony and Elizabeth Cady Stanton <u>were</u> extraordinary women; they <u>were</u> geniuses.*	*Susan B. Anthony and Elizabeth Cady Stanton were extraordinary women; <u>they</u> were geniuses.*
Compound Subject: one entity despite appearing to be two subjects (N=S)	*Ben & Jerry's <u>makes</u> the best ice cream.*	*Do you like Ben & Jerry's? <u>It's</u> my favorite!*
Subject separated from verb can confuse	*The winner amongst all the contestants goes to the Caribbean.* Or, *The winners of the race go to the Caribbean.*	*The winner amongst all the contestants goes to the Caribbean. He or she will be happy.* *The winners of the race go to the Caribbean. They will be happy.*
Indefinite Pronoun	<u>*Each*</u> *of the contestants <u>gets</u> a new car.* Generally Singular	*Each of the contestants gets a new car. <u>He or she</u> will select a model.*
Correlative Conjunctions: Neither...nor Either... or	Verb agrees with number of the subject closest to it (or the 2nd subject) *Neither the stockholders nor the <u>CEO seems</u> concerned about the sudden dip in profits.*	Pronoun agrees with the antecedent closest to it. *Neither the stockholders nor the <u>CEO seems</u> concerned about the sudden dip in the profits of <u>his</u> company.*
Collective Nouns (N=S) Generally Singular	*The committee <u>announces</u> the much awaited decision today.* *Economics is a tough subject as is statistics.* *Measles/mumps <u>keeps</u> you in bed.*	*The committee announces <u>its</u> much awaited decision today.* *Economics gets <u>its</u> bad reputation from its many false predictions.*
Postponed subject: subject follows the verb Verb agrees with subject (not complement)	*At the end of the corridor is a <u>small door.</u>* *The <u>real power</u> is the men behind the scenes.*	*At the end of the corridor is a small door, <u>it's</u> black and tan.* *The real <u>power</u> is the men behind the scenes, hidden though it is, it's what really makes things happen*

(continued on next page)

Table 6.10 Verb Agreement *(continued from previous page)*

Who, which, that can confuse	*Lucinda is the <u>one</u> who resc<u>ued</u> the bird.* *The boys want to be on the <u>team</u> that sco<u>res</u> highest.*	
Gerund phrase: a gerund with object Gerund phrases take singular form	*<u>Following speeding cars</u> is a dangerous thing to do.*	*Following speeding cars is dangerous. Doing <u>it</u> is a foolish thing to do.*

Voice: Active and Passive

English strongly prefers that the subject come first, followed by the verb, then by the object or recipient of the actions, or, if a linking verb, by a subject complement or an adjective.

> *The batter hit→→the ball hard.*

> *The Academy of Film Arts gave→→Julia Roberts an award.*

This pattern with the subject going toward (with the verb) the object (formula, S+V+O) is the *Active Voice*.

However, writers sometimes (correctly, often incorrectly) use the *Passive Voice*. This reverses the formula, O+V+S, making a sentence with the object of the verb first, then the verb, and finally, the subject.

> *The ball was hit hard by the ←batter.*

The action is turned around, the subject, *batter*, fades and the focus is on the object, the *ball*. In short, the passive voice puts the object in the limelight, and it weakens both the act (the verb action) and the subject (the doer). By contrast, then, the active voice highlights the subject and emphasizes that she/he is the doer. So, when is it correct to use the passive voice? Answer: when the object is more important than the subject. Consider:

> *Julia Roberts was awarded an Oscar for her performance in* A Civil Action.

Or in the active voice:

> *The committee awarded Julia Roberts an Oscar.*

The first sentence is preferred because the fact that Roberts won the Oscar is more important than the committee that did the awarding. Now let's examine the structure of that passive voice: *Julia Roberts* is the object, *was rewarded*, the verb, and the subject has so faded from importance that it isn't even in the sentence!

Was rewarded also shows us the formula for a passive voice verb = to be + past participle.

> *The* Mona Lisa *is considered a Renaissance masterpiece by most art critics.*

Is (to be) *considered* is the past participle of *consider*. In this case the doer is nowhere to be seen. A much stronger, active sentence is:

> *Art critics consider the* Mona Lisa *a masterpiece.*

Here's another case: *This is to inform you that your application has been rejected.* By who? As a rule, the active voice is the most effective, and it's always more concise and less wordy.

While in a few instances, using the passive voice is fine, and, more rarely still, preferred, in the vast majority of instances, the passive voice is discouraged for two good reasons: the passive voice is weaker because the subject as actor is backstage–if at all, in the rear rather than up–front. Thus, "the action" is muted and diluted. The passive voice is more wordy–always. Count the words in the two sentences above. Count them in the two following sentences.

Active: *The instructor discussed the requirements and the time schedule for this semester's class.*

Passive Voice: *The requirements and the time schedule for this semester's course were discussed by the teacher.*

Adjectives and Adverbs

Adjectives are words that describe nouns or pronouns. We use adjectives a lot in speech and writing; many common ones pepper our conversations. For example: *a good day*; *a soft sound*; *a yellow car*.

Adverbs have more possible roles than the adjective. Adverbs can describe verbs (*he spoke slowly*); they can describe adjectives (*His face had a sickly yellow look. She is very sad.*); they can describe adverbs like *themselves*; they can describe infinitives (*he was urged to go quickly.*)

Adverbs often answer the question *how*? How did he go? *Quickly*.
Adverbs often end in *–ly*: *quickly, smoothly, sleepily, coldly*

Those adverbs that don't end in *–ly* are often those that refer to time and frequency:

> *today, yesterday, often tomorrow, soon, never, always, never, sometimes*

Grammar Highlight: Remembering that adjectives modify nouns, and that, contrarily, adverbs modify verbs, adjectives, or another adverb will help you to identify what a prepositional phrase is doing in a sentence.

Prepositions

"Never end a sentence with a preposition!" But what's a preposition? We use them very frequently (look at the list below), but defining them clearly is difficult. Prepositions, for instance, are words that connect a noun to other parts of its sentence. Or, prepositions are words that express space (on the table), time (at the appointed hour), and direction (towards the North Pole). There are two kinds of prepositions—simple, one-word prepositions, and group prepositions.

It's easier to get a handle on the simple, one-word prepositions by identifying them in the prepositional phrase (where they most often are to be found, except when they end a sentence by themselves!). You will find the preposition before a noun or a pronoun, and it will almost always be working as an adjective or an adverb, modifying a part of the sentence of which it is itself a part. The most common:

> above, behind, except, off, toward
> above, below, for, on, under
> across, beneath, from, onto, underneath
> after, beside, in, out, until
> against, between, inside, outside, up

along, beyond, into, over, upon
among, by, like, through, with
around, despite, near, throughout, within
at, during, of, to, without

Group prepositions are made up of more than one word:

in addition to	in place of
next to	in front of
as well as	along with
according to	due to
in conjunction with	because of

Infinitives: The word *to* is one of the most used prepositions. When you find it, you are fairly sure that it is the first word in a prepositional phrase. However, another important construction using the word *to* is the ***verb infinitive***, the base of a verb preceded by *to*. Infinitives: *to go*; *to see*; *to believe*; *to investigate*. All verbs have this simple infinitive form.

In a sentence, the infinitive can be a noun, both subject:

> <u>*To read*</u> *is heaven on earth to Julia.*

or an object,

> *Julia likes <u>to read.</u>*

An infinitive can be the subjects complement:

> *It is the responsibility of all expert detectives to investigate a crime for as long as it takes.*

Conjunctions

Conjunctions come in four basic varieties. They work to join parts of sentence, to join together words, or phrases, or clauses, or even sentences. *And* is probably the most used conjunction—observe how frequently we use it to join words: *apples and oranges*; *work and play*; *sing and dance*; *toys and hobbies*; *Bill and Sally*.

And is also one of a group of **coordinating conjunctions**: <u>for</u>, <u>and</u>, <u>nor</u>, <u>but</u>, <u>or</u>, <u>yet</u>, <u>so</u>, otherwise know as **FANBOYS**. We'll use that term throughout the book when we refer to these coordinating conjunctions. These FANBOYS help create compound sentences, and when they serve this role, a comma comes before their use.

Correlative conjunctives: Remember these by their "relatives." These are twins such as *neither/nor*, *either/or*, *not/only*, *but/also*, *both/and*.

Subordinating conjunctions are

after	if	so that
although	in case	than
as if	in that	though
as though	insofar as	unless
because	no matter	how until
before	now that	when, whenever
even if	once	where, wherever
even though	provided that	whether
how	since	while

Conjunctive adverbs—make brain connection with semi–colons and commas.

however, then	*She went to the film; however, I didn't go.*
therefore, hence	*It rained hard and fast; therefore, we stayed home.*
also, consequently	*The book focused on a popular topic; also, its central character was controversial.*
thus, nevertheless	*The importer pays the taxes, then sells the articles at an inflated price; thus it is the consumer who ultimately pays.*

Interjections: These are odd-balls in that they almost contradict our definition of a part of speech as defined by its function to other words. This is because they do not really function in relationship, but rather stand outside the grammatical connections. An interjection is strong expression, a powerful emotion, a cry from the soul that sometimes is barely a word:

O Heavenly Father, help us in this time of hardship
Oh, she cried
Yikes!
Help!

When we spill over in exasperation, we are likely to express ourselves in interjection:

oh hell; fine; drop dead; scram

Articles: These are so numerous in that we want to give them a special focus even though they are not one of the eight parts of speech. *A, an, the*: Meet the articles–they always come before a noun. General vs. specific noun: *A* or *a* functions to identify a noun referring to something in general: *a book*; *a door*; *a cat. The* functions to identify or point to a specific: *the book, the cat, the door.* Spelling articles: *a* is used when the noun it identifies starts with a consonant: *a book, a door, a cat. An* is used when the noun starts with a vowel: *an elf, an apple, ice cream cone, an ox, an ulcer.*

THE SENTENCE

The previous section reacquainted you with grammar or syntax: the laws of relationships and the function of the components of English, the eight parts of speech. This section focuses on the sentence: what it is (definition); what it does (function); what it's made of (structure and criteria); its four forms (meanings), its four types (variations in structure); and the punctuation that sentences use to fulfill their function: to express a thought! In this section we will also identify the major grammatical and punctuation problems related to sentence structure.

What defines a sentence? Basically it is a complete thought–that is, it's a grammatical unit that is composed of one or more clauses. Clauses are units of words that form a complete thought. The function of a sentence is to express an idea, a fact, or a desire.

Examples: *I want an ice cream.*
             We left the restaurant at midnight.

Table 6.11 Sentence Function

Type	Example	Grammar Rules
Declaratory Sentence: States, expresses a point <u>Thesis statement</u> is a declaratory sentence.	*Logan, the adorable pit–bull, licked his owner's face.*	All sentences begin with a capital; declaratory sentences end with a period.
Interrogatory Sentence Asks a question	*Did Logan lick her face?*	Begins with a capital; interrogatory sentences end with question marks.
Imperative Sentence Gives an order or a direction to another	*Lick her face and jump all over her.*	Begins with a capital; ends usually with a period, but sometimes with an exclamation point. The subject is often hidden, or "understood." The subject is whoever is being given the direction (Logan, you) *lick her face, jump all over her—right now!*
Exclamatory Sentence Expresses emotion!	*What a handsome dog!*	Begins with a capital; often exclamatory sentences end with exclamation points. Writers are urged to use such sentences and punctuation only rarely. Overuse takes away their expressive power.

As we speak, the listener knows when our thought is complete by our inflection, by the tone of our voice, or by our body language. In writing, two signals, "tell" the reader: "Mission accomplished!" The capital marks the start, the ending punctuation (period, question mark; exclamation point) in effect, says, "I'm done." When we incorrectly give the signal telling the reader that we are finished, but it isn't a complete thought–we cause confusion. This signal malfunction creates a ***sentence fragment***. To qualify as a sentence, and earn its punctuation marks, a group of words must meet three criteria:

1. it must have a subject.
2. it must have a verb (and often has a verb <u>predicate</u>, verb + other words).
3. It must be a complete thought (this is the criteria that a fragment does not meet!).

Table 6.12 Sentence Fragments

Fragment	Analysis	Corrective Sentence	Structure
Seeing you in the supermarket.	No subject (actually no verb either as you will see in the section on phrases). *Seeing* is a gerund.	*I saw you in the supermarket.*	Subject (I) verb (saw) predicate (you in the supermarket)
In the produce section at the back of the store.	No subject. No verb. Two prepositional phrases	*I saw you in the produce section at the back of the store.*	Subject (I) verb (saw) predicate (you in the produce section at the back of the store)
Since it rained last night.	Subject (it) Verb predicate (rained last night.) Complete thought? No!	*Since it rained last night, we cancelled our stargazing appointment.*	The additional words complete the thought and meet the criteria Subject (we) verb (cancelled) predicate (our star gazing appointment)

Sentence Patterns

English sentences tend to fall into patterns, and represented as formulas. The following are the **major ones**.

Pattern 1

Formula	Subject (noun or pronoun)	Intransitive Verb (no object)
S+V	*The population*	*has tripled.*

Pattern 2

Formula	Subject	Transitive verb	Object
S+V+O	*The thunder*	*awakened*	*the children.*

Pattern 3

Formula	Subject	Linking Verb	Complement
S+V+C	*The effects of climate change*	*are*	*catastrophic.*
	The children	*must be*	*tired.*
	The leader	*is*	*General Mottard.*

Pattern 4

Formula	Subject	Transitive verb	Indirect object	Direct Object
S+V+IO+DO	*The Professor*	*gave*	*Julie*	*a good grade.*

Pattern 5

Formula	Subject	Transitive Verb	Direct Object	Object Complement
S+V+DO+OC	*The critics*	*proclaimed*	*the film*	*a triumph.*

Table 6.13 Four Sentence Types

Structure	Grammar & Punctuation	Meaning	Style
Simple: One independent clause: Subject (S) + Verb/ predicate (V)	Do not use commas to separate S from V	One idea, point, statement, or question is expressed	Too many create choppiness and disconnection amongst the ideas/ points
Compound: Two or more–independent clauses that are connected to form one sentence	Two connectors only: 1. FANBOYS preceded by comma 2. Semi–colon **Not** by comma (cs)! Comma after conjunctive adverbs: *therefore, however, thus, hence,* etc. $\Rightarrow$	Each of the independent clauses is an idea/point and connecting them expresses that they are of equal value. Points that are **not** related and/or are not of equal value should not be compound sentences. *The storm raged; therefore, school was cancelled.* *Logan is a pit-bull mix; however, contrary to myths, he is a gentle fellow.*	Helps reader see connection between ideas; fosters the feeling of "flow" Semi–colon is a powerful link with dramatic meaning In a compound sentence, linked with a semi–colon, followed by a conjunctive adverb, place comma after the adverb:

(continued on next page)

Table 6.13 Four Sentence Types *(continued from previous page)*

Complex: one independent clause plus one or more dependent clauses	Dependent clauses function as modifiers: 1. Adjective clauses 2. Adverb clauses 3. Noun Clauses <u>Subordinate clauses</u> connect a related but less important idea to the main idea expressed in the independent clause. Commas when clause begins sentence Commas only for <u>nonrestrictive</u> clauses	The point in the independent clause is in some way <u>modified</u> or <u>qualified</u>, rather than equivalence as in compound *If you go to the movies, we will meet you there.* *Keena, <u>who mothered our five pups</u>, won the Westminster,"Most Adorable Dog" trophy.* *The boy <u>who threw the rock</u> will be expelled.*	Help reader make accurate connection between ideas Readers need a break from too many in a row
Compound–Complex: two or more independent clauses and one or more dependent clauses	1 + 2 above	Number of idea or points connected is increased	Readers **need** a break from too many in a row

Simple Sentence: doesn't mean short, nor does it mean is non-complex. Rather, it refers to its structure—to what its parts are. A simple sentence can be very long, but it will have only one **independent clause**.

Independent Clause: is a synonym for sentence. Another way of saying this: A sentence is an independent clause, or it is made up of more than one independent clause. Whenever you come across the phrase *independent clause*, think–it meets the three criteria for a sentence. We'll examine clauses in the paragraphs below. Here is a short simple sentence.

> *Proust and Gide are the best known French writers of the 20th century.*

Here's another a little longer.

> *Both Proust and Gide wrote for a 20th century audience and yet retained their relevance for readers of the 21st century.*

And longer still:

> *In the end, against our wishes, in opposition to all advice, <u>our son,</u>* <u>*John, and the neighbor's daughter, Janice, dropped* out of school, *left*</u> *all their friends and family, and <u>embarked</u> on a trip across country despite the poor weather and the high cost of fuel.*

Note: the underlined sections identify the skeleton of the one independent clause: compound subject and compound verb (three of them). The rest of the sentence is primarily prepositional phrases.

Compound Sentence: is one that has more than one independent clause, and no dependent clauses.

Examples:

> <u>*The children baked three pies*</u>, *and <u>they took all of them to the patients</u>.*
>
> <u>*Barack Obama began the presidential campaign of 2008 behind*</u> <u>*Hillary Clinton*</u>, *but <u>he still managed to win</u>*

Look closely at each of the underlined sections. Think back on the sentence pattern. Identify how each has a subject + verb predicate, and each is a complete thought. Therefore, each of them <u>could be</u> a separate sentence. As the examples demonstrate, **compound sentences** connect independent clauses into one sentence, rather than allowing them to stand alone. They do this in **two** ways **only**:

1. With a **coordinating conjunction** (FANBOYS = *for, and, nor, but, or, yet, so*), and, as the two sentences illustrate, a **comma before** the coordinating conjunction.

2. **Compound sentences** are also linked with semi-colons.

> *The victor is the quickest; Jane Levin's the sure winner!* Or:
>
> *Wealth is often coarse; poverty is frequently refined.*

> **Grammar Highlight**: a most common comma error stems from not differentiating between the and connecting two independent clauses (requiring a comma) from the and, or, but, that is connecting a compound verb (no comma):
>
> *John scored well below his average level of performance, but he still passed the test.* (Compound Sentence)
>
> *John scored well below his average level of performance but still passed the test.* (Simple sentence with one subject, John, and a compound verb: scored 1 passed)

When do you choose a FANBOYS connection, or the semi-colon? The semi-colon is often used to pull the two independent clauses closer together for dramatic effect. Consider the dramatic difference between these two sentences:

> *John studied hard, but he still failed.*
>
> *John studied hard; he still failed.*

Or imagine how much less dramatic with a FANBOYS:

> *He came; he saw; he conquered.*

> **Grammar Note:** Linking **two independent clauses** is generally the **only** correct use of a semi–colon in the middle of a sentence. When you see a semi–colon, check on each side for a sentence that could stand alone. Other, less frequent semi–colon use is to separate items in series, when the items have internal punctuation.

The next sentence type is the ***complex sentence***. They contain one independent clause plus one or more dependent clauses (IC+DC, or IC+DC+DC). Let's look at a complex sentence with more than one dependent clause:

> <u>*When the ship comes in,*</u> *he will get a handsome paycheck* <u>*even though he never lifted a hand in actually delivering the goods to port.*</u>

This combination of one or more dependent clauses in a sentence with an independent clause forms a ***complex sentence***. Let's examine how dependent clauses in a complex sentence function:

> *Linguists have discovered at least three ancient languages.*

This is a **simple sentence: one independent clause**. However, we change it to a ***complex sentence*** by adding a dependent clause:

Linguists have discovered at least three ancient languages <u>that may be the origin of all others</u>.

Complex–compound sentences are made of at least one dependent clause (making it complex) and two or more independent clauses (making it compound):

> **Because Gene has always been a big eater**, <u>no one was sur-prised at his obesity</u>, and <u>his congestive heart diagnosis also came as no surprise</u>.

The underlining identifies the two independent clauses. The phrase in bold is the dependent clause. It's <u>not</u> the length of the sentence but its <u>structure</u> that makes it a **compound-complex sentence**–at least two independent clauses plus at least one depen-dent clause (2 IC+DC). Here's another example:

> *Since Susan B. Anthony was such a staunch proponent of justice in the long struggle for women's suffrage, <u>the U.S. Post Office finally, and justly, issued a stamp in her honor; we can only hope</u> that such recognition will follow quickly for Elizabeth Cady Stanton; after all, <u>Stanton and Anthony were indivisible beings</u>, in a partnership that transcended space.*

The underlining identifies the three independent clauses; the bold identifies the three dependent clauses that make up this **compound-complex sentence**. Note that the depen-dent clause adds more information to the complete thought of the independent clause. This addition of more information is called *modifying*.

> <u>*Since Susan B. Anthony was such a staunch proponent of justice in the long struggle for women's suffrage, the U.S. Post Office finally, and justly, issued a stamp in her honor.*</u>

Clauses

Let's begin our discussion of clauses by examining the simple sentences from the van-tage of clause language:

> <u>*Proust and Gide(A)*</u> <u>*wrote(B)*</u> *for a 20th century audience and yet* <u>*retained(C)*</u> *their relevance for readers of the 21st century.*

*Proust and Gide (A) are the subjects, a **compound subject** because it has more than one actor.*

(B) and (C) are the clause's **compound verb**. Both *wrote* and *retained* belong to the **subject**, *Proust and Gide*. Take away all the other words, and you see the skeleton pattern (S+V) clearly: *Proust and Gide wrote and retained*.

Grammar Highlight: Comma errors often occur in sentences with compound verbs. The writer mistakenly places a comma before the *and*, thus separating the verbs that must, for clarity, remain together. Consider this sentence:

Dublin, the awesome pit–bull who lives down the street, habitually barks at, and chases cars.

The sentence reads much smoother if we take out the comma after *barks at*.

Dublin, the awesome pit-bull who lives down the street, habitually barks at and chases cars.

Let's examine a sentence with a ***simple subject*** (one) and a ***simple verb*** (only one):

In the afternoon, after our long hike, *we <u>took a very long nap</u>.*

We is the subject; the underlined words are the verb predicate (S+VP). It is a complete thought. This is a simple sentence. The words indicated in **bold** are two prepositional phrases.

   Summary: An ***independent clause*** is a group of words that has a subject, a verb, and is a complete thought. Since it meets all the criteria of a sentence, it can be one! It's independent, then, because it is capable of standing alone as a sentence—with a capital and an ending punctuation. However, as in **compound sentences**, independent clauses are sometimes connected, so that there are two, or three, or even, four, or five of them in one compound sentence.

   Dependent Clause as the name suggests needs "someone to lean on" because even though it has a <u>subject</u> and a <u>verb</u>, it does not meet the 3rd criteria of a sentence: it is not a complete thought!

Whenever a new discovery is made. (S=discovery, V= is made.)

But, *what* happens when a discovery is made?

> *If we go to church.* (S=we, V=go)

Yes? *What* if we go to church?

In fact, in their current formation (incorrectly telling the reader they are sentences with the capitals and periods), they are **sentence fragments**. However, we can use them if we complete the thought:

> *Whenever a new scientific discovery is made, <u>society</u> inevitably <u>benefits</u>.*

Look at the description of dependent clauses below to see the different ways that dependent clauses add information to, or modify their independent partners in a complex sentence.

Table 6.14 How Clauses Modify

Clause Type	Example	Typical Words	Grammar
Adjective Clause: modifies noun or pronoun	*The idea <u>that girls can't do math</u> discourages female achievement.* *He <u>who is without fault</u> should cast the first stone.*	**Relative pronouns**: *that, which, who, whom, whose, whoever*	*That* is often 'understood': The values (that) I most appreciate.
Adverb Clause: modifies verb, adjective, or another adverb	<u>*Since the women's movement of the 60s and 70s*</u>*, many women are keeping their maiden names.* *Names are powerful <u>because they bestow existence</u>.*	**Subordinating conjunctions**: *since, when, although, if, before, in order that, while, after* ⟹	When subordinate clauses begin a sentence, always follow them with a comma. When they come at the end, a comma is often not used.
Noun Clause: does all a single noun does: • Subject • Object	<u>*What we force ourselves to forget*</u> *often returns through an underground leak.* *I cannot forgive <u>that you wished me harm</u>.*	How, who, which, who, whomever, whether, Whose, why, what whatever, where, that	Do not use comma after a noun clause subject.

Restrictive and Non-Restrictive Clauses, Misplaced Modifiers, and Parallelism

Identifying the grammar problems of these three issues depends greatly on the ability to identify the clauses we have just studied. These three are also very frequent problem areas for students, so understanding them is especially important.

Identifying the difference between <u>restrictive</u> and <u>non–restrictive</u> clauses will also tell you when to use **that** and **which**. **Restrictive clauses** are necessary to the sentence's meaning therefore use **that**. **Non–restrictive clauses** are not necessary to the main meaning so you would use **which** plus **commas**. Here is a **complex** sentence with **restrictive clause** underlined:

> *The poet <u>who served as England's Laureate throughout Victoria's reign</u> was none other than Alfred Lord Tennyson.*

Why is that clause necessary to the meaning? Because if we did not have this information, we wouldn't know which poet is being discussed. Here's another example of a restrictive clause in a complex sentence:

> *The buildings <u>that are scheduled for demolition</u> are marked with red paint.*

Try taking that restrictive clause out. Note that without the information in the **restrictive clause**, one cannot identify why the buildings are painted red and, therefore, cannot identify which buildings need to be removed.

Non-restrictive clauses add some information too, but their information is not vital to the main point of the independent clause in which they are embedded:

> *John Wilkes Booth, <u>who was an actor</u>, shot Lincoln in a theatre in front of the players and the audience.*

The commas tell the reader: *here's a bit of interesting information.* But knowing that Booth was an actor is not necessary to the main meaning–that he shot Lincoln in full view of the audience and actors. Here's another to reinforce that **which** is preferred over **that** in a non–restrictive clause:

> *<u>Lost</u>, the television series, which was created five years ago, won three prizes at last night's award ceremonies.*

In the examples below, *which* is selected to head the clause in the second sentence because the clause gives the reader additional information. Unlike the first sentence, the information does not alter the meaning, nor is the correct understanding of the sentence dependent upon it.

> *The revolution that dramatically changed the form of Russian society began in 1905 with a bread strike.*
>
> *The Russian revolution, which to this day has worldwide reverberations, began in 1905 and dramatically changed Russian society.*

Who*, *whom*, *whoever*, *whoever are often confusing to writers. The key to using them correctly is **pronoun case**. Review the pronoun case chart previously displayed in the chapter. *Who* and *whoever* are **subject case** and *whomever* and *whom* are **object case**. Remember, too, that in speaking we commonly are ungrammatical. It's ok in speaking, but not in writing!

> *Who killed Abraham Lincoln and altered American history?*

Ask yourself what is the subject of "killed and altered"? It is *who* and thus the choice is correct.

> *To whom is much given and thus is much expected?*

In this case the presence of the preposition, *to*, would require the objective *whom*. In addition, *to whom* is the indirect object of the verb *given*.

> *The law decreed that whoever violated the letter would be exiled forever.* (Who violated the law?)
>
> *The book would belong to whomever won the spelling bee.*

Phrases

Phrases look different from clauses—they do **not** have both a subject and verb. And, they do **not** determine sentence type as do the presence of independent and dependent clauses.

Major Types of Phrases

1. Verbal phrases (those made with various verb parts).
2. Prepositional phrases
3. Appositive phrases

Verbal Phrase. A *verbal phrase* uses a form of verb but the new form <u>doesn't</u> function like a verb (to show action, to help, or to link). Instead, depending on the type, they function as nouns, adjectives, or adverbs.

Table 6.15 Verbal Phrases

Types of Verb Phrase	Structure	Function	Example	Grammar
Gerund	Verb base –ing *singing*	*Noun, and like a noun, a gerund can be subject or object*	*Beautifully pitched <u>singing</u> is her trademark. She was applauded for her <u>singing</u>.*	Almost always require singular verb or pronoun form.
Infinitive Phrase	to + verb base *to sing*	Functions as a noun, an adjective, or an adverb	*To sit for hours is boring. She has many books <u>to read.</u> They design casinos <u>to make</u> people want <u>to spend</u> money.*	adjective modifying the noun, *books to make* modifies verb, *design;* to spend is noun object of *want*
Participial Phrases	present participle/ or past participle: *sleeping frightened*	adjectives, often right after the noun	*The Judge, <u>looking stern</u>, emphatically delivered the death sentence. The dogs, frightened by the sirens, hid under the bed Frightened by the sirens, the dogs hid under the bed.*	**Commas** often around them when in the middle of a sentence, or after them when they come before an independent clause

Table 6.15 Verbal Phrases *(continued from previous page)*

Absolute Phrase	A noun or pronoun,+ participle + any modifiers that go with these	Modifies the whole remainder of the sentence	*His voice rising to a shriek*, the teacher scared the students with his sharp criticism.	Note that unlike the participial phrase above, this one has a subject (*his voice*).
			The tower, its bells ringing loudly, announced the ceremony's start.	**Commas** follow an absolute phrase that comes at the beginning, surround one the comes in the middle, and precede one that comes at the end of a sentence.
			The squad used the cover of night to infiltrate the town, surrounding and containing everyone residing there.	

Prepositional Phrases begin with a *preposition* and they end with a *noun*. In the sentence below the underlined words are all prepositional phrases. But note that *to buy* is an infinite–*to* with the verb *buy*.

All *of the children* ran *to the corner store* to buy candy *for the movies*.

Prepositional phrases are always working as either an *adjective* or an *adverb*. Prepositional phrases that are functioning as adjectives are almost always right after the noun or pronoun they modify. Ask the question after *all* (indefinite pronoun) *what*? Or after *candy* (a noun), *which candy*? The candy *for the movies* answers the question. On the other hand, *to the corner store* modifies the verb *ran*; its functions, then, as an adverb, answering the adverb question, *Where did they run*?

Grammar Highlight: Remember that adjectives modify nouns, and that, contrarily, adverbs modify verbs, adjectives, or other adverbs. They will help you to identify what a prepositional phrase is doing in a sentence.

Appositive Phrases are nouns that *describe* another noun or pronoun.

Abraham Lincoln, the 16ᵗʰ President of the U.S., is considered by many the greatest of our leaders.

What makes this a phrase? First, it's more than one word; second, the main definition or defining word is the **noun**, *President*. Appositive phrases nearly always require commas. If one comes in the middle, then commas are placed around the phrase.

> *American track-and-field athlete Jesse Owens, <u>the winner of four Gold Medals at the 1936 Olympic Games</u>, was a Black man.*

If one comes at the beginning of a sentence, then the comma follows.

> *<u>A big thief without a doubt</u>, Madoff deserves life in prison.*

Parallelism (//)

Language shares much with music, beginning, of course, with its basic reliance upon sounds and being heard. **Parallelism** requires that elements in a sentence that are <u>in series</u> or that are being <u>compared or contrasted</u> be expressed in the same grammatical and syntactical form.

Let's look at parallelism <u>in series</u> construction: *it's only a <u>hop</u>, <u>skip</u>, and <u>jump</u> away.* All three items are nouns, and this makes the sentence flow. Contrast the effect of violating parallelism: *it's only a <u>hop</u>, <u>skip</u>, and <u>jumping</u> away.* The switch from a simple noun to a gerund phrase sounds awkward and it confuses the meaning. Consider, again, the difference:

> *Government of the people, by the people, for the people.*

Perfect parallelism such as this is a masterful rhetorical style. Note that each item in the series is a prepositional phrase. In contrast to:

> *Government of the people, by the people, and with the needs of the people foremost.*

Changing the 3rd item of the series from one prepositional phrase to two alters the rhythm and flow of the phrase, significantly damaging its impact. Sentences that violate parallelism disturb the reader like a note off key disturbs a listener; both jolt and distract. The smooth flow of meaning is stopped until the reader can remove the blockage.

Table 6.16 Parallelism in Sentences

Structures	Non Parallel	Parallel
Items in series	Hobbits also love adventures, traveling, and dream of becoming heroes with swords.	Hobbits love adventure, traveling, and dreams of heroism.
Comparisons Comparisons such as those made with **correlative conjunctions** that commonly come in pairs: *either…or; not only…but also; whether…or.*	*The Hobbits were not only fearless warriors but also their friendship was something you could rely upon.* *He is neither a scoundrel nor does he aspire to dominate others.*	*The Hobbits were not only fearless warriors but they were also loyal friends.* *He is neither a scoundrel nor a tyrant.*
Lists and outlines	*I will do three things to improve my listening skills:* *Avoid interrupting* *Eliminate noise* *Eye-contact*	*I will do three things to improve my listening skills:* *Avoid interrupting* *Eliminate noise* *Maintain eye-contact*

Misplaced and Dangling Modifiers

Modifiers are words or phrases that describe, identify, and specify another part of a sentence. We have examined adjectives, adverbs, adjective clauses, and adverb clauses—how they are used, how they are punctuated. How they are located in a sentence is another major concern. As the term indicates, a **Misplaced Modifier (mm)** is one not correctly positioned in its sentence. These are often the cause of unintended humor–and lack of clear meaning!

> *I saw the sick skunk <u>driving down the street.</u>*
>
> *He wore a red beret on his head, which was much too small.*

The underlined modifying phrase/clauses are placed next to the wrong nouns. The sentences need to be revised to place them next to the nouns they do modify:

> *Driving down the street, I saw the sick skunk.*
>
> *He wore a red beret, which was much too small, on his head.*

Dangling Modifiers (dm), too, are often sources of humor and twisted meaning:

> <u>Although exhausted and demoralized</u>, the coach kept insisting on another lap.

> <u>Hanging by one toe from the rope 300 feet above</u>, the performance was the most exciting of the circus.

The underlined modifiers are problematic because they refer to a subject who is either absent from the sentence or whose identity is unclear. In the above, the track team is missing as is the high rope performer. Revision is required:

> *Although the track team was exhausted and demoralized, the coach insisted on another lap.*

> *Hanging by one toe from the rope 300 feet above, the high rope expert gave the most exciting performance of the circus.*

Here's one in which the subject of the modifier is present but unclear:

> <u>With only a 3.0 GPA</u>, Rutgers's graduate school nonetheless accepted Sarah.

As it is, Rutgers has a 3.0 GPA requirement. Revision:

> *Sarah, with only a 3.0 GPA, was accepted by Rutgers.*

Squinting Modifiers occur when a modifier is placed between two words, either one of which could be its anchor. This confuses:

> *We were certain <u>at noon</u> our trip was cancelled.*

Does the writer mean: *At noon, we were certain our tip was cancelled, or that our trip was cancelled at noon?*

Placement of adverbs: *Only, just, merely*

Proper placement of these adverbs can determine and alter the **meaning** of a sentence.

For instance, consider the different meanings of:

> *I eat only one dessert per day.*
>
> *I only eat one dessert per day.*

Again:

> *Only I can eat the ritual meal.*
>
> *I can only eat the ritual meal*
>
> *I can eat only the ritual meal.*

Finally:

> *I can see merely the shadows*
>
> I can merely see the shadows.

PUNCTUATION, MECHANICS, AND USAGE

Basic Rules and Conventions, Major Errors

This section focuses on the most important and most frequently occurring punctuation and mechanics errors—most important because they have negative effects on the clarity of meaning. Some are repeats and because they are often difficult to identify, the repetition should help you learn to "see" them more readily.

Sentence Fragments (frag) A **sentence fragment** is a group of words wrongly punctuated as if it were a sentence. The group starts with a capital and it ends with a period, question mark, or exclamation point. But it is not a sentence because it lacks one or more of the three ingredients: subject + verb + expression of a complete thought.

Fragments confuse readers who expect a complete thought but who get a partial product causing them to try to "figure it out." Thus, fragments undermine the purpose of writing, clear communication, and they frustrate readers who do not want the burden of puzzle solving.

The most common configuration you will find is illustrated as follows (from a student paper):

After everyone takes their* (pn agr) share, I refuse to take treasure; instead, I offer it to my good friend, Gandalf. <u>Which shows how good natured I am</u>. frag

The underlined fragment (dependent clause) comes after a correct sentence. The fragment expresses a point that is related to the sentence, but it is a dependent clause. Note: dependent clauses are often the most difficult for students to identify because they meet two criteria of a sentence; they have a subject and a verb. They are not, however, complete thoughts.

Grammar Highlight: Reading out loud will frequently make the reader hear the incomplete thought. "*When I get home.*" Hearing that voiced will make the listener say, "When you get home, what?" Encourage students who habitually write fragments to read aloud—not under their breath!

---

*Note this student's pronoun error.

Run-on (fused) Sentences (run) and Comma Splices (cs)

Like the fragment, these errors violate the rules of sentence structure. In this case, it's about connections and misconnections. A railroad analogy helps explain this common error. Imagine that sentences are railroad cars. Now, like them, sentences or separate cars can be linked together—or coupled; they don't have to be separate. Often to get an idea communicated most effectively, as to transport materials across the country, linking is the most effective method. But how?

To begin with, there <u>must</u> be a link. Just as you can't expect to connect by placing two cars next to one another without a coupling mechanism, so, too, the writer cannot simply place two sentences (independent clauses) together without a link, as in:

> *The evening showers were soft and <u>warm they</u> made the night enchanting.*

> *Dublin, king of his breed, strutted as he patrolled his <u>yard his</u> posture blared his dominance through every street and alleyway.*

The underlining identifies where two independent clauses have been fused, or run on, without a coupler. **Note**: in the second example of a run–on sentence, there are two possible ***independent clauses***.

> **Grammar Highlight:** a run–on sentence is not about length; rather it's about structure. A run-on lacks the coupler (FANBOYS, or semi-colon) necessary to link independent clauses.

Comma splice is the second type of fused sentence. Again, it's a problem of connection. You can't link two railroad cars with rubber bands; they are not strong enough. You can't link two independent clauses with a comma—it's not strong enough to do the job of communicating clearly.

> *The evening showers were soft and warm, they made the night enchanting. cs*
>
> *Dublin, king of his breed, strutted as he patrolled his yard, his posture blared his dominance through every street and alleyway. cs*

ONLY the FANBOYS or the semi-colon can do the communication job:

> *The evening showers were soft and warm, and they made the night enchanting.*
>
> *Dublin, king of his breed, strutted as he patrolled his yard; his posture blared his dominance through every street and alleyway.*

Semi-colons are confusing to many students. Yet their correct usage is straightforward and very limited. There are three grammatical situations which require them.

Table 6.17 Requirements for a Semi-colon

1	Compound sentence link: *"One is not born a woman; one becomes a woman," wrote Simone de Beauvoir*	**Note** how the semi–colon is selected over the FANBOYS to emphasize the relation between the two independent clauses
2	***Before a transitional phrase or conjunctive*** adverb that comes between two independent clauses(*for instance, therefore, thus, however, as a matter of fact, as a result, for example, in addition, in conclusion, in fact, on the contrary*) *Dr. Holmes tried valiantly to save the ill ferret; however, the bacteria resisted treatment.*	**Note** that a comma comes after the transitional phrase
3	To separate items in series with internal punctuation *The office ordered five boxes of stainless–steel, galvanized staples; two cartons of multi-colored, one letter, one legal size; and a gross of pens.* Underlining is of the internal punctuation (in most cases, a comma)	**Note** commas are usually used to separate items in series except when one of the items (or more) also has a comma.

DON'T	ERROR	REVISION
Do not use to introduce a list or series, or quotation	There are three points to emphasize; (1) *The king's exact words are; "Total submission."*	There are three points to emphasize: (1) *The king's exact words are: "Total submission."*
Do not use to separate subordinate clause from the main, independent clause of a complex sentence	*If the weather holds; we will go sailing.* *Finally, he settled down; because the medication was powerful.*	*If the weather holds, we will go sailing.* *Finally, he settled down because the medication was powerful.*
Do not separate appositives with semi–colons	*Gates; the highest ranking official on the team; spoke well of General Tremor.*	*Gates, the highest ranking official on the team, spoke well of General Tremor.*

Commas

I have spent most of the day putting in a comma and the rest of the day taking it out.

Oscar Wilde

Wilde's wry observation about comma choice highlights two important points: First, and this guides you in editing your and others' writing, that placing commas where they don't belong is a bigger problem with students' writing than failing to use them where they do belong; two, that while we do have rules to guide these decisions, it is often not clear–cut when a comma is necessary.

The uses and misuses of commas are probably the single most troubling punctuation question. Perhaps this is because there are so many situations that do require them and also so many situations in which they are incorrectly used. The correct use of commas is crucial to communicating meaning and also to the coherence of writing. Readers are ornery; they don't like to be confused; they do like the sensation of smooth flowing writing—that's what coherent writing produces.

One guiding principle for all comma use is your best tool. That principle simply is that commas help the reader keep the various parts of a sentence in their proper places. Consider, for instance:

After leaving his friend John made his way to his mother's apartment.

When you read the above sentence, you probably experienced a moment of confusion because your brain connected friend to John, which is not the meaning of the sentence. Rather:

After leaving his friend, John made his way to his mother's apartment.

Here, the comma helps the reader; it "tells" the reader, "pause to meet John, who is the person who left his unnamed friend." As for writing that is incoherent, consider this:

Since Alice hadn't cooked the family decided to dine out.

To which the reader does a double-take: did Alice cook the family? After a confusing moment, the reader may succeed in getting it right—but not without some annoyance. The correctly placed comma avoids the confusion:

Since Alice hadn't cooked, the family decided to dine out.

Now let's look at a different comma problem. Consider: *John took a walk, and talked with Mary about their engagement.* This illustrates a frequently made error: placing a comma to separate a **compound verb**. The comma both breaks the flow of the verb action, putting a brake on the forward movement of walk and talk, and it confuses the meaning, suggesting that walking and talking are being compared, or that they happened at a different time. It's important to foster this understanding with students.

Table 6.18 Comma Dos and Don'ts

Do Use Commas	Don't Use Commas
To separate **introductory clauses** and *phrases* from the main clause: *Since she got her degree, Jeanne has held several challenging positions.* *Travelling at the speed of sound, the jet emits a deafening sonic boom.* *To the extroverts, tourists are a boon; to introverts, they are a curse.* *Having been disappointed in love before, Kate was reluctant to admit that she liked her blind date*	**Omit** when the dependent clause **follows** the main sentence and a comma pause would interrupt the flow of the statement. *When I was a boy, people were afraid when the stream that ran past the factory didn't change <u>color, because</u> that meant that lay-offs were coming. X*

(continued on next page)

Table 6.18 Comma Dos and Don'ts *(continued from previous page)*

Do Use Commas	Don't Use Commas
To separate the independent clauses of a compound sentence linked with a correlative conjunction (FANBOYS) *Dr. Holmes spoke firmly to the distressed client, and she quickly calmed down*	**Not** after the FANBOYS *Dr. Holmes spoke firmly to the distressed client and, she quickly calmed down. X* **Not** to separate independent clauses *Dr. Holmes spoke firmly to the distressed client, she quickly calmed down. (cs)*
In direct *quotations* separate the subject/speaker from his/her statement: *Dr. Holmes emphatically said, "I will excuse a mischievous pet, but I will not tolerate a bad pet owner."* *"No pets allowed for any reason!" The sign over the entrance says.*	*Be careful not to create a comma splice:* *"I don't want to hear about the dunes," I said, "tell me about the experiment."(cs)* *"I dont want to hear about the dunes," I said. "Tell me about the experiment."*
Do use comma for contrasts: *I agree with his facts, not with his interpretations of them.* **Do** use comma after both city and state, or city and country: *In Rome, Italy, we had the best meals of our trip.* *Portland, Oregon's population is twice that of the state.* **Do** use commas with dates and numbers In December 31, 1775, Washington…	Do **not** separate compound subjects or compound verbs: *Both the House of Representatives, and the Senate passed the economic stimulus bill. X* *Today, both the House and the Senate voted for, and passed the bill. X*

Pronouns: Case, Agreement, and Reference

These frequent problems involve the all-important connection between a pronoun and the word to which it refers–its antecedent. As we have previously discussed, confusion in this relationship will obstruct meaning. Pronoun agreement is a very frequent error!

Agreement (agr): Does the pronoun match (agree) the number (singular/plural), gender (male/female), and person (1st, 2nd, 3rd) of its antecedent?

Examples:

Athletes frequently suffer injuries to their bodies.

Athletes, the antecedent is **plural** in number, **neutral** in gender, and in the **third** person. *Their* is plural in number, neutral in gender, and in the third person.

> *A reader must focus his/her attention sharply in order to see the minis-cule marks in the margins.*

A reader, the antecedent, is singular in number, either male or female, and in the third person. So, too, are *his* and *her*.

To be inclusive, whenever an antecedent can be either male or female, you need to use both *his* and *her* (so as not to exclude either the female or the male). However, too many of these constructions in a piece of writing make for awkwardness. To avoid these gender constructions often requires creating different sentence formats. For instance, changing the antecedent to plural removes the awkwardness because the plural doesn't have different gender form.

> *Readers must focus their attention sharply in order to see the minis-cule marks in the margins.*

Agreement Challenges: Once the basic "mirror relationship" is understood, it seems easy to follow the agreement rule. However, there are several words and grammar constructions which cause difficulties.

Collective nouns—that is, nouns that refer to more than one person such as *team, jury, committee, army.* Note these words are singular in form; they therefore require a singular pronoun as in this example:

> *The committee left the boardroom and announced <u>its</u> decision to the court.*

Sometimes, however, a writer does mean to describe the <u>separate</u> members of a collective and in this case, since the reference is to more than one, then the pronoun should be plural.

> *The committee left the boardroom and went to <u>their</u> offices to cast their votes for the proposal.*

Personal pronouns called indefinites because they don't specify gender or number take the **singular**.

> *Everyone is responsible for his/her belongings and must take precautions to secure them.*

> *Anybody can apply by submitting his/her qualifications and years of experience.*

> *Each student has his/her own computer.*

> *Every book must be returned with its cover.*

Commonly used Indefinite Pronouns

Everything	anyone	something	nothing	each
Everyone	anything	someone	nobody	every
Everybody	anybody	somebody	no one	

Faulty or unclear pronoun reference (ref)

Consider the pronouns in the sentence:

> *Jane hit the ball so hard that she sent it flying twenty feet over the fence.*

We understand this because we clearly understand that the antecedent of *she* is *Jane* and that the antecedent of it is ball. This clear relationship is sometimes ambiguous or incorrect

> *Claudia threw the vase at the window and broke it.*

It is ambiguous; is it the window or the vase that was broken?

> *The Andersons told the next door neighbors that their children were chasing the chickens.*

> (Whose children—the neighbors' or the Andersons'?)

Pronoun Case (case)

Subjective case is for pronouns functioning as subjects.

Examples: *She purchased every bottle the store had. (subjective, singular)*
We purchased every bottle the store had. (subjective, plural)

Objective case is for pronouns functioning as objects

Examples: *They called him from the pay phone. (objective, singular)*
They called us from the pay phone. (objective, plural):

Possessive case is for pronouns functioning to indicate "belonging to."

Examples: *Gloria Gaynor sang her disco hits. (possessive, singular)*
The Bee Gees sang their hits from Saturday Night Fever. (possessive, plural)

Table 6.19 Pronoun Case

Pronoun Type	Subjective Case (Nominative)		Objective Case		Possessive Case	
Personal Pronoun	I you he, she, it	we you they	me you him, her, I	us you them	my, mine your his, hers, theirs its	our, ours yours, their
Relative Pronouns	who	whoever	whom	whomever	whose	whosever

When you struggle to decide between using *I* and *me*, or *who* and *whom*, you are grappling with pronoun case. The right answer is in the rules above. However, two situations can make pronoun case difficult. One is because we often violate these rules in speech, so much so that the correct use sounds unnatural or pedantic as in "*Whom did he call?*" Yet, this is correct because whom is the object of the verb call. Second, there are several grammatical formats that cause confusion and make it tricky to determine whether the case we need is the subjective or the objective. Knowing these confusing formats helps you identify the most common problems students have with pronoun case.

Table 6.20 Common Problems with Pronoun Case

Challenging Case Usages	Examples
Compound subjects with a **pronoun** require the **subjective case**	*Mary and I went shopping together.* ≠ *Mary and me went shopping together.*
Appositives with **pronouns** need to agree with the case of the word they re–name	*The Smiths, both he and she, attended.* ≠ *The Smiths, both him and her, attended.* *They photographed only two actors, the lead man and me.*
The items being compared (*as, as much as, than*) with need to match each other in case.	*I run faster than she (does)* ≠ *I run faster than her.* *The Professor graded us all as hard as (he graded) him.* *We liked nobody else as much as her* *We felt as bad as she*
A **pronoun** referring back to the subject after a linking verb is in the **subjective case**	*It was I (≠ me) who rang the bell.* *The principal announced that the essay winners were he and I. (≠ him and me)*
Who and *whom* are problems generally I subordinate clauses or in questions. *Who* or *whom* depends on its function in the subordinate clause that it starts In questions, usage depends on whether he pronoun is the **subject** or the **object** of the question	*The student (who will address the class) asked for a stipend.* The subordinate clause in the () = who (subject of will address). *The woman (whom he gave the ring to) is the one he will marry.* *Who got to the finish line first?* *Whom did you recommend for the reward?*
We or us before a **noun** is in same case as the noun	*We students want more fairness in grading.* *The supervisor wanted to fire us teenagers*

Plurals and Possessives

Forming plurals

Most nouns can be singular or plural. The usual plural form adds –*s* to the end of the word.

desk   desks   book   books

However, there are exceptions to this guideline. After a *–y* preceded by a consonant, the *–y* changes to *–i* and *–es* is added.

    sky skies   secretary secretaries

If the final *–y* is preceded by a vowel, no change is made, and the plural is formed by adding *–s*.

    decoy decoys   attorney attorneys

If the last sound in the word is a sibilant–a word ending in *–s*, *–z*, *–ch*, *–sh*, or *–x*, or *–z*, add *–es*.

    churches, sashes, masses, foxes, quizzes (however, with words ending in *–z*, it must be doubled before adding the *–es*)

    class classes   branch branches

However, if the *–ch* is pronounced *–k*, only *–s* is added.

    stomach stomachs

Often the final *–fe* or *–f* in one-syllable words becomes *–ves*.

    half halves
    wife wives

There are exceptions, of course.

    chief chiefs
    roof roofs

Many nouns have plural forms that are irregular or the same.

    child children   mouse mice
    woman women   series series

For nouns ending in "o," it depends on the word whether you add –*s* or –*es* to form the plural. These spellings must be memorized individually.

potato, potatoes   hero, heroes

Finally, there are a number of foreign words that have become part of the language and retain their foreign plural form. There is a trend to anglicize the spelling of some of these plural forms by adding –*s* to the singular noun. In the list that follows, the letter(s) in parentheses indicate the second acceptable spelling as listed by *Webster's New Collegiate Dictionary*.

datum   data
medium   media
crisis   crises
parenthesis   parentheses
criterion   criteria
phenomenon   phenomena (s)

As you can see, there are many peculiarities associated with plural formation. It is advisable to have a dictionary on hand to check plural forms.

Possessive nouns (those that own something, or to which something belongs) use apostrophe plus an s (*s'*) as in,

Eleanor Roosevelt's husband was perhaps the most famous president of the twentieth century; or,

The classroom's ceiling is too high to be energy efficient; or,

Charles Manson's behavior has become synonymous with modern psychosocial disorder.

If the noun showing possession is plural that ends as most plurals do with an –*s* (boys, girls, and engineers) then only an apostrophe is used:

The engineers' computers are left on even during the evening when they are not around.

The girls' attitudes made them a delight to work with.

However, there are nouns that do not use an –*s* to form their plural. These non –*s* ending plurals—such as children, men, women—use an apostrophe and an –*s* to show possession:

> *The women's hats are all different colors.*
>
> *The children's playground is across the street.*

Joint Possession: In situations where two nouns "possess" something together, add the *s* apostrophe (*s'*) to the last noun owner:

> *John and Mary's Mercedes Benz is frequently borrowed by their son
> for dates.*

Be careful, however, if the subject nouns "own" separate and different things, then each require an *'s*:

> *Although they are married, John's and Mary's bank accounts are in
> different banks.*

Possessive Pronouns (review the pronoun case Table 6.3) do not use any form of apostrophe *s*. They are possessive in themselves and require no special sign:

> *The tree cast its shadow across the field.* (Not *it's*, which means it is;
> not *its'*: It's not a word!)

Table 6.21 Singular and Plural Possessives

Number		Possessive	
Singular	Plural	Singular possessive	Plural possessive
idea	ideas	*The idea's power,* or *the power of the idea*	*The ideas' power,* or *the power of the ideas*
girl	girls	*The girl's jacket,* or *the jacket of the girl*	*The girls' jackets,* or *the jackets of the girls*
army	armies	*The army's position,* or *the position of the army*	*The armies' positions,* or *the positions of the armies*
class	classes	*The class's objective,* or *the objective of the class*	*The classes' objectives,* or *the objectives of the classes*

(continued on next page)

Table 6.21 Singular and Plural Possessives *(continued from previous page)*

child	children	*The child's mind,* or *the mind of the child*	*The children's minds,* or *the minds of the children*
man	men	*The man's thoughts,* or *the thoughts of the man*	*The men's thoughts,* or *the thoughts of the men*
potato	potatoes	*The potato's color,* or *the color of the potato*	*The potatoes' blight,* or *the blight of the potatoes*

Special Uses of Apostrophes

When referring to plural words *as* words, there are both italicized and the apostrophe used to indicate plural:

> The author uses many *if's* and *but's* in this article. A review of this book will demonstrate all the times we italicize words when we are *using apostrophes in this manner.*

When referring to plural lowercase letters:

> *John could write his as perfectly clearly but he had difficulty with his a's.*

Note how the omission of the apostrophe in the lower case plural would confuse the reader (is it *as*?).

Contractions use an apostrophe to show that letters have been omitted, frequently in auxiliary verb constructions such as does + not = don't, have + not = haven't, and the one often misused as a possessive, it + is = it's.

Faulty Predication (fp) occurs when the subject (the 'who' or "what" of the verb) doesn't fit with the predicate:

> *Writing is where I have my greatest problems.* (The subject writing is not a place (where)).

> *Horses are the activity she most relishes.* (The subject horses is not an activity)

Revision:

> *I have my greatest problems with writing.* Or, *writing is my greatest problem.*

In the second example, note that "my greatest" uses subjective case because it is the complement of a linking verb (to be).

Revision: *Horseback riding is the activity she most relishes.*

Table 6.22 When to Use a Colon

Yes	Examples	No!	Incorrect
After salutations	*Dear Mr. Rodriguez:* *Dear Sir:*	Not following the verb *to be*	*Her flaws are: greed, envy, and sloth.*
Before a list introduced by *such as, the following, a number*	*The essay covered the following topics: customs, rituals, play, and dance.* *From the many ideas the Professor discussed, she emphasized three: feudal relationships, courtly romance, and knighthood.*	Not following a preposition	*The lecture was about: medicine, surgery, and massage therapy.*
Before a long quotation *Note the capital letter after the colon. This follows APA manual; MLA and CMS do not capitalize (see research)	*The Senator emphasized the crisis:* *"In troubled eras, when tumult and confusion seem normal, and peace, an illusion, great leaders shine like beacons in a dark night."*	Not following a linking verb	*The children's faces seemed: pale, thin, and sharp.*
Between two sentences when the second one explains or re-states the first one	*The truth will set you free: It undoes the shackles on your mind.*		

(continued on next page)

Table 6.22 When to Use a Colon *(continued from previous page)*

Dates, titles, ratios, chapter and verse of Biblical citations	*Affirmatives outperformed negatives 2:1.* *June:2007; 1:15; John 5:3* *"The Fictional Detective: A Psychological Study"*		

Quotations and Quotation Marks

Quotation marks are necessary with **direct quotes**, which are words that someone else exactly said or words exactly as they are written or spoken from a source such as a book or film.

> *Mary gave me very precise directions. "Do not," she urged, "enter the kitchen, and do not open the door to the basement."*

> *According to the philosopher, Hannah Arendt, "Evil is banality."*

Indirect quotes are reports on what someone said, summarizing or paraphrasing it. They do not take quotation marks.

> *Sarah said that yesterday had been the worst of her life.*

> *The historian Barbara Tuchman claimed that World War I was an unnecessary mistake.*

Note: the word *that* is generally a sign that you are dealing with an indirect quotation. To indicate someone's exact words, not the writer's, requires quotation marks as when a character in a short story makes a statement:

> *John turned to Mary and confessed, "I quit my job."*

In essays, however, most quotations are to acknowledge another writer's words on the subject of the essay; and in an argumentative/persuasive essay, we often use quotations as evidence to support our arguments.

Quotation Mechanics and Punctuation

Where and when to capitalize, to place quotation marks and punctuation marks such as period, question marks, and exclamation points is largely dependent upon the position of the quotation.

If it is at the beginning, the quotation starts with a capital, and ends with a comma inside the quotation marks. The same is true for question marks and exclamation points.

> *"I have loved you since we were children," Mary admitted to John.*

> *"Did you really love me all along?" John asked. "Yes!" Mary exclaimed.*

If it is at the end of the sentence, place a comma after the source of the quotation, a capital letter for the first word, and the terminal punctuation if a period, question mark, or exclamation point inside the quotation marks.

> *Wendell Phillips says, "The Tree of Liberty requires constant pruning to maintain vital and true."*

The **broken quotation** is a bit more complicated. Let's examine the varieties:

> *"The unexamined life," says Socrates, "is not worth living."*

Note: The beginning follows the same format as noted above. The second part, which is a continuation of the first, is not capitalized, needs a comma after the source, and follows the same rules for placing the period inside the quotation marks. If, however, the quotation consists of two sentences with its source in the middle, note the changes:

> *"The unexamined life is not worth living," says Socrates. "It is the life of the beast, not of the man."*

Quotation marks for titles

Colons and Semi-colons go outside of the quotation marks:

> *The document stressed the accident's "special circumstances": It insisted that the holiday atmosphere changed normal behavior.*

> *The killer coldly confessed that he "felt nothing at all"; then, he leaned back in his chair and yawned.*

> **Grammar Highlight:** Commas, periods, question marks and exclamation points are inside the quotation marks; colons and semi-colons are outside of them.

However, there are some tricky situations: Sometimes a quotation is not itself a question or an exclamation, but it's part of a larger sentence that is a question or exclamation. In these cases, the question mark and exclamation point go outside the quotation marks.

> *Does Mr. Babbitt think he is alone in thinking that new courthouse is "a monument to injustice more than a temple of justice"?* (It's not Mr. Babbitt's question)

> *Samson didn't have to go so far as to call the defendant "disreputable, heartless scoundrel"!* (It's not Samson who is outraged at these words)

Embedded Quotations: When quotations are part of the larger sentence, note that there are no commas:

> *I pointed out to Jason that his belief that "all abuse cases should be treated the same" would lead to an abuse in justice.*

> *The Judge concluded that the defendant is "a total psychopath incapable of redemption"; no doubt, his sentence will be harsh and invoke the maximum penalty the law permits.*

Ellipses are used to indicate that material has been omitted from a quotation:

> *The author stated that his work "is meant to entertain, to instruct...but not to preach."*

If the omitted material comes in between two sentences in a quotation, add a period:

> *The author stated that his work "is meant to entertain, to instruct, to promote good values...."*

Italics

Word processing has made this font style easier and thus replaced underlining in many instances. However, there are still some style manuals which encourage underlining of titles, for example.

Major use	Example	
Books	*Gone with the Wind*	
Magazines	*Newsweek*	*Wired*
Plays	*Cats*	*The Glass Menagerie*
Newspapers	*The Boston Globe*	*The San Francisco Chronicle*
Ships, planes	*Mayflower*	*The Spirit of St. Louis*
Films	*The Exorcist*	*Terminator*
TV shows	*American Idol*	*Lost* *The Situation Room*
Radio shows	*Democracy Now*	
Music	*Sentimental Journey*	
Art works	*Mona Lisa*	*David* *Starry Night*
Web sites	*Google*	
Electronic databases	*InfoTrac*	

Table 6.23 Italics and their Uses

Italics	Examples	Do not use (common errors)
titles	See list above	Not with article titles or book chapters. These are indicated with quotation marks Not to the title of your papers.
Words, letters, or numbers that identify themselves not what they commonly mean	To celebrate his invention of the telegraph, Edison named his children *Dot and Dash.* Gerunds are formed by adding *–ing to the verb base;* *A*dverbs by adding *–y* to an adjective	
Names of specific diseases	*Congestive Heart Failure; Alzheimer's; MS*	Not general disease types: Cancer; paralysis; a fever
Foreign words	I was *enchante* to have made his acquaintance	Not words foreign originally but now part of English: laissez–faire economics; or pot–porrei

CAPITALIZATION

A very important element of writing is knowing when to capitalize a word and when to leave it alone. When a word is capitalized, it calls attention to itself. This attention should be for a good reason. There are standard uses for capital letters. In general, capitalize (1) all proper nouns, (2) the first word of a sentence, and (3) the first word of a direct quotation. The following lists outline specific guidelines for capitalization.

What Should Be Capitalized

Capitalize the names of ships, aircraft, spacecraft, and trains:

Apollo 13
Boeing 767
DC–10
HMS *Bounty*
Mariner 4
Sputnik II

Capitalize the names of divine beings:

God
Allah
Buddha
Holy Ghost
Jehovah
Jupiter
Shiva
Venus

Capitalize the geological periods:

Cenozoic era
Neolithic age
Ice Age
late Pleistocene times

Capitalize the names of astronomical bodies:

Big Dipper
Halley's comet
Mercury
the Milky Way

North Star
Ursa Major

Capitalize personifications:

Reliable Nature brought her promised Spring.
Bring on Melancholy in his sad might.
She believed that Love was the answer to all her problems.

Capitalize historical periods:

Age of Louis XIV
Christian Era
the Great Depression
the Middle Ages
Reign of Terror
the Renaissance
Roaring Twenties
World War I

Capitalize the names of organizations, associations, and institutions:

Common Market
Franklin Glen High School
Girl Scouts
Harvard University
Kiwanis Club
League of Women Voters
Library of Congress
New York Philharmonic
Pittsburgh Steelers
North Atlantic Treaty Organization
Smithsonian Institution
Unitarian Church

Capitalize government and judicial groups:

Arkansas Supreme Court
British Parliament
Committee on Foreign Affairs
Department of State
Georgetown City Council
Peace Corps

     U.S. Census Bureau
     U.S. Court of Appeals
     U.S. House of Representatives
     U.S. Senate

A general term that accompanies a specific name is capitalized only if it follows the specific name. If it stands alone, comes before the specific name, or is used on second reference, it is lowercased:

     Central Park, the park
     Golden Gate Bridge, the bridge
     the Mississippi River, the river
     Monroe Doctrine, the doctrine of expansion
     President Obama, the president of the United States
     Pope Benedict XVI, the pope
     Queen Elizabeth I, the queen of England
     Senator Dixon, the senator from Illinois
     Treaty of Versailles, the treaty
     Tropic of Capricorn, the tropics
     Webster's Dictionary, the dictionary
     Washington State, the state of Washington

Capitalize the first word of a sentence:

     Our car would not start.
     When will you leave? I need to know right away.
     Never!
     Let me in! Please!

When a sentence appears within a sentence, start it with a capital letter:

     We had only one concern, "When would we eat?"
     My sister said, "I'll find the Monopoly game."
     He answered, "We can only stay a few minutes."

The most important words of titles are capitalized. Those words not capitalized are conjunctions (*and, or, but*) and short prepositions (*of, on, by, for*). The first and last word of a title must always be capitalized:

     A Man for All Seasons
     Crime and Punishment

Of Mice and Men
Rise of the West
Strange Life of Ivan Osokin
Sonata in G Minor
"Let Me In"
"Ode to Billy Joe"
Rubaiyat of Omar Khayyam
All in the Family

Capitalize newspaper and magazine names:

The New York Times
the Washington Post
National Geographic
U.S. News & World Report

Capitalize radio and TV network abbreviations or station call letters:

ABC
CNN
HBO
NBC
WBOP
WNEW

Capitalize regions:

the Northeast, the South, the West
Eastern Europe
but: the south of France, the east side of town

Capitalize specific military units:

the U.S. Army, but: the army, the German navy, the British air force
the Seventh Fleet
the First Infantry Division

Capitalize political organizations, and in some cases, their philosophies, and members:

Democratic Party, the Communist Party
Marxist
Whigs
Nazism

Federalist (in U.S. history contexts)

But do not capitalize systems of government or individual adherents to a philosophy:

democracy, communism
fascist, agnostic

Do not capitalize compass directions or seasons:

north, south, east, west
spring, summer, winter, autumn

Capitalize specific diseases:

Alzheimer's
Swine Flu

DON'T capitalize general diseases:

cancer
flu
heart disease

Capitalize search engines, names of computer programs, internet service providers, websites, electronic databases:

Google
Yahoo
Microsoft Word
America Online
HotWired
LexisNexis
InfoTrak

Numbers, the basics

When to spell out a number and when to use the numeral (ten, or 10)—that's the question! Unfortunately, there's no simple answer because the experts differ: some say spell out numbers between one and ten, and use numerals for all above ten: *Only 59 students out of 100 passed the test.* Some experts, however, recommend spelling out all the numbers from one to ninety nine. So chose whichever you like best, but be consistent.

There are some clear cut guidelines however. Never begin a sentence with a number—it must be spelled out:

> Correct: *Fifty-nine out of 100 students passed the test.*
> Incorrect: *20 students flunked the exam.*

Do not spell, rather use numbers for any requiring more than two words:

> Correct: *We sent out 157 invitations.*
> Incorrect: *We sent out one hundred fifty-seven invitations.*

If two numbers are next to one another, spell out one and use a number for the other:

> Correct: *John ran three, 50 yard races.*
> Incorrect: *John ran 3, 50 yard races.*

Percentages, statistics, distances, money are not spelled out, unless they begin a sentence!

> Correct: *Recycling removes 25% of waste from landfills.*
> Incorrect *25% of the population recycles.*
> Correct: *Twenty-five percent of the population recycles.*
> Correct: *We drove 10 miles out of the way to find a Starbucks.*
> Correct: *The sweater cost $59.99.*

Commonly Misused Words and Phrases

Note that many of the confusions involve parts of speech.

A lot/a lot: a lot is informally used a lot. But it is incorrect.

> *"A lot" is a much used informal phrase; do not use it in your writing.*

Advice/advise: advice is a noun; advise, a verb.

> *I never asked for your advice.*

> *The counselor advised me to research the biotechnology field.*

Affect/effect: *affect* is a verb meaning "to influence, or have impact upon"; *effect* is a noun meaning results of; effect can also be used to mean influence, or impact but not as a verb: The effects of nuclear radiation are radiation sickness, soil contamination, and global pollution.

> *Poverty affects the incidence of animal neglect. When people are short on cash, they sometimes abandon their pets.*

> *My paper concerns the effects of television violence on children's behavior.*

All ready/already: *all ready* means fully prepared; *already* is an adverb meaning previously or before

> *I was all ready to leave for my trip when I got the surprise cancellation.*

> *By the time I arrived home, the family had already eaten.*

Bad/badly: *bad* is an adjective and thus modifies nouns and pronouns; *badly* is an adverb

> *John looked bad after his accident*

> *John was badly hurt in the accident.*

Breath/breathe: *Breath* is a noun; *breathe* is a verb

> *I was all out of breath by the time I reached the summit.*

> *She was so frightened that she couldn't breathe.*

Capitol/capital: A *capitol* is a building wherein a legislative body meets. A *capital* is either a political center as in, Boston is the capital of Massachusetts, or it refers to the uppercase letter that must begin all sentences. Capital can also mean goods, assets, cash.

> *Madoff bilked many investors of their capital.*

Complement/compliment: *complement* means to go along with, to match; *compliment* means "to flatter. Both can be either nouns or verbs.

> *The professor complimented the class on its stellar performance.*
>
> *As one of the class members, I felt honored by his compliment.*

Conscience: the part of mind that experiences right and wrong

> *After lying to his girlfriend, Jim's conscience bothered him.*

Conscientious: an adjective meaning very careful, attentive to requirements

> *He is a very conscientious teacher; lectures are always well-prepared.*

Conscious: an adjective meaning aware or deliberate

> *Irena is often not conscious of how alienating her behavior can be.*

Continual/continuous: *continuous* refers to something that never stops; *continual* to something that happens frequently but not always.

> *The continuous force of evolution means that change is inevitable.*
>
> *Rainfall is the result of the continuous cycle of evaporation and condensation linking the waters of the earth and the clouds of its atmosphere.*
>
> *The college students in the apartment above us have frequent parties that continually disturb us in the middle of the night.*

Council/counsel: *council* is a noun and signifies a group; *counsel* is either a noun or a verb meaning advice or to advise

> *Four magnificent mutts, Dublin, Logan, Molly, and Sasha elected me to the Council of All Beings.*
>
> *The council debated heatedly before finally deciding to whom the prize was awarded.*
>
> *The therapist counseled my best friend to leave her relationship.*
>
> *When I met her partner, I gave her the same counsel.*

Desert/dessert: *desert* is an arid land; *dessert* is a delicious sweet food.

> *Arizona contains many deserts.*
>
> *Dessert is the best part of the meal.*
>
> *Mnemonics: As a desert lacks water, so the word lacks an s.*

Every day/everyday: *every day* is a phrase, two words meaning "happening daily"; *everyday,* one word, meaning ordinary, usual

> *Every day I go to the gym to work out.*
>
> *Arguments at dinner are everyday affairs.*

Farther/further: *farther* refers to physical distance, while *further* refers to difference in degree or time

> *The restaurant is about two miles farther down this road.*
>
> *His shifting eyes were further proof of guilt.*

Good/well: *good* is an adjective; *well* is an adverb. Hence,

> *I may look good, but I don't feel well.*
>
> *He cooks very well.*

Hanged/hung: unless you are referring to stringing someone up by a rope, use *hung.*

> *The stockings were hung on the chimney. The clothes hung on the line.*
>
> *The vigilantes hanged John Dooley for his thievery.*

Its/it's: *its* is a possessive form of *it*– a pronoun; *it's* a contraction of it is.

> *Our town must improve its roads.*
>
> *It's time to leave the zoo.*

Like/as: *like* is a preposition; *as* is a conjunction that introduces a clause. Hence, if a statement has a verb, use *as*; if not, use *like.*

> *Dorothy drank as heartily as a thirsty camel.*
>
> *Her muscles were strong and ropey like a weight lifter's.*

Loose/lose: *loose* means "not attached," the opposite of tight; *lose* means to misplace

> *He has been accused of having loose lips: don't trust him!*
>
> *If I lose these keys, I'll be in serious trouble.*

Passed/past: *passed* is the past tense of the verb, *to pass,* meaning to move by, or succeed; *past* is a noun meaning before the present time

> *We passed two hitchhikers on Route 22.*
>
> *In times past, people enjoyed much richer social lives.*

Principal/principle: *principal* means a supervisor or something of major importance; *principle* refers to a value, an idea.

> *The principal of Sunnyside High was fired for fiscal irresponsibility.*
> *Some pal!*
>
> *The fired principal was evidently not a man of high principles.*

Proceed, proceeds, precede: *proceed* is a verb meaning to carry on, to go forth; *proceeds*, a plural noun, meaning revenue raised; *precede* is a verb, meaning to be ahead or in front of, or earlier than:

> *"Proceed, counselor," bellowed the judge, "or be fined for stalling."*
>
> *In the Easter procession, the Bishops, priests, and other clergy precede the parishioners.*
>
> *The proceeds from the raffle are going to the Food Bank.*

Quote/quotation: *quote* is a verb; *quotation* is a noun

> *I chose a quotation from Karl Marx to summarize the negative effects of capitalism upon family ties.*
>
> *I quoted Karl Marx to emphasize the adverse effects of capitalism on family ties.*

Raise/rise: *raise* means to elevate, or to increase. Past tense is regular, *raised*; *rise* means to stand up, to get up. Past tense is irregular *rose*.

> *The State Department of Education is charged with raising academic standards.*

The reform effort has successfully raised student achievement.

"All rise for the benediction," the minister directed.

The congregation rose for the benediction as surely as the sun rises every day.

Real/really: *real* is an adjective; *really*, an adverb.

He is a real artist, in my opinion, contrary to the hacks employed in advertising.

He is a really good artist, despite his large commercial appeal.

Set/sit: *set* means to put down or to adjust; its past tense is also *set*. *Sit* is a verb meaning to place oneself in a sitting position; the past is *sat*.

John set his hat on the bureau.

After setting his hat on the bureau, John sat in his favorite chair.

Than/then: *than* is a comparison word; *then* is an adverb referring to time

The politics of health care are more complicated even than those of public education.

I got up at 8:00 AM and, then, five minutes later, I was on my way to the office.

Their/they're: *their* is a possessive pronoun; *there're* is a contraction for they are.

The Smiths can be annoying; they're always late for dinner.

Their habitual lateness annoys their friends.

Used to/use to: *used to* is the past tense phrase to express a former action/state; *use to* is simply incorrect.

When American artists migrated to France in the 1920s, they used to gather at the Café Metro in Paris.

Who/whom: *who* is the nominative case; *whom*, the objective case (Review pronoun section)

The first person who reaches the goal post wins the prize.

Ask not for whom the bell tolls: It tolls for thee.

Who's/whose: *who's* is a contraction of who is; *whose* is a possessive pronoun

The student who's voted the most likely to succeed wins a full scholarship.

The student whose GPA is the highest wins a full scholarship for graduate school.

Your /you're: *you're* is a contraction of you are; *your* is a possessive pronoun

The neighbors dislike that you're an environmentalist who doesn't cultivate a lawn.

The neighbors dislike your choice of herbs and stones for your front yard.

Teaching Tip: Mnemonics is an effective tool to help students with confusing words and spelling problems. Making up ways to remember can be an entertaining and instructive class exercise. For instance, remember that *principal* is a pal (person).

SPELLING

Many of the easily confused words we study are different in spelling such as, advice/advice. Many stem from confusing phonetics (how a word sounds) with how it is spelled, a real problem since English contains many words spelled very differently from how they sound. There are some rules to help us. For instance, the jingle that many of us learned:

I before e except after c, or when it sounds like "ay" as in neighbor, eighteen, weigh.

Unfortunately, there are exceptions such as *seize, leisure, height*.

Plural formations are another area in which some general rules help:

Recall from the section above that discusses nouns that most nouns form plural by adding *s*: (flower/flowers; car/cars). However, if a noun ends in a *–y* that follows a consonant (country), then drop the *y* and substitute *ies*, as in *country/countries* or *story/stories*. However, the *y* is kept if it follows a vowel (*day/days*), or if it ends a proper noun (*Barney/Barneys*).

What's a person to do? Given the many exceptions that characterize English, here are two practical strategies:

- Do not rely on spell-check alone for there are some words it simply cannot pick up.

- Familiarize yourself with the typical problem situations (such as *ie/ei*), pay attention to them, look them up in a dictionary if you are not sure. The following are common words prone to spelling errors:

    Occurred
    Heroes
    Parallel
    Laboratory
    Preferred
    Preference
    Grievance

PRACTICE EXERCISES

1. Put a double line under the sentence's main (independent) clause; put a single line under its dependent (subordinate) clause.

    While the writer wanted to create a sense of mystery, he did not succeed.

2. Working with the sentence below, construct two compound sentences using two different connectors.

    Since the day had turned cold and rainy, we decided to skip our walk and to go to a movie instead.

3. Underline all the prepositional phrases in the sentence below. What type of sentence is it?

To her great disappointment, Sarah did not get into the school of her choice, but to her credit, she immediately re-applied for admission to next year's class.

4. Name the underlined group below. What part of speech is it functioning as?

   Seeing you so upset was disturbing to me.

5. Double underline the 2 main (independent) clauses; single-underline the dependent clause. What type of sentence is this?

   The car that Jack sells gets forty miles per gallon, and it costs under $20,000.

6. Double underline the main (independent) clauses; single-underline the two dependent clauses. What sentence type is this?

   Except that she is overweight, Sandra met all the physical requirements for the firefighters' union, although that one problem may keep her out.

7. Both of these sentences have the same problem. What is it? Construct two sentences that correct the problem.

   Jeff wants either to go to college or a cross–country trip. If he takes the trip, he plans to take his dog, his father's RV, and to camp in National Parks.

8. Underline the main (independent) clause in the sentence below. What type of sentence is this?

   In their parents' absence, Tim and John have had to clean house and cook dinner every night for the past two weeks.

9. The sentence below is a(n)
   (A) compound sentence.
   (B) complex sentence.
   (C) simple sentence.
   (D) absolute phrase.

The truck in the backyard is filled with rickety furniture and rusty appliances.

10. The following describes or shows the correct punctuation of the sentence below.
    (A) place a comma before *but.*
    (B) place a comma before and after *but.*
    (C) place commas around *into the evening.*
    (D) do nothing; it's correct as it is.

    Sarah studied long into the evening every night for a week but she still failed the test.

11. The underlined section of the sentence below is a(n)
    (A) independent clause.
    (B) prepositional phrase.
    (C) dependent clause.
    (D) appositive phrase.

    <u>*After the dust settled and feelings were calmed*</u>*, we could speak logically and resolve our differences.*

12. The three criteria for a sentence are
    I.   a subject
    II. a verb
    III. an independent clause
    IV. a complete thought
    V.   a predicate
    VI. a direct object

    (A) I, III, VI
    (B) II, VI, V
    (C) I, II, IV
    (D) V, VI, II

13. Which of the following statements is most accurate?
    (A) A fragment is a phrase that is not a complete thought.
    (B) A fragment is a dependent clause incorrectly punctuated with a beginning capital and an ending period.
    (C) A fragment is a dependent clause attached to an independent clause.

(D) A fragment is two or more clauses incorrectly connected to one another.

14. The underlined phrase in the sentence below is most fully described by as a
    (A) modifier of *difficulty*.
    (B) prepositional phrase with a gerund functioning as an adverb modifying *difficulty*.
    (C) prepositional phrase with a verb that modifies the adverb, *difficulty*.
    (D) gerund functioning as an indirect object.

    Leonardo da Vinci could paint exquisitely, but he had great difficulty <u>*with writing*</u>.

15. Which of the following statements BEST describes the sentence below?
    (A) It is a well-constructed complex sentence.
    (B) It is a sentence beginning with a participial phrase that is correctly punctuated with a comma.
    (C) It is a sentence with a dangling modifier.
    (D) It is a simple sentence with a gerund phrase.

    Failing to pass the test, all the potential benefits were lost

16. Which of the following BEST describes the sentence below?
    (A) The sentence opens with a misplaced modifier and needs to be revised.
    (B) The sentence opens with a dependent clause, is attached to an independent clause, and is a complex one.
    (C) This is a compound sentence incorrectly punctuated with a comma.
    (D) This is a simple sentence that contains two gerunds.

    Hiding in the dark shadows cast by the trees, the searchers had a difficult time seeing the wandering livestock

Practice Exercise Answers

1. <u>*While the writer wanted to create a sense of mystery,*</u> *he did not succeed.*

2. *The day had turned cold and rainy, so we decided to skip our walk and to go to a movie.*

   The day had turned cold and rainy; therefore, we decided to skip our walk and to go to a movie

3. *To her great disappointment, Sarah did not get* into the school *of her choice, but to her credit, she immediately re-applied for admission to next year's class.*

    Compound sentence connected with one of the FANBOYS.

4. *Seeing you so upset was disturbing to me.*
    1. gerund phrase
    2. noun (subject of the verb 'was'.)

5. *The car that Jack sells gets forty miles per gallon, and it costs under $20,000.*

    *The car that Jack sells gets forty miles per gallon,
    and it costs under $20,000.*

6. *Except that she is overweight, Sandra met all the physical requirements for the firefighters' union, although that one problem may keep her out.*

    Complex sentence

7. Both are weakened by lack of parallel structures

    Jeff wants either to go to college or to take a cross-country trip.
    If he takes the trip, he plans to take his dog, to drive his father's RV, and to camp in National Parks.

8. *In their parents' absence, Tim and John have had to clean house and cook dinner every night for the past two weeks.*

    Simple Sentence

9. (C) Simple sentence with only one independent clause.

10. *Sarah studied long into the evening every night for a week but she still failed the test.*

    (A) Comma always comes before a FANBOYS in a compound sentence.

11. (C) A dependent clause since *we could speak logically and resolve our differences I* makes no sense on its own.

12. (C) A sentence requires a subject, verb, and a complete thought.

13. (B) Since a phrase can be a complete thought (A) is not correct. And both (C) and (D) are not necessarily true, (B) is the correct answer.

14. (B) is the only possible answer.

15. (B) It is a sentence beginning with a participial phrase that is correctly punctuated with a comma.

16. (A) The sentence opens with a misplaced modifier and needs to be revised.

Application of Writing Skills to the Classroom

DEVELOPING WRITING SKILLS

Writing skills enrich our personal lives and our careers. By the time we reach middle school, success is closely tied to writing particularly in the language arts, history, and the social sciences. In the more demanding fields of higher education, writing skills become more important and expand significantly in business and science careers.

The workplace also highly values writing skills. The job ads are filled with requirements for "excellent communication skills." Rightfully so! Your future students may be seeking jobs in business, where they will write emails daily, correspond frequently, and prepare reports often. Grant applications, reports, and publications fund and advance scientific careers. In short, all professional and technical jobs require good writing skills, and all jobs require good communication skills.

But we are more than our jobs; our personal and social lives are equally important to us. Effective writing enriches these, too. We communicate with those close and closest to ourselves when they are away, or when we need to express our feelings, or when we have conflicts to resolve. We want to help our children with their essays; we want to express ourselves with a letter to the editor; we want to defend ourselves against a complaint or we want to ask for a total refund and apology.

Books about writing often neglect these interpersonal and social parts of life; more rarely still do they discuss how writing fosters self-development. We all have a relationship to ourselves. We harbor feelings and thoughts of which we are often unaware or aware of only dimly. Many writers speak of how writing helps them know themselves better; they claim that by writing daily they benefit from emotional and mental development even healing and improved health. As the ancients urged, "Know thyself; it is the beginning of all wisdom."

Finally, we are judged on our writing skills. People value and respect the effective writer. But they also judge us harshly when we fail to demonstrate good writing skills. We come across as *illiterate*, a generally negative assessment of all our abilities.

The message: Writing is empowering in all aspects of our lives; it's worth the effort to develop!

> **Teaching Tip:** Explore the importance of writing skills to students' vocational, professional, and personal lives. Motivate students to want to learn.

Writing Takes Time and Effort

Writing an essay or a paragraph, or a good sentence, is a sophisticated mental and physical accomplishment. This is why we have written this book, and why you are reading it. Knowing the basics and practicing them is how we become effective writers; writing demands learning and effort. There is no shortcut!

In contrast, speaking is learned effortlessly, simply in the course of living and interacting with other human beings. By the age of three, children have mastered the basic grammar of their native languages, and by the age of five, they command the vocabulary to live fully functional lives in their societies. The development of speech is certainly extraordinary, and certainly not simple. But learning to speak does not require study. However, no one learns to write without instruction and study. Writing is a learned activity that builds upon, but goes far beyond, speech.

The evolution of human beings provides an interesting analogy to individuals' acquisition of speech and writing. Anthropologists, for instance, trace the first written activities and artifacts—the existence of physical marks on some material—not yet even an alphabet, to approximately 6000 BCE. Yet it took another thousand years before an alphabet was developed. Human societies and human beings who spoke a language have been traced back to nearly 30,000 BCE. But our species spoke for tens of thousands of years before being capable of the written language.

The message: There is nothing natural about writing; it is a cultural creation, acquired only with concentration, effort, practice.

Why stress this point?

Many people hold the false idea that "some" are good at writing and "some" just aren't—it's in the genes. This myth discourages the effort and the confidence that students need to develop into effective writers. Writing is the application of learned, specialized knowledge. With guidance and effort, we all can learn to become effective writers though relatively few of us will become artists.

Indeed, the best analogy for setting an apt learning expectation for students is that between writing and playing a musical instrument. Both require knowledge, application (practice), time, and effort! Anyone can learn to play the piano decently, but only a few will become virtuosos. We don't need to be artists to communicate accurately and to win the appreciation of our teachers and colleagues. But no pianist simply learns to read music and then sits on a bench and plays Beethoven, or even "Silent Night." No, even the simplest song requires practice or all the knowledge is futile to actual performance.

> **Teaching Tip:** Use sports as an analogy to emphasize the important of "doing" writing, the time first to develop competence, then to strive for finesse.

Many students fail to produce clear writing because they wait till the last day to write their papers. Typically, they then write "off the top of their heads," meaning, driven by the pressure, they write what comes into their mind, read it (maybe) to catch any glaring errors, and then put it between a fancy cover.

Nothing could be more unproductive; it neither produces good writing, nor—and this is most damaging—does it provide the opportunity for the development of skill through practice and effort.

Developing an effective composition takes time–in that time, one plans, organizes, and revises. Each of these steps has its own objectives; yet, each is also connected. The writer is constantly going from part to whole and back again, from sentence to paragraph, from paragraph to thesis, etc. The objective is a whole that harmonizes all the parts. The writer achieves this only through time.

The Approach

Just as the pianist may practice one chord over and over, or the beginning trumpet player will practice the scale before being capable of playing a whole musical composition, so, too, the writer learns the notes and chords, and practices these, with the objective of putting it all together in an essay.

As instructors to ourselves or to others, we develop effective writing by examining and practicing writing notes, chords, and principles of connection (rhythm, harmony etc.).

Of course, the names differ: sentences, paragraphs, unity, development, coherence; but the process is similar. We can learn and practice the parts so that we may put them together effectively into the whole piece.

Thus, in this section, we start with the paragraph "part" before moving on to the essay that equals "paragraph + paragraph + paragraph." In the previous section, we examined the sentence "part," but from the viewpoint of grammar and punctuation. Now we view it as in connection to meaning and message. We also go to the smallest parts words and practice their role in the whole. Finally, we take apart the process itself, dividing it into five stages that, again, proceed over a period of time.

The Application

By examining the parts and practicing their laws, we carve out a manageable task demanding less time than the whole essay. Most important because the laws and principle of the parts are the same as those for the whole, even as we learn effective paragraph writing, we are learning effective essay writing.

The five stages of writing sort out the mental steps that must be taken to compose an essay. Just because they are stages, the model emphasizes the time factor.

Teaching Tip: Provide exercises to practice the parts and the laws of writing; structure assignments over time. The outline is due one week, the first draft the next, etc.

Paragraph Structure and Organization

To compare writing a composition to constructing a building emphasizes the key point that effective writing is created with principles and laws. An essay is built with words connected to each other and organized in accord with rules and laws just as the architect's house is built with materials—cement, lumber, metal—which are organized together in accord with the laws of mathematical relationships, mechanics, and hydraulics. Without obeying the basic laws, the building falls apart—and the paper fails to communicate.

We all want to be clear writers, to get our words on paper to say what's in our heads. Thus, we must become architects of the word and masters of the basic knowledge of clear thinking and clear writing. Of course, as we emphasized in the introduction, one needs to **apply** this knowledge for it to matter.

Structure and Laws of Paragraphs and Essays

Structure refers to the parts of a paragraph or an essay; *laws* refer to the principles that govern the **relationships** of the parts to each other. Examining these two organizational principles, we discover how tightly knit effective writing is: a paragraph is in many ways a microcosm of an essay; it has a very similar structure (parts), and it uses the same organizational laws.

We are starting with the microcosm, the paragraph, but the same laws govern the essay to which the paragraphs belong: at every level of writing, like a hologram, the three laws are operating.

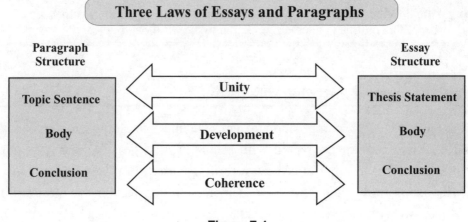

Figure 7.1

Unity

In a well-crafted paragraph the sentences will be servants to one main idea and that idea will be formulated in one of the sentences, the *topic sentence*. There are many metaphors that express this organization. For instance, consider the topic sentence as the navigator of a ship with a specific destination; his/her role is to direct that vehicle to the destination (getting across the main idea); the role of the crew (the supporting sentences that comprise the body) is to follow the line charted (keep to the main idea).

Thus, the crew member who strays from the charted course, breaks the unity, takes the ship off course. The readers are like passengers on a misguided ship, they find themselves unpleasantly surprised by twists and turns, annoyed at the waste of time and energy (the shortest distance is a straight line, or keep to the point!), and confused about just where the ship is taking them: what's the point of this paragraph?

The topic sentence tells readers where they are going, so as the journey progresses they are able to make sense of the various points. Without a topic sentence or with only a weak one, the readers are as on the sea without direction. Read the following paragraph:

Revision 1: the missing topic statement

> *"If I could read," one peasant said in explanation of his difficulties, "I should have four eyes, but now I see nothing." Illiteracy, coupled with the language barrier, meant Italians were frustrated in their ability to compete in America's growing industrial society. Italians came to America mainly as unskilled laborers and were amongst the nation's lowest-paid immigrant groups. In 1905, Boston households headed by*

the language barrier, meant Italians were frustrated in their ability to compete in America's growing industrial society. Italians came to America mainly as unskilled laborers and were amongst the nation's lowest-paid immigrant groups. In 1905, Boston households headed by Southern (the poorest) Italians, who accounted for about 80% of all Italian immigrants at that time, earned an average of $360 annually, far below German, Swedish, and Irish immigrants, and slightly below Russian Jews, all of whom had a much higher literacy rate. In the North end the figure was far lower, about $338 annually. (Polio 2007)

Now insert the topic statement at the beginning and examine how it provides direction and meaning:

<u>Illiteracy</u> proved the most <u>serious handicap</u> for Italians to overcome.

Revision 2: breaking unity, the wandering crew

Sometimes, as in the example above, paragraphs need revision because they lack a topic statement; more often in student writing, the paragraph violates the law of unity: one or more of the supporting sentences veers off the path, introducing or digressing into a topic different from the main idea:

In the past ten years, many newcomers have entered our neighborhood and are changing it. They buy a vacant lot, for instance, where we kids like to play, and then they build a fancy big house that makes our homes look like shacks. If they don't build something new, they purchase an apartment house and turn it into condominiums where few children live. Then they put a gate around the yard and shut us off from our playfields. I just hate what they are doing. It makes me and the other kids really angry. Sometimes we even hide behind bushes and throw rotten apples at the newcomers' cars. It's not that we dislike them; what we hate is how they are changing our neighborhood. Not only do they construct fancy houses that make us look bad, but they never come out of their houses the way we do. We talk to each other; we hang out on our porches and in our yards, and none of them are enclosed and decorated with "private property" signs.

Revision:

In the past ten years, many <u>newcomers</u> *have entered our neighborhood and are* <u>changing</u> *it*. The underlined words identify the main points. The writer starts by correctly giving examples to develop that point, but about midway, the writer's feelings erupt, and a new idea—not in the topic statement—intrudes to break the unity:

> *It makes me and the other kids really angry. Sometimes we even hide behind bushes and throw rotten apples at the newcomers' cars.*

Teaching Tip: Students need exercises to help distinguish between ideas and points that are <u>related</u> to the main idea, but are **not** developing the main idea. Yes, it's because of the changes that kids are angry, but that's not in the topic statement.

Revision 3: a weak topic sentence.

There are poor, good, and better topic sentences. The qualities of an effective *topic sentence* are the same as those of an effective *thesis statement*. This likeness is logical because, as we said above, the paragraph is a mini-essay. Thus, as the topic sentence expresses the main idea of the paragraph, the thesis statement expresses the main idea of the essay. Like the effective thesis statement, the best topic statements are **specific** (not vague and general).

Examine the following paragraph; see if you can identify the weakness of the topic sentence.

> *Angry drivers can be dangerous. The best thing to do is to move away from them, especially if they are behind you. If you can, signal, and then allow them to pass.*
>
> *If you're on a road that doesn't permit passing, consider pulling over and stopping so they can go ahead. Should this not be possible and the angry driver begins honking and tailgating, do not give back any angry signals. These might provoke the assailant to greater heights of anger, and, as we have all seen, road rage can result in very destructive actions. Don't take a chance; even if the odds are with you, you don't want to be the victim of an irrational adult.*

Revision note: The key point is underlined: *Angry drivers can be dangerous*. This would lead us to expect a paragraph describing and giving examples of the dangers posed by angry drivers. Instead, the supporting sentences concern **strategies for avoiding** angry drivers.

A more effective topic sentence: *Because they are so dangerous, it's wise to avoid angry drivers.*

Or: *My experience with angry drivers has taught me to avoid them at all costs.*

On Paragraph Structure: Topic statements can be in the middle or at the end of a paragraph, but it is best to encourage student writers to place them as the first sentence in the paragraph. In this position, it can serve as a guide, keeping the writer focused on the main point.

> **Teaching Tip:** In the revision process, highlight the topic *sentence* and underline its signal words as the previous examples have demonstrated. This simple practice helps sharpen thinking, create effective topic statements and unified paragraphs.

Development: The Body/Supporting Sentences

To develop, to get across to readers, their points, writers need to "say enough" so that the reader "gets it." This involves such developmental strategies such as defining, explaining or analyzing the points, and giving examples. Look at the paragraph above and note how the writer gave examples, explained, the signal phrases *avoiding angry drivers*—that is development.

Let's explain (that is, develop!) this law further by comparison and contrast, starting with the latter. Suppose students are writing on the subject of self-esteem. The following paragraph illustrates problems with development instructors typically find in student writing.

> *Self-esteem is really powerful. In fact, it's what makes most people successful because if you feel good about yourself, you have the kind of positive attitude that leads to winning. People with self esteem are the winners in life. Everyone should try to develop self-esteem.*

What are some of the problems with too little development?

- Too much *repetition* of the same idea: *people with self-esteem are successful*
- Use of *general words* that lack definition; e.g. self-esteem: what is it? And, how is it powerful?
- Lack of *specific examples* of success? Who?

By contrast, examine the following:

> *Self-esteem has a <u>large effect</u> on <u>how</u> a person <u>sees</u> the world. Whether a person feels good about him/herself or feels poorly about self will show in how he or she sees or interprets other people's behavior. People who have low self-esteem don't value themselves, so they perceive others as not liking, or not respecting or caring about them. Thus, if a friend walks by, distracted by some personal problems, and looks distant, the person with low self-esteem is likely to perceive his friend's failure to say hello as rejection. He then feels terrible about himself inside as he receives (creates!) this dispiriting message. By contrast, the woman who feels good about herself, is more likely to "wonder what's up with her friend" than to suffer any rejection. In most instances, people who don't feel good about themselves will see the glass as half-empty; while they who like themselves perceive the "same glass" as half-full. They tend to enjoy a fuller cup of life because they participate in pouring it for themselves!*

Let's now identify the developmental strengths. Repetition is replaced by development. That is, the writer gives a clear description of self-esteem with examples; and with comparing, and contrasting to illustrate. The writer is also specific about the examples of how people perceive and how they feel about themselves. The generalized language is replaced with more concrete language: a story, thoughts in someone's head; images of full and empty glasses and cups.

Note, too, that the topic statement is also a better guide and navigator because it is more specific and pointed than the first paragraph's vague and general: *Self-esteem is powerful.*

Teaching Tip: Students have much difficulty with development, and need to experience and examine the differences between well and poorly developed paragraphs.

Coherence

Coherence accounts for the feeling that "it flows." Coherence gives readers a smooth ride. They move down the stream, without any snags to catch their clothes and hold them back, without any boulders grinding the ride to a halt.

Writing is free of snagging branches and rocks that slow down and interrupt, when:

(1) All the parts of the paragraph (topic sentence + supporting sentences + concluding statement) are in an <u>order</u> that makes sense;

(2) When the sentences within the paragraph are <u>connected</u> to each other with appropriate transitional phrases and transitional devices. (See common examples of these below).

Coherent Order or sequence prevents the confusion readers experience if a group of ideas is out of order. Basically, there are <u>three</u> frameworks of order in a paragraph–time, space, and logic.

Time sequence is the easiest to illustrate. For instance, if a writer is describing an accident, then he/she wants to explain it in the temporal order that makes it clear:

> *I was driving down Sycamore Street, approaching the intersection at Main Street. I noticed that the light had turned yellow. I saw a red truck on my left that was also approaching the intersection. I stopped at the red light. The light had changed to red well before I reached the stop line. The light changed.*

> *It went through the light. The nose of my Volvo was already well into Main street. The truck hit me hard.*

Coherent Connections: A smooth ride also requires that the separation between sentences, the gap between periods and capital letters be bridged for the reader. Transitional phrases create those bridges. Examine how the illustration above is made <u>more coherent</u> by the addition of the underlined transitional phrases and words:

> *I was driving down Sycamore Street, approaching the intersection at Main Street. <u>As I approached</u>, I saw the light turn yellow, <u>so</u> I immediately began to slow down, preparing to stop. <u>At the same time</u>, I saw a red truck on my left that was also approaching the intersection on Main Street. <u>Shortly after</u>, I stopped because the light had turned red before I reached the stop line. <u>Then</u>, the light changed quickly back to*

green, and I slowly started across the intersection. Soon, the nose of my Volvo was well into Main Street. Then, the truck hit me hard.

Spatial order as the word indicates moves the reader in space so that he/she can best visualize what the writer is communicating. Again, the coherence aspect of "best visualize" is the spatial order. Imagine you have moved to a home in an area that your reader knows and you wish to describe your new home. An example of weak development would be:

> *The house is a multi-color single family about half-way down Shaffner St. It's got a front porch and shutters and is medium sized.*

An example of incoherent development:

> *The house is a multi-color single family about half-way down Shaffner St. It's got a front porch and shutters and is medium sized. The kitchen and a half bath are on the first floor in the rear of the house. They have been nicely remodeled. But the front porch is my favorite; the deck in the back is great, too, but I have always wanted a large front porch.*

The spatial order is wacky. The reader steps into the rear of the home, then goes back to the front porch, then to the rear of the house, then back to the front. This is rough riding for the reader!

Compare both of the above with the much improved (coherent, well-developed, with specific words to aid the visualization):

> *Take a right onto Shaffner, and start looking to your left for a warm green Victorian with beige and grape trim. About half-way down, the color will draw your eye right to the large stained glass window that faces the driveway. Pull in, and walk up the stone stairs onto the wraparound porch with its corner columns and its filigree millwork. In front of you, take in the doors. These double doors are the original carved wood and glass, and I installed the brass fixtures to enhance the antique look. You will walk into a small foyer, about 4x6, but note the clothes' closet on the right and the windows on sides—storage, plus light! I also love that the foyer is separated from the inside by yet another original carved wood and glass door that brings you right into the inner foyer, looking straight at a cozy fireplace with a carved wood mantle of oak, capped with a long beveled mirror. Don't turn around, yet. But look to your left and through the French door into the living room and right at that gorgeous stain glass window you parked in front of.*

Note how the writer is taking the reader into the house in a spatially natural, orderly manner. That's **coherent order**. Note, too, the description and the use of concrete words that help the reader see and even feel the home. That's **development**—in order to develop fully though, the writer would have to continue on through the front living room into the dining room to its right and from the rear of the dining area to the kitchen, etc.

Logical Order: this could be from general to specific, from most important to least important, or from the cause, to the effect. Common transitional words are *first*, *second third, etc.*; *accordingly, consequentially, thus.*

In the following, note how the paragraph develops the topic that lobotomies create people different from whom they were before the operation. The main transitional words are underlined.

> *Emotionally disturbed patients who undergo lobotomies (removal of the front part of their brains) lose their disturbances, but become very different people than who they were.*
>
> *Two English doctors reported on a number of such cases. <u>One</u> patient continued to lead his normal life, but, lost all relationships with even the closest members of his family and showed no interest whatever in his children. <u>Another</u> seemed to exist in a sort of vacuum; no friendship was possible with him. A <u>third</u>, a skilled mechanic still considered an excellent craftsman, lost the ability to undertake a complicated task. He stopped studying and resigned himself to being a routine worker. An unemployed clergyman didn't seem the least concerned that he was out of work. He left all decisions to his wife and was completely passive when it came to planning for the future.* (Flesch 13)

Transitional words, phrases, and devices create coherence. The following table provides the major transitional words and phrases.

Table 7.1 Major Transitional Words and Phrases

Device	Word Or Phrase
To connect	*in addition, likewise, also, furthermore, moreover, similarly*
To contrast	*however, but, in contrast, instead, on the other hand, contrarily, on the contrary*
Cause and Effect/Logical	*therefore, first... then, thus, first...second...third, accordingly, finally, consequently, as a result*

Example	*to illustrate, for instance, for example*
Time coherence	*after, then, subsequently, previous/previously, soon, meanwhile, next, recently, shortly, immediately, date (On July 1ˢᵗ, in May), season (in the summer)*

There are other **coherent devices** that <u>relate</u> sentences to one another and give a smooth ride. Here are some *dos and don'ts* for strengthening coherence.

Don't Shift Verb Tense, or Person

- **No** Shifts in Verb Tense (**t**):
  Do not change verb tense in the same passage or paragraph(s). For instance:

  > *John practiced his golf every day. He drives powerfully and accurately.*

Note the writer starts with <u>past</u> tense, *practiced*, and then switches to <u>present</u> tense, *drives*.

- **No** Shifts of Person

  > *All students need to study hard because you can't pass this course without great effort.*

Note: the sentence switches from 3ʳᵈ person (students, *they*) to 2ⁿᵈ person (*you*).

> **Teaching Tip:** Be on the lookout for the use of "you" in student writing. It is a common error either because it is a shift as in the example above, or it is used incorrectly as the general "you," or both. *You* is only correctly used when the writer is directly addressing the reader, as when one writes a letter to someone. In very rare cases, an essay does directly address the reader, but in 99.999% of student writing this is not the case.

- **Use parallel sentence structure**. Have students' skim their papers, pausing at the words "and" and "or." Have them check the phrases on each side of these words to see whether the items joined are parallel if not, make them parallel.

  > *We shall fight on the beaches. We shall fight on the landing grounds; we shall fight on the fields and in the streets. We shall fight in the hills. We shall never surrender.*

- **Look for Sentence Variety**. Suggest students <u>vary the rhythm</u> by alternating short and long sentences, simple and complex sentences. Another suggestion is for students to vary <u>sentence openings</u> too many sentences begin with the words *The*, *It*, *I*, and *This*. Different beginnings to sentences not only change the structure of the sentence, but can also add emphasis.

Introductory Paragraph: The Psychology and Style

Neither as readers and often not as writers are we fully conscious of the ways that writing "gets into the head" of the reader. As we discussed in Chapter 6, the writer doesn't want to annoy or frustrate the reader by causing unnecessary confusion and/or interrupting the smooth flow of attention with confusing grammar and mechanics. Best to think of the reader as a sensitive creature who needs stroking, who is somewhat lazy and doesn't like difficulties in the path of a "good read," and, finally, one whose loyalty requires that you interest and engage his attention.

The introduction needs to be crafted with this psychology in mind. Communication researchers claim that peoples' attitudes towards others are established within the first five seconds of meeting, highlighting the importance of the first impression. In the writing context, the introduction is essential for "hooking" (interesting) and informing the reader (clearly informed of the purpose and main idea of the essay: the effective thesis!) if he is to commit the energy and time to read on.

Benefits of the funnel organization:

- It provides students with a template to "fill-in" (grabber; from general to more specific; ending with the thesis statement)

- Ending with the thesis statement makes it easier to transition smoothly to the first paragraph of the essay's body

---

Teaching Tip: While there is no hard-and-fast formula for how an introductory paragraph is organized, for teaching and learning, it is a good idea to use the popular funnel structure.

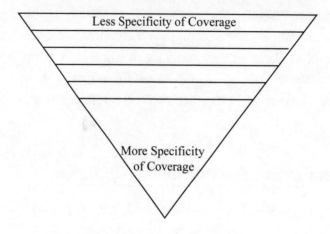

Figure 7.2 Funnel Structure

Identifying the Parts: Examine this funnel-shaped introduction to an essay that analyzes the writings of Stephen King, the popular author of horror:

> [1]*Stephen King, creator of such stories as* Carrie *and* Pet Sematary, *stated that the Edgar Allan Poe stories he read as a child gave him the inspiration and instruction he needed to become the writer that he is. Poe is the master of the horror, and his short stories are filled with nerve-racking shrieks, creepy dark vaults, diabolical madmen, and nightmarish twists and turns.[2] Poe, as does Stephen King, fills the reader's imagination with the images that he wishes the reader to see, hear, and feel. Thus, it's not surprising that following in the footsteps of his ghoulish mentor, King's grotesque novels are stamped with vivid, concrete* imagery *and* symbols *to create settings that pulse with emotion, and take us into mental caverns to reveal the* psychologies of dark personalities.

Modeling Revision: Use the chart on the next page to examine each part of the paragraph above. Does the first sentence introduce us to the subject in an interesting way? Well, it certainly lets us know the writing is about Stephen King and it does somewhat tantalize the reader by reference to Edgar Allan Poe —"quote the raven, nevermore!"

However, there's always room for improvement. Perhaps the writer could draw on the provocative imagery both of these authors use to fashion an even more powerful grabber.

> *Who does not feel a chill remembering Jack Nicholson's crazed eyes, an axe over his shoulder, and his insane mocking promise, "Daddy's coming…" to his son, both of them, the center of a grotesque violation of parent/child love played out in a barren, remote land of snow and ice and isolation and in a dwelling whose doors and hallways periodically*

spill and over flow with blood.

Or a shorter revision that also brings in Poe:

Of all the dark personalities that populate King's imaginary world, there is none darker than the insane writer played by Jack Nicholson who is reminiscent of the cast of diabolically clever madmen who populate Edgar Allan Poe's work.

Table 7.2 Revision Guidelines for Introductory Paragraphs

Guideline	Example
Grabber: an opening designed to interest the reader to continue. • **A number or statistic** • **A dramatic event** • **An intriguing question that leads into the paper's subject matter** • **A provocative quotation**	*Every year in the U.S. eighty thousand people are harmed, even killed, by doctors' poor handwriting and its consequence—wrongly filled prescriptions.* *"The fact is women are in chains, and their servitude is all the more debasing because they do not realize it."* Susan B. Anthony *How many people realize that it took a century, 100 years, of unremitting fighting for women to gain the right to vote?*
General background leading up to the thesis statement	**Review the paragraph on Stephen King**
The thesis statement: a declarative sentence that expresses the purpose and the main idea of the essay (highlight or underline the key phrases in the revision process)	*Three simple <u>operations</u> will make anyone a <u>master</u> at using the <u>IPOD</u>.* Process essay to explain three tools to help IPOD users effectively navigate this popular high-tech gadget. *The <u>costs</u> of litigating and carrying out the death penalty, connected to the evidence that it does <u>not deter</u> violent crimes are powerful reasons for abolishing the <u>death penalty</u>.* Argument essay to persuade reader to abolish the death penalty because of its economics and its failure to prevent crime. Never **announce: "This paper will show how to use ...," or "in this paper I am speaking about"**

Either the original opener or the more graphic revisions will do, but onto the next part. Does the paragraph proceed to give the reader background that leads up to the thesis statement? Yes, it gives more specifics about the relationship of Poe's writing to that of King. In particular it focuses on Poe's signature use of dramatic images and symbols.

Finally, does the thesis do its job? It does: It is a declarative sentence that promises the reader an essay on Stephen King's writing, focused <u>specifically</u> on its imagery, and its use of symbols that explore the mental states and inner thoughts of King's cast of disturbed characters like Jack Nicholson.

Consider *by contrast* how less effective a vague and general thesis such as: "Poe's use of language makes him a powerful writer of horror." What kind of language? Powerful? How?

Teaching Tip: Providing students the opportunity and the examples to compare and contrast effective and less effective openers and thesis statements is necessary to guiding the development of writing skill.

Try it out with the following introductory paragraph to an expository essay on the role of Susan B. Anthony and Elizabeth Cady Stanton, the pioneering leaders of the nineteenth century's Suffrage Movement:

> *Only because of the persistent efforts of activists in the 1980's and 90's, a marble sculpture of three women has taken its rightful place in the rotunda of the Capitol in Washington, D.C. Lucretia Mott, Susan B. Anthony, and Elizabeth Cady Stanton are depicted in vivid detail by the sculptor, Adelaide Johnson, who finished the 14,000 ton monument in 1925. Stenciled on its base, a lengthy tribute to the significance of their work begins with, "The three great destiny characters of the world whose spiritual import and historical significance transcend that of all others of any country or age." Yet, after one day on display in 1925, the statue was moved to the basement of the capital where it remained for seventy-five years awaiting the renewal of a women's movement and the efforts of women who finally succeeded in getting the monument out of the basement and into a place of honor on Mother's Day, 1997. This neglect is a historical question unto itself: Susan B. Anthony and Elizabeth Cady Stanton should be larger than life icons in American history, as well known as Patrick Henry or Paul Revere because these two leaders of the American Suffrage movement—inseparable partners on behalf of a revolution affecting millions as they dedicated their lives to the cause of women's right to vote and the inherent dignity of that privilege—<u>were individuals</u>*

of gigantic intellectual achievement, of political genius, of steel-hard, unflagging commitment to a cause larger than self.

Compare the much less specific thesis statement:

> *Susan B. Anthony and Elizabeth Cady Stanton, two nineteenth century women, played a major role in the Suffrage movement.*

The Concluding Paragraph

Essays require a concluding paragraph that, as the term suggests, gives the reader a sense of finality—it's over! To do this effectively, the conclusion must contain two parts:

1)   A summary or a restatement of the thesis; and

2)   A closing that expresses finality, possibly a bang!

Let's examine a concluding paragraph for an essay on the death penalty.

> *Finally, the facts speak loudly in favor of abolishing the death penalty. There's not a shred of evidence that this practice prevents crimes of violence, and, as study after study demonstrates, far from saving taxpayers' money, the legal costs of implementing a death sentence are double and in some cases even triple those of an average life imprisonment bill. Thanks to science, the evidence gathered from DNA testing puts the nail in the coffin of this primitive practice. If failure to deter and astronomical costs weren't enough to convince us, then surely the certainty that in the future, as in the past, at least 5% of persons who "get the chair" will be innocent victims must give us pause. Since I'm not one iota safer, and I'm definitely carrying less of my hard earned money I certainly don't want the blood of even one innocent on my conscience. Who does?*

Analysis: First, note the transitional phrase that opens the paragraph. The second underlining illustrates that the position of the writer has been re-stated. Then, the writer has re-stated the three main points that have been argued to persuade the reader. And the last two sentences actually re-state these again in a dramatic fashion, to end with a claim to the reader's conscience, and a "direct" question that puts the reader "on the spot."

The conclusion in a persuasive paper can be compared to the defense attorney or the prosecutor's final case to the jury: the writer wants to emphasize the main points and to end with a new twist.

Hour Glass Essay Structure

In the final analysis, the structure of any well-organized piece of writing resembles an hour-glass (see Figure 7.3 below).

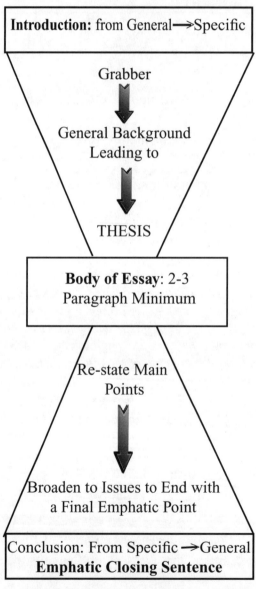

Figure 7.3 Hourglass Essay Organization

Patterns of Organization and Development

Rhetoric is the systematic study of how to communicate clearly, persuasively, and forcefully—in both speech and writing.

Rhetoric is a form of communication science. Its basic questions are how do humans think and feel, and how do they communicate ideas and feelings to one another? Rhetoric includes laws of oral and written communications, and these have somewhat different application.

Rhetoric is the science of how humans think, and in applying its laws, rhetoric seeks to teach how language can be put together to best communicate to others. Rhetoric offers formulas which writers in the laboratories of their brains, can use to express ideas and feelings. Rhetoric formulas include specific language, figurative language, parallelism.

Rhetorical Organization Patterns are frames for organizing paragraphs, for developing key points (hence they are things writers do to meet the law of paragraph development), and they can even be the organizing framework of an essay.

Process Pattern development focuses on explaining, describing, analyzing the "how to" or "how it happened" of a subject—how to change your car oil; how to edit photos in Adobe Photoshop. Or: how deregulation of the markets in the 1990's led to the current global recession; how unsafe sex leads to AIDS epidemic; how lowering the speed limit will save lives and energy. The following describes the process of keeping one's mind fresh:

> *Find a way to introduce yourself to new concepts and new ideas. Just following the same terrain will take you to the familiar places and lead you to the familiar conclusions. To reach a new or exotic destination requires taking a different route. Go outside your comfort zone! Occasionally read different publications or take a field trip to visit businesses you've never been too before.*

> *Schedule a regular time for thinking. Pick a location conducive to thinking where you will not be distracted or interrupted. Schedule 15 to thirty minutes to think (it's harder than you think). Be sure to write down your insights. (Sanborn, 38)*

> **Teaching Tip:** because "how to" approaches are easily broken down into steps, they are excellent for teaching and practicing logical organization.

Narrative Pattern: If you want to get a point across, tell a story. For example, the author Sanborn wants to explain the person who has a positive attitude and chooses this story:

> *A family has two sons who are very different—one is very negative and critical, and the other is positive and optimistic. The parents decide to see how far this difference would go, so for Christmas, they bought the negative child most desirable gifts–a new bike, a train set, and many board games.*
>
> *But for the other child, they got a box of manure.*
>
> *On Christmas morning, the negative child entered the room with all his presents displayed and looked dismayed. When questioned, he explained that his bike would get dirty after the first ride, and the other gifts would wear out in time.*
>
> *The other child was excited as he discovered his box of manure. The puzzled parents asked why. "Well," the smiling boy explained, "with all this manure, there's got to be a pony somewhere!" (Sanborn 37)*

Description Pattern development's purpose is to make the reader "see" the subject, object, or topic. Description highlights the importance of **specific** language in effective writing. Consider the difference between: *The man looked poor.* And: *His clothes were worn, torn, and dirty and his face was thin and drawn.* The reader of the first has to invent his own picture; that of the second "sees" the man in question much mo re clearly as the writer intended.Descriptions call upon the five senses: What it look like; what it feels like; what it smells like; what it taste like; what it sounds like.

Definition Pattern development highlights the importance of explanation in writing. The following section could be part of an essay that promotes educational reform by fostering service learning. But first, the writer needs to <u>define</u> it:

> *Service learning fosters academic learning, sparks student interest and motivation to learn, develops character and social awareness, and gives to the community. Some examples speak for themselves: Take the middle school in Washington that organized social interactions between classroom and kids living in the local homeless shelter. As a*

result the students wrote and illustrated children books, used computers, and desktop publishing software to publish books that they gave the shelter. Or, think of the excitement and skills of the elementary and middle school in Burlington who live in a now run-down historical, that has also become immigration center; the schoolkids are learning research, sociology, how to gather date, as they are collectively developing a history and a study of the neighborhood's demographic history. The power and gut level obviousness makes the agonizing dilemma of how to improve seem disingenuous, the extravagant waste of the testing fad painful: Service learning would revolutionize education.

It can be useful to learn the types of **definition** (note how this is classification pattern):

- **Descriptive**: what it looks like

- **Functional**: what it does

- **Logical**: how one category differs and/or is similar to another

- **Etymological**: the word or historical origin, as in the original meaning of the word *radical* is "at the root of."

<u>**Comparison Pattern**</u>: Making a comparison to get an idea across is a longer simile. The following explains rhetoric by comparing it to chemistry.

Rhetoric, like science, seeks to identify the laws and organization of phenomena. Chemists have identified the molecular structures; they discovered the two parts hydrogen and one part oxygen that make up basic water. So, too rhetoricians identified mental structures involved in communication both oral and written, how they were the same, how different, what are basic formulas— the H_2O—of getting, receiving and expressing ideas and feelings to others. Rhetoric is the science of how humans think, and in applying its laws, rhetoric seeks to teach how language can be put together to best speak to others. Rhetoric names several formulas which writers in the laboratories of their brains use their ideas and feelings.

<u>**Contrast Pattern**</u>: Showing how your subject is different from some other idea or object is another basic way of communicating:

Most of the so-called defining moments of our lives really aren't. College graduation, marriage, retirement are often called defining moments. In reality they are commemorative moments. Graduation commemorates how you spent the last four years. Marriage commemorates the courtship leading up to it. Retirement commemorates a life at work. In each instance, the person has been defined long before the moments occurred.

What are the moments that define you? They are right now. Each moment we live helps define us. People who act as leaders in their lives, and in the lives of others, understand this, and choose to live intentionally. (Sanford, 48).

Compare and Contrast Pattern development involves identifying the **similarities and the differences** between two or more objects, subjects, ideas, experiences.

Managers and leaders differ from one another is at least one crucial way. Managers are focused on themselves; leaders look more to enable their team members, and to use their powers to maintain a productive environment. As someone said: "Managers take the credit; leaders take responsibility." Managers are concerned with getting the objectives met tomorrow; leaders are planning towards the future.

Or:

Drifting and waiting are very different things. Waiting is an intentional choice. It requires patience and deliberation. Drifting takes away your power of choice. When you wait you believe that something will happen, although you may not know when. Instead of acting rashly or impetuously, you pause to gather information or to gain insight. Drifting results from rudderlessness and lack of direction. When you drift it doesn't even take particularly large waves to capsize the boat. (Sanborn, 43)

Classification Pattern development involves grouping and subdividing larger categories into their sub-parts. **High School, College,** and **Professional sports are three very different games**. This topic sentence sets the stage for a classification pattern paragraph or essay.

Or the introductory paragraph below prepares us for a classification of **citizenship** into three qualities.

We all throw around words as if we know what they mean: freedom, justice, even free trade. So, too, the phrase good citizen, and the injunctions that "thou should be one." But I am sure if a study were done it would find that there are different, even opposing, and, certainly many vague undigested thoughts about what this, we are asked, "is." It's my belief that there are three attributes that qualify a person to call him/herself a good citizen.

Teaching Tip: Because this development is crucial in the pre-writing process, it's a good exercise to have students practice, beginning with tangible subjects such as football, basketball, or restaurants, or movies, and moving towards more conceptual subjects such as political systems.

<u>**Cause and Effect Pattern** development</u> is showing how one thing leads to another. Sometimes this can be very dominant in experience writing; often in college essays it is the kind of development or paper type that requires a lot of evident and good logical, critical thinking.

MORE BASICS OF EFFECTIVE WRITING

<u>Words, Phrases, and Sentences.</u> The right choice of words is one of the most important aspects of effective writing. That selection is particularly important in English since it has more words than any of the 5000 languages in the world. So, you logically ask, on what basis does one choose the best word?

After the obvious answer that the word has to mean what we want to say, we confront the real issue of choice—that is, there are many words that mean the same thing. For instance, think of the words, *look, see, view, watch, observe, perceive, and notice.* They all mean roughly the same, yet one or the other would be better depending upon the writing situation. For instance, if the audience is children, we would probably select *look* or *see.*

That's a relatively simple example of how word choice can depend upon audience. However, the issue gets more sophisticated. Consider that words fall on a spectrum. One end of the spectrum is *abstract*, and the opposite end is *concrete*.

Specific and Concrete Language vs. Abstract language

That language falls on a scale that ranges from concrete (very grounded and specific) to airy (vague and general) is a concern crucial to effective writing. Abstract language is likely to go along with insufficient development; conversely, using specific and concrete language is likely to produce well-developed writing.

Abstract is more conceptual; concrete is more sensual. Abstract expresses ideas; concrete communicates through the five senses, especially the visual sense because it is dominant in us humans. The degree of abstraction or specificity is relative, and words or phrases fall on some point in a continuum. The more abstract a word, the less we are able to use our senses to grasp its meaning, or being; the less abstract a word, the more it elicits our senses. Abstract or general language is less clear (more opaque), less expressive (says less), and more ambiguous (more likely to misunderstand) than more concrete and specific language.

General words or phrases are those that refer to many, or broad things or concepts. By contrast, specific words zero in more on particulars. At this point, you, the reader, are dealing with a lot of abstract words–*general*, *concepts*, *meaning*, *etc*. As soon as we change style and use more concrete and specific language, you will experience a greater clarity of meaning:

Consider, for example, how the general word *animal* differs from the word *dog*. When the reader processes *animal*, there's no saying how individuals will interpret it. You might "see" an elephant, a giraffe, or a cat; I might "see" a tiger, a cat, and a ferret. Neither one of us may have gotten what was inside the head of the writer when he/she wrote; *I saw the animal cross the street last night*. If she wanted us readers to get it, she should have been more concrete: *I saw the dog cross the street last night*. Then if she wanted us to see even more like how she saw, she would use even more concrete language; *I saw the brindled, tan pit-bull cross the street last night*.

When we hear or read the word *animal*, a variety of vague forms come to mind; when we encounter *dog*, the mental images are more specific; but, when we read *pit-bull*, we have a particular picture in mind. It is more vivid, more particular. Of course, we could make the image more specific still by sharpening its details:

> *Logan, my deep, rich tan pit-bull with his tight barrel chest, his muscle ribbed legs tipped with white paws, and his deep-set chocolate brown eyes, looked longingly at Midge, his new female companion, and with his one ear droopy and the other stiff and upright as a sentinel, and his whip thin twitching tail, he seemed more a clown than a Casanova.*

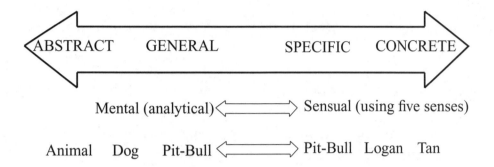

Figure 7.4 Abstact vs. General Language

Helping students to appreciate the difference between this last passage, and something more general such as *Logan, my brown pit-bull, can be a funny dog,* is crucial to developing effective writing.

In *argumentative* or *persuasive* writing, abstract words are to be avoided—especially in thesis statements. Words or concepts which can mean many things are abstractions—that's why they are more open to misunderstanding and less clear. For instance: *Jim is a good kid.* Try asking different people what it means that Jim is *good.* Is he good because he is polite or because he has high moral standards? Is he good because he has a tender heart or because he obeys his teachers and his parents?

Pushing student writers to make their ideas more specific is crucial in persuasive paper assignments. For instance, the tentative thesis: *Pollution is harmful and should be strictly regulated.* The student should be guided to ask, "What kind of pollution? Air, water? That which is harmful to the earth or to people? How should it be strictly regulated? Banished? New filters on cars and treatment plants? Legislation that caps emissions?"

Photography provides a good analogy to the continuum between abstract and concrete, between general and specific language, far away (hard to see) and close-up. Think about an aerial photographer, relatively close to the ground at 1000 feet, and taking pictures of your house. The pictures from this distance would be indistinct. One would not see the colors, the porches, the flowers surrounding the properties. Now take that picture on the street, in front of your house. Which would make a better description of your home?

The General Rule: Concrete words are better communication vehicles than abstract words.

Figurative Language

Special use of words that uses comparisons called similes and metaphors generally expands the sensual quality of words from the visual to the other four senses (smell, touch, sound, taste).

Simile and metaphor are two major types of figurative (vs. literal) language that enrich communication and provide tools of development. Both similes and metaphors compare two unlike things in order to deliver a more concrete message: *"my love is like a red rose."* This is so familiar, it is a cliché. However, consider this for describing a person: *Katee is as emotionally deep as a flounder is wide.*

A metaphor also compares but without the use of *like* or *as*:

> *My father, a brick layer for thirty years, was the family's beast of burden.*

Sometimes one word alone functions as a metaphor: As a teacher, my role is <u>*to plant*</u> the ideas in students' minds.

> **Teaching Tip:** Students need to develop an understanding of figurative language (especially for studying literature) and the ability to incorporate it into their own writing).

Denotation and Connotation

The difference between the dictionary definition of a word (denotation) and the emotional and psychic associations (connotation) many words carry provides a helpful approach to raising students' awareness of words, their complex dimensions, and how the choice of words can have vital impact on the meaning.

Exercise: Take the word, *spider*: without looking it up in the dictionary, simply take a minute yourself, or if with a class, write it on the board, and ask for what comes to mind. Without a doubt, the result will be similar to: *creepy, poisonous, evil, black, sinister, crawly.* Of course, there may be a budding entomologist in the group who loves spiders, but for the most part, spiders in our society connote creepiness.

Now look the word up in the dictionary, and you will find some definition as much as possible devoid of emotional overtones and bias–a definition of *spider* such as: "any of an order of arachnids having an abdomen…" This is what *spider* denotes.

Even more abstract words carry connotations. Consider (or do an exercise with): *democracy, liberal, fascism, slavery*. Try more current words such as *rap, pig, cool,*

Active and Passive Voice

The "natural" order of English is subject-verb-object. That is, the subject *acts on* the object: *Jack hit the ball*—This is the active voice.

When this order is reversed and the subject is the receiver of the action, we create the passive voice: *The ball was hit by Jack*. In fact, the doer is not even present in many passive voice constructions: *The ball was hit over the fence*.

While in a few instances, using the passive voice is fine, and, more rarely still, preferred, in the vast majority of instances, the passive voice is discouraged for two good reasons:

- Passive voice is weaker because the subject as actor is left backstage—if present at all—in the rear rather than up-front. Thus, "the action" is muted and diluted.

- The passive voice is more wordy—always. Count the words in the two sentences on the previous page. Now, count them in the two following sentences.

Active: *The instructor discussed the requirements and the time schedule for this semester's class.*

Passive Voice: *The requirements and the time schedule for this semester's course were discussed by the teacher.*

Choppy Sentences and Sentence Variety

Writing can be both monotonous and hard to read if it lacks sentence variety. This is a common problem with student writing. Consider this paragraph from a student: Read it out loud for the best appreciation.

> *I don't only have weaker traits, but I have very strong traits, and let me tell you they help me throughout the adventure. My tookishness is*

one of the main reasons why I went on the Quest. I bet you are wondering what is Tookishness? The Tooks are from my mom's side of the family. Unlike normal hobbits they have a special kind of magic to them. There is a rumor that I have fairy blood in me. I wouldn't find it strange if I really did. I like every other Took have a love for beautiful things. We also love adventures, traveling and dream of becoming a hero with a sword. The Tookishness in me helps me. I preserved it throughout the Quest.

You will hear the "choppiness" as you have to stop frequently as you move from terminating punctuation to terminating punctuation. Too many simple sentences is the root of the problem. However, the choppy feel is not the only weakness of this style. The lack of relationship between the ideas also makes the writing unclear. This passage would be improved by making relationships using more compound and complex sentences and using more *transitional devices*. Recall that these strategies transform choppiness into coherence:

I don't only have weaker traits, but I have very strong traits. Let me tell you how they help me throughout the adventure. My tookishness, for instance, is the strength that led me to the Quest. I bet you are wondering what is Tookishness? Some background will help you understand: The Tooks are from my mom's side of the family, and, unlike normal hobbits, they have a special kind of magic to them. In fact, there is a rumor that I have fairy blood in me, and I wouldn't find it strange if I really did because I, like every other Took, have a love for beautiful things. And I, like the Tooks, love adventure, travel, and dreams of becoming a hero with a sword. Because the Tookishness helped me, I preserved it throughout the Quest.

STAGES OF WRITING: THE FRAMEWORK

Effective tools and approaches to developing writing skill are based in the statement: *Writing is a process*. Writing is not a *thing*; rather it is an *activity*. It's not Scrabble, the board and tiles; it's <u>playing</u> the game. Furthermore, it's an activity that occurs over a period of time. Of course, this period varies greatly depending on the type of writing. A book can require years; by contrast, a memo describing a company's new vacation policy may require twenty minutes.

The time varies, but <u>need</u> for time and planning doesn't; it's shorter, or longer. Whether it's a thirty page report, a two page letter, an essay for school, or an email to the staff or a colleague, the plan must include the *what*, *to whom*, and *how of* the message(s), the audience, the organization, and the format.

These two chapters focus on what students in K-12 and in higher education are learning and need to develop to write effectively. Of course, the 7th grade student will be writing different assignments than college students, but the laws and principles of effective writing are the same no matter the level.

We also address an audience who will be assisting others to improve their writing. Thus, we include recommendations on how to apply this learning to teaching/coaching, an example of how writing is shaped by consideration of its audience. Here's a tip: a major goal is to get students to act upon the writing process. So, let's lay out the steps that give some grounding to this process, the commonly used five stages of writing.

The Five Stages of Writing

The five stages of writing method depicted on the next page is a valuable tool in that it systematizes several important aspects of writing: time and the process of evolving towards the finished product; and, the distinctive activities that bring an essay towards its final form. However, a fine-tuned understanding of this model is important to avoiding frustration.

First, and most important, the model could obscure the reality that writing is a *recursive process*–it's back and forth…back and forth–until its right. It's <u>not</u> a one-way progression from stage one, to stage two, then three–with no turning back. We have tried to indicate this in the graphic with arrows going in both directions.

For teaching purposes, the stages are very clear-cut. However, in reality, individuals use them differently. Some people do simple scratch outlines; others do sentence outlines. Some writers like to compose a concluding paragraph before writing the introduction, etc. **Key point**: use the model flexibly.

Plan to devote most time, however, to Stages One and Three, because, one, students must expect that developing even a <u>tentative thesis</u> takes time and effort; two, students often confuse *editing* (focused on grammar and punctuation) with *revision* (much more complicated, focused on organization and the three laws of unity, development, and coherence). Both cases emphasize the importance of time management and planning.

Stage One, Pre-Writing

Don't be confused: this step requires writing; it's just not formal, organized writing. In fact, it's writing to help get to organized writing. The crucial end of pre-writing is selecting a focus (**tentative thesis**) and an initial organization (**outline**). "Initial" is important because what one starts with at the end of this stage might not be what he/she ends up with.

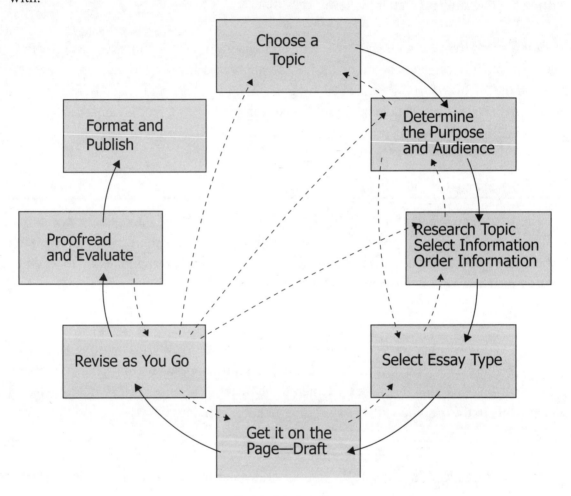

Figure 7.4 Recursive Stages of Writing

But let's get to it by asking, what are we pre-writing about? Well, the topic, you say. And this leads to one problem that people frequently express: "I don't know what to write about." So you respond: "Write about something that you have strong feelings about," and, "something that interests you a lot."

Yet as basic as these recommendations are, the would-be writer still looks at you with anxious eyes. Some barrier stands in the way of putting pen to paper.

Invention/discovery Strategies: brainstorming, free writing, clustering and mapping.

The following strategies work by overcoming the barriers to thought flow. By freeing the mind from structure, each of these tools allows the writer to by-pass fear and self-consciousness, by going around the conscious mind and plunging into the sub- and preconscious parts of our brains. Then the juices flow.

Of course, not everyone is hampered by fear, and still these methods are useful for getting what's inside the writer's head out onto paper so that it can be assessed. Which method is best? There is no one right way. Individuals will gravitate to what works best for them. The key is that you as mentor stress the importance of this thinking/getting down on paper/and coming up with a starting point for the next stage of writing–*drafting*.

Teaching Tip: students need the opportunity to try out a variety of pre-writing strategies on an individual basis, in teams, and as part of a group process.

Brainstorming is the best method for the free flow of ideas. You can do this by yourself. As a teacher, you can help an individual student who is blocked, or you can use it with a class. It's best, however, to jump start the activity with a subject or topic. If the activity is going to lead to a specific writing assignment, the jump start needs to be related to that. For instance, if the class is working on descriptive writing, phrases such as, *automobiles in American life*, *favorite people*, *favorite places*, and *friendship* would trigger the flow.

Free Writing is another powerful release mechanism. It's more structured because the writer is asked to put the flowing lava fragments into sentences rather than simply jotting down words or phrases as with brainstorming. It draws upon the tendency for sentences (ideas) to lead to, or follow one another in the mind and hence on paper (or computer).

The method for this exercise is also more structured, and very important to follow:

- First, a time needs to be set (5-10 minutes) and strictly adhered to.

- Then, the rule: you must keep writing during 10 minutes no matter what jumps into your head. No judgment that this doesn't fit; or "I can't say this!"

- Most important, if you get stuck, just keep your pen on the paper, and continue to write.

Focused free writing uses an actual subject/topic, thereby providing the starting point as opposed to simply putting pen to paper without a given and subject and going with whatever comes up from the depths of consciousness. For instance, students were asked to free-write on their favorite place, and the following emerged from one of them:

> *Lakeside, Ohio is the <u>most peaceful place</u> I have ever known. As soon as you enter the western gate, a huge white archway that spans the road, life slows down. When I pass through those gates (I can imagine it and conjure the feeling even now), I allow a <u>peace</u> to flow through me that I never let in on the outside. I came to Lakeside when I was 15. I was a camper falling immediately in love with the Victorian homes, the streets dominated by bicycles and walkers, where cars were made to poke along behind us. When you walk the streets of Lakeside at night, everyone sits on their porch and greets passersby – there are no TVs <u>blaring</u> and video games to play. Every day you walk down to the dock and play shuffle board or putt-putt. Families hang around the park, ride bikes, and swim. It is a safe place for children. People you meet can become friends for life. There is no sound like the sound of the lake lapping up on the huge rocks. If I walk down to the end of my street, I look across the water at Putney Bay.*

Shaping the Raw Material

The raw material next needs to be <u>organized</u> with organization being the single most important quality of effective writing, and perhaps the most challenging. There's unfortunately no formula for achieving a working order, but there are tools that help.

The process involves <u>sorting</u>, <u>eliminating</u>, <u>adding to</u>, and <u>grouping</u>. One begins to sharpen focus, like turning the focus ring on a camera and one organizes the materials harvested in the free writing or brainstorming. In this stage one is likely to eliminate some of the raw material as irrelevant; then to identify a big idea or point, and connect other images, examples, or points to it. In short, the process is working towards identifying the *topic sentence* if it's a paragraph or a *thesis statement* if it's an essay.

It's hard to talk about this in the abstract, so let's examine the passage on Lakeside.

Sorting:

• *Identify repeated words, phrases, ideas, or feelings*: The underlining was done after the free writing. Note the feeling word, *peaceful*

• *Identify sense words:*

Sights: huge white archway, people walking and bicycling, swimming, the dock, playing shuffleboard or putt-putt, Victorian homes, looking across the water, people sitting on porches greeting, cars poking

Sounds: lake lapping against huge rocks

Textures, tastes, smells: there are none

• *Identify ideas and points*: safety, friendly, people interacting, history: the first time I came; friends made who last for life

Grouping:

• *Compare and contrast*: no blaring radios or video games vs. quiet and children/families playing together; cars are poking, not speeding; people are walking and bicycling, not driving; children alone with video games vs. families and children together

• *Connecting similar*: history, passing through gates of time, Victorian homes, cottages, people on porches, families together, long-lasting friends; quiet and walking, cars poking, no blaring radios; lapping water; togetherness; peace : quiet, lapping water

• *Eliminating*: safety for children

A topic statement: The writer focuses on peacefulness of an earlier age with its slower pace, quieter atmosphere, and simpler technology. The first sentence connects these into a topic sentence, and then the details are organized to develop the main idea of the peacefulness of an earlier time:

When I pass under the great white archway and through the gate into Lakeside, Ohio, I return to the peacefulness of an earlier age. The Victorian homes and humble cottages are part of the time warp, but it's so much more. It's the sights, for example: people walking and bicycling; families playing shuffle board on the court; children laughing and playing putt-putt. If a car appears, it's poking along, and the people sitting on their porches are waving to the driver, to the walkers, and the riders–a friendly place where lifelong friends can be made like my friend Doris. But if the sights are pictures of its peace and quiet, the sounds of Lakeside are its music; its instrument is Lake Erie. Sometimes, when it storms, its waves crash against the huge rocks of the shore, or even overwhelm and submerge the long dock where people stroll or fish on calmer nights and normal days. Mostly, the lake laps the rocks and sloshes over the sands of the beaches, a background whisper. When I am far away from Lakeside back in the fast-paced world and need to calm my nerves, I close my eyes, I walk from my cottage, down through the park, and place myself under one of the big old oaks, on the banks of Lake Erie, and cast my eyes across its huge expanse to the far away speck that is Island, my spirit is calmed and settled by the sights and sounds of the waves whispering softly to the shore and reaching yearningly towards the setting sun.

Now you try it before looking at one way of sorting and grouping the following—free-write.

Global warming leads to confusion and misunderstanding. People think it is only about warming days. But global warming is actually associated with greater cold and stronger storms and other extremes that are far from what warm means. It's an example of difference between cause and effect. People confuse these and thus we find faulty thinking and wrong conclusions especially this is important to policy decisions that have serious consequences. Church placard: Global warming…Yeah, dripping with sarcasm between the border of Icicles and the mountains of snow surrounding it. Eliminating or mitigating carbon dioxide for instance and weighing costs benefits is very affected by ignorance or knowledge. Economic calculations are an especially influential debating point. Conservatives are always ridiculing the economic devastation that wrongheaded environmentalists who make up the fantasy of global warming recommend. This is a good example of short-sightedness plus ignorance. Katrina is a good counterexample that suggests the devastation economically of not mitigating global warming and of erroneously confusing the cause with the effects. This is the tip of the iceberg.

Clustering and Word Maps

An article in a recent issue of *The Boston Globe* provoked a discussion between two friends on the proposal that the Catholic Church build a monument to the victims of priests' sexual abuse. One decided to write her paper on this subject, and she explored her conflicting feelings in a word map.

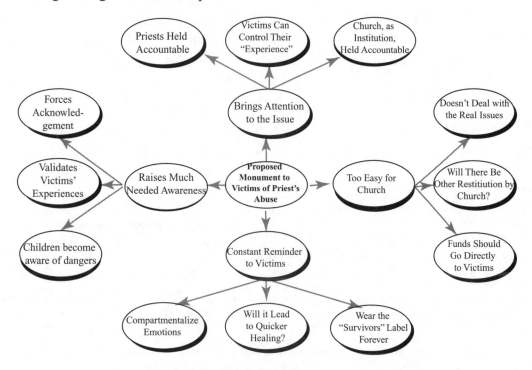

Figure 7.4 Word Map

Method

The process opens with placing the topic being explored in a circle and then letting the ideas flow but organizing the flow into sub-topics as illustrated in the graphic.

Teaching Tip: Have students use color pencils for drawing their subtopics; also use these in the sorting and grouping stage. The color helps reinforce the grouping and organizing processes.

After generating this map, the student needed to develop a tentative thesis, and submitted the following:

Tentative Thesis A

> *The movement amongst victims of sexual abuse to create monuments acknowledging their abuse raises significant issues for the survivors as well as for the rest of society who gave witness to the emotional aftermath of these tragedies.*

The instructor then pushed the student's thinking by asking her to decide which side of the controversy she agreed with (for or against the monument); the student then <u>sorted</u> her raw material so she could assess the pros and cons. She used a simple T graph:

PRO	CON
Raises awareness	Prolongs pain, becomes a barrier to healing
Even children may learn and thus defend themselves against abuse	"Glorifies abuse" encourages "victims"
Makes perpetrators accountable	Uses resources better used for prevention or counseling
Recognizes existence of invisible dangers, brings out the hidden	Too easy for church
Victims can visit the "experience" in a controlled way	Never have to face real issues stemming from abuse—gets rid of the problem

> **Teaching Tip:** T graphics are also useful for brainstorming about a controversial issue either for individuals or groups and classes.

After considering the pros and cons, the student decided to argue against the monument and constructed another tentative thesis:

Tentative thesis B

> *While the issue of clergy committing sexual abuse against children is a difficult, painful, often life-shattering subject, the concept of acknowledging such violations with a permanent memorial will encourage a waste of precious resources, allow victims to wallow in their victimhood and channel energy away from the vital work of preventing future crimes.*

Let's use these theses, A and B, to understand the major purposes that compositions/essays serve, and the role of the thesis statement and the outline (the finish lines of Stage one) in all essays— no matter their stance or purpose.

Rhetorical Stance and Thesis Statement

The Four Stances (Puposes) of Essays

1. *Narrative: Sometimes writers are asked to write a story as in, "write about an event that changed you". The major purpose is to tell the story; it's a narrative essay*

2. *Descriptive: Sometimes an essay can be devoted to describing a place, or a person, or a pet. The major purpose is to get the reader to "see" the subject; it's a descriptive essay.*

3. *Expository: Sometimes an essay is concerned to explain or give information about a subject,- for instance, the causes of the Civil war, or the best diet for weight loss, etc. The major purpose is to inform or educate the reader; it's an expository essay.*

4. *Argumentative /Persuasive: Sometimes the writer wants to express his/her position on a controversial topic such as the death penalty, constructing a monument to victims of sexual abuse, lowering the high way speed limit, etc. The major purpose is to persuade the reader to accept the writer's position; its an argumentative or persuasive essay.*

A thesis statement is the main idea of the *essay* as the *topic sentence* is the main idea of a *paragraph*. The thesis is the writer's compass; it's the reader's map: it keeps the writer on topic; it shows the reader where he/she is going.

Consider the thesis statement for an argumentative essay on the death penalty:

> *Contrary to the claims of its supporters, the death penalty neither saves taxpayers' money, nor does it protect them from criminal behavior; contrarily, it does result in killing significant numbers of innocent people, and it disproportionately victimizes Black Americans. With such a record, the death penalty <u>must be repealed and replaced with</u> a more just, effective, and less costly approach to handling violent crimes.*

An effective thesis statement is a powerful defense against distraction and disorganization.

With this "map," readers know the writer's position (an argument to abolish the death penalty), and they know the main points (costs, deterrence/non-deterrence, racial injustice, wrongful conviction). Now that they know where they are going, they can sit back and take in the scenery—evaluating the worth and strength of the main points as the writer develops them.

With this compass, the writer is equally well-served; the thesis tells her exactly what she needs to cover. Should she find herself veering off course (getting off topic into the morality of killing, or the eye for an eye), a quick check with the compass reminds her that this is not on the way! The thesis says nothing about morality and revenge! Either go back and re-draw the map (the thesis) to include morality in the trip, or get back on course.

A well-organized essay is unified. All the paragraphs develop the thesis statement; anything not in the thesis is not included in the essay. An effective thesis statement foreshadows, or may preview the organization of the essay:

> *The death penalty neither saves taxpayers' money, nor does it protect them from criminal behavior; contrarily, it does result in killing significant numbers of innocent people, and it disproportionately victimizes Black Americans. With such a record, the death penalty must be repealed and replaced with a more just, effective, and less costly approach to handling violent crimes.*

Paragraph 1–costs more

Paragraph 2–does not deter crime

Paragraph 3–more black Americans incarcerated

Paragraph 4–innocents killed

The Effective Thesis Statement:

- *States the writer's position* (if an argumentative paper), or the writer's purpose (if an expository paper)

- *Expresses the main idea* and purpose in specific language that tells the reader exactly what the writer will cover

- *Describes a main idea* that is neither too broad, nor too narrow

- Accomplishes all of the above in one (possibly two) declarative sentence(s)–not as a question!

The Ineffective Thesis Statement:

*   Statement of Fact. *The Patriots are the best team in the NFL.* Presumably this is because they have won more games, but there's nothing of interest here, and nothing to write about. *DNA analysis has established the innocence of 5% of inmates on death row.*

*   Announcement. *In this paper I describe the causes of the Civil War* or *This paper is about listening skills.* Students often use these clunky announcements. Discourage them from doing so.

*   *Vague and General.* *The death penalty is wrong.* Contrast this to our theses above, and apply the criteria for an effective thesis. Where is the position? Wrong how? Another example: *The U.S. needs to make big changes in education to maintain its place in the world.* Again: All of education? What big changes? What place?

*   *Too Broad.* *The Tax system needs to be overhauled.* This is far too big for an essay. Consider all the different forms of taxes, for instance: federal, state, sales taxes, property taxes, excise taxes, etc.

Applying the Criteria

Tentative Thesis A:

> The movement amongst victims of sexual abuse to create monuments acknowledging their abuse raises <u>significant issues</u> for the <u>survivors</u> as well as for the rest of <u>society</u> who gave witness to the emotional aftermath of these tragedies.

Underlining the key words and phrases provides an X-ray of the main idea (thesis) stripped of extra words. The stance is expository: the writer wants to explain and to inform the reader; there is no position as for an argumentative stance.

But *significant issues*? Too vague: What are these? Well, the writer has generated them in the word map, and now needs to select which to develop. Selection involves dealing with the positives and the negatives, and thus a decision: Will I describe only the positives, only the negative, or both? Which of the several issues, both plus and minus, will I develop?

Then, there are the two agents affected by the significant issues: the victim and society, and this requires some further sorting of the word map, and perhaps some further brainstorming to identify the impact on society more specifically.

As the writer <u>evolves</u> the ideas through the processes we have described, it is helpful to select an organization strategy and to incorporate it into the thesis statement. The raw material lends itself to a classification strategy, for instance:

The prospect of a monument to sexual abuse victims raises three fundamental concerns, both positive and negative, for both the victims and for society at-large—concerns that range from psychological health to wise management of human resources.

Note that the organization for the outline unfolds from the "three fundamental causes," two of which are identified in the thesis.

Two large concerns—psychological and ethical—affecting both the victims and society-at-large are raised by the proposal to construct a monument to sexual abuse survivors.

Thus, in the above thesis statement, the main focus has properly shifted to explaining the psychological and ethical concerns of both the victims and society-at-large.

The Evolutionary Process Summarized

The two examples demonstrate that there is not a right or wrong thesis. Rather, the raw materials create the possibilities of numerous choices. The final selection depends upon many factors including order of importance, the amount of material available for developing the various points, the interests, and values of the writer, etc.

Getting to the thesis is a process of generating ideas, selecting, organizing, thinking, and deliberating. As a compass guides a journey, so the criteria of the specific and the orderly form of expression provide the goal of the thinking process. When the writer gets "there," the thesis provides an excellent template for the organized development of the essay because the process is not simply about finding the effective expression. Rather, the writer finds the effective expression because he/she has clarified to herself what she thinks. Thus, effective writing is always based upon clear thinking!

Tentative Thesis B, an argumentative thesis:

> *While the issue of clergy committing sexual abuse against children is a difficult, painful, often life-shattering subject, the concept of acknowledging such violations with a permanent memorial will encourage a waste of precious resources, allow victims to wallow in their victimhood and channel energy away from the vital work of preventing future crimes.*

Sorting the raw materials in the word map allowed the writer to come to a decision and to define the main reasons for his/her position.

But what is the position? It is implied but not stated. The writer needs to state a <u>position</u>, using a declarative statement–*should*, *should not*, *must*.

> *A memorial to sexual abuse victims <u>should not</u> be constructed because....*

The remainder of the thesis is, however, clear and specific and the outline thus "writes itself."

Thesis Statement: *A memorial to sexual abuse <u>should not</u> be constructed because it <u>wastes resources</u>, allows victims to <u>wallow in victimhood</u>, and channels energy away from the vital work of <u>preventing future crimes</u>*

I. Wastes of precious resources
   A. Money
   B. Space
II. Encourages wallowing in victimhood
   A. Past event rather than future orientation
   B. Past becomes primary focus in daily living
   C. Future devalued
   D. Victimhood promotes self-indulgence
III. Channels resources away from prevention
   A. Victims spend time focused on pain and not on prevention
   B. Community members are drawn away from prevention activities by the consuming nature of constructing the memorial

Given its power and importance, it should not be surprising that creating an effective thesis takes time and thought. Generally, it doesn't pop into one's head, but instead it comes into shape as the writer thinks, perhaps researches, perhaps discusses the subject matter with friends (all of which are highly recommended methods!).

Table 7.3 Essay Stances

Stance	Thesis Format	Revision Questions	Example
Argumentative/ Persuasive Essay	A declarative sentence expressing the writer's **position** Not an announcement: *In this paper, I will...* OR *This paper will discuss why advertisements featuring thin models should be censored.*	Is it a statement of the position, or **simply a fact**? Is it too vague/general and lacking specifics?	**Eating disorders are seriously harmful to health.** **Eating disorders are caused by the media.**
Expository Essay: To educate and inform	A declarative sentence expressing the writer's **purpose** Not an announcement: *In this paper, I will...*	Is it too broad to be adequately covered? Is it too vague/general and lacking specifics?	*The cause, effects, and treatment of eating disorders require explanation and input from medical doctors, psychiatrists, and marketing/public relations critics.* *There are known methods of preventing and treating eating disorders.*

Instructional Guidelines

Respect the reality that crafting the thesis statement takes time and effort: build it into a schedule, conduct activities to bring perspectives and materials that can assist students to develop theses. Students should study/practice identifying the qualities and constructing effective thesis statements. Peer groups are excellent formats for developing these skills.

> **Teaching Tip:** Use the funnel structure to guide student writing. The thesis statement is the last sentence in the introductory paragraph after the general subject has been introduced–with a "grabber." This is **not** a hard-and-fast rule. The thesis can come first or in the middle, but placing it at the end helps students make a transition into the body of the paper.

Essay Purposes and Types

We distinguish four major purposes in writing an essay: one is to <u>persuade</u> the reader to agree with the writer on a <u>controversial</u> topic (*argumentative essay*); the second is to <u>inform, or educate</u> the reader (*expository essay*); three is to tell a story, (*narrative essay*); and four is to describe a person, place, or event (*descriptive essay).*

We focus on one and two because the large majority of writing in education is of an expository or persuasive type. Despite their differing objectives, both need a *thesis statement*–a single sentence at the beginning—usually in the *introductory paragraph*—that expresses the main idea(s) of the essay.

Outline

The final task of the pre-writing stage is the **outline.**

Writing is a process; writing *well* is <u>thinking clearly</u> and using the grammar of language to express that thought to others.

Developing an outline illustrates both the process and the importance of clear thinking. First, consider the process: the outline unfolds from the thesis statement. If the thesis is effective, designed to include all the main points very specifically, the metaphor *unfold* is very apt.

Thesis and outline: a recursive process

In most writing experiences the writer doesn't come up with the best thesis statement first, then proceed to the ideal outline next in a linear, step-by-step movement. No, that linear movement is not the usual.

Most writing, in contrast, develops *recursively*. The writer, that is, goes back and forth somewhat like a painter who checks her new line by looking back at the posing model, finds it off, goes back to the canvas, makes a change, then returns her eyes to the model, finds the change still not quite right, and returns to the canvas, back and forth, until the painting captures the desired image.

So, too, in the writing process, the development of an outline unfolds from a thesis statement; however, that statement is most likely first a tentative *thesis*—a place to start—rather than the finished product. As the writer develops the outline, a recursive process most likely takes place: *unfolding* the outline from the thesis reveals the weak spots. Let's examine two thesis statements to illustrate this recursive process:

Tentative Thesis Statement:

> *Given its failures and its high economic and human costs, the death penalty should be abolished.*

The writer should start by highlighting the key words as is illustrated. *Failures*? To develop the outline, the writer asks, *What do I mean by this? Economic costs* will probably pass because they are specified by *high*, but *human costs*? The writer meets the problem of the vague and general.

The thesis statement is altered to address these weaknesses: *failure* means it doesn't decrease violent crime; it doesn't deter; *human costs* mean the likelihood that innocent people will be wrongly executed. Now we have a thesis from which the outline readily unfolds because in order to develop the outline the writer was forced to be more specific.

The writer has now changed the thesis to be more specific. Notice how the outline easily unfolds from the revised statement that shows the writer exactly what needs to be developed:

Thesis Statement:

> *Since its costs are astronomical, its deterrence purpose non-existent, and, as science has now revealed, its victimization of innocents an intolerable fact, the death penalty must be abolished.*

Outline of Essay

I. Deterrence not proven (The hard data on violent crime reveals that if the purpose of the death penalty is to deter, this policy is a failure.)
A. Explain deterrence
B. Provide evidence
   1) FBI data
   2) NYC and LA reports
   3) Data and anecdotes from studies of crimes of violence

II. Economics of the death penalty (Many people think that the death penalty is less costly to the taxpayer than long-term imprisonment)
   A. Explain the myth
   B. Compare and contrast the economics of life imprisonment and the death penalty
   C. Cost analysis of long-term imprisonment
   D. Cost analysis of the death penalty

III. Human consequences (Recent advances in DNA research have led to the realization that many innocent people have been put to death by society)
   A. Profiles of men on death row at present
   B. Cases in which DNA analysis has revealed innocence
   C. Statistical applications to the past
   D. Studies and conclusions on the number of mistaken executions

IV. Conclusion

Teaching Tip: The sentences in parentheses are topic sentences for the ideas—actually examples of how the paragraph for its section could start. When outlines are done in this format, they are called *sentence outlines*. Because they are further developed (thought-out more) than the simple phrase (*deterrence not proven*), they will not be the first version of the outline. It is, however, a good exercise to guide students from a topic outline with phrases to translating these into topic sentences. This, too, is likely to start a *recursive process of improvement*.

The function of the **outline** is to organize the way the writer will develop the thesis—logically; visually represent the main ideas, their development, and their order; and provide a map which guides the writing of the first draft.

Outline Format

The format: Alpha-numerical is the most commonly used. The model above illustrates the flow of general, larger categories of thought to more specific sub-groups, from roman numeral I,II,III,IV, to capitals (A,B,C,D), to numbers (1,2,3,4), and if we were to go further to lower case (a,b,c,d) and if subdividing those, we put parentheses around numbers.

Principles that govern outlines:

- *Division*: this reflects that outlines are visual representations of sorting and classifying, and of arranging from general to specific, from whole to part of the whole.

Common Problem to identify: There must be more than one subdivision. If A is subdivided, there must be at least A.1 and A.2, or, if I, or II are subdivided, there must be at least I.A and I.B, II.A and II.B, and so forth.

However, the division needs to be logically consistent, so the writer must pay attention to:

- *Coordination* requires that the parts and subparts of an outline be of consistent equal value. This is best understood by example:

Teaching Tip: Provide exercises for students to practice movement from abstract to concrete, from general to specific, from whole category to sub-division. These are linguistic and logical operations crucial to the writing process and particularly to organization that the outline requires.

Table 7.4 Coordinated and Non-coordinated Outlines

Non-coordinated	Explanation	Coordinated	Explanation
A. movie genres 　1. dramas 　2. comedies 　3. horror B. *Mrs. Doubtfire*	A and B are not coordinate (equal). A is about different types of movies; B is a specific movie, a much small class (Non-equal).	A. movie genres 　1. dramas 　2. comedies 　3. horror B. classic comedy: 　*Mrs. Doubtfire* A. movie genres 　1. dramas 　2. comedies 　3. horror B. classic comedy 　1. *Modern Times* 　2. *Some Like It Hot* 　3. *Mrs. Doubtfire*	Both examples illustrate the consistency between the parts (A and B) and the subparts (1, 2, 3).

- *Subordination* reflects the logical relationship between the whole and the parts into which it is divided.

Parallelism: Parallelism describes the use of the same grammatical structures in certain communication situations: When comparing two or more things, when describing something in series, and in preparing lists and outlines.

Thus in B.1, in Table 7.5 just below, you find the same grammatical form—nouns: *plot types*, *characters*, *Mrs. Doubtfire*. Check it out: each of these could be the subject of a sentence. However, had we found nouns—*plot types, characters, how to analyze comedy*—in addition to showing faulty coordination, the third statement would also be non-parallel because it is a clause, not a noun.

Again, note the parallelism in the outline on the death penalty found on page 264, II.A. and B: *Explain*; *Compare and contrast*. Each of these is the same grammatical form: 2nd person verbs.

Table 7.5 Subordinated and Non-subordinated Outlines

Non-Subordinated	Explanation	Subordinated	Explanation

A. Movie Genres
  1. Dramas
  2. Comedies
  3. Horror
B. Comedy
  1. Plot Types
  2. Characters
  3. *Mrs. Doubtfire*
	#3 is the name of a specific comedy.
	
	By contrast #'s 1 and 2 are elements of comedy
		A. Movie Genres
		  1. Dramas
		  2. Comedies
		  3. Horror
		B. Comedy
		  1. Plot Types
		  2. Characters
		C. Classic Comedies: *Mrs. Doubtfire*
		Or,
		A. Movie Genres
		  1. Dramas
		  2. Comedies
		  3. Horror
		B. Comedy
		  1. Plot Types
		  2. Characters
		C. Classic Comedies
		  1. *Mrs. Doubtfire*
		  2. *Modern Times*
			The first version of correction makes the movie, Mrs. Doubtfire, the sole subject of B. Apparently it is going to be analyzed as a model for all comedy.
			
			Example 2 reflects a different thought/main idea, that is, two specific movies will be discussed to illustrate the form of comedies.
			
			In both, the ideas are properly subordinated.

Stage Two Drafting

In this stage, the writer is elaborating the map to the form necessary to communicate to a reader. Since he has a map to depend upon, he is free to give himself completely to explaining each point as if speaking to someone. He doesn't have to worry about the order. It's important to take advantage of this support. And here's how:

First, put a time limit on the draft. Forty-five minutes to an hour and a half. Of course, this will vary, but the key is to create a framework that encourages the writer to write freely, relatively quickly, and to finish the map.

Second, to aid this process, write the draft without concern for correctness. Do not focus on grammar or punctuation. Do, however, write complete thoughts or sentences.

Stage Three Revision

Last-minute writers neglect this stage. Yet this is the most critical stage to creating an effective piece. Because the draft has given the writer the structure to **expand** ideas, he may find that he has become distracted and gone off topic (**Cut**). But wait, he may have uncovered a point not considered before (**Add**). Then, he is likely to realize that he needs to explain a point more thoroughly and more clearly (**Add**); or that he needs to put his ideas or examples in a different place (**Move and reorganize**).

Revision entails analysis about **unity**, **development**, **and coherence**. It is generally far more time-consuming and mentally taxing than editing, stage 4.

Revision guidelines

1) The thesis is the main point: underline or highlight it. Examine it for the qualities of an effective thesis. Compare the thesis to the concluding paragraph: is the thesis re-stated in the conclusion?
2) Examine all of the paragraphs against the thesis statement. Analyze the paragraphs. Underline or highlight the topic statement (Does it support the thesis statement?).
3) Examine the supporting sentences: Does each of them describe, explain, give evidence to the topic statement (Is the paragraph unified?)
4) Does the topic statement need to be changed or revised to better communicate the main idea and to more effectively connect it to the supporting sentences: is it specific enough? Does it include all aspects of the main idea? Does the main idea need more explanation, description, evidence? (development)
5) Are the explaining, supporting, and descriptive sentences in the correct, logical order (coherence)? Are each of the sentences a complete idea? Each sentence needs to be connected to the next to help the reader move smoothly. These connections are often formed by transitional words or

phrases. Sometimes connecting two or more sentences into a compound or a complex sentence can bring about the knitting of sentences.

6) The concluding sentence: Does it still relate to the main idea, and does it also transition, or lay the groundwork, for transition to the next paragraph?

7) Examine the concluding paragraph. Does it transition smoothly from the previous paragraph? Does it summarize, with emphasis, the thesis? The conclusion should remind the reader of how all of your points relate to your thesis. What have you proven? Why does it matter? Broaden back out to show the relevance of your essay in a larger context. Like a snake with its tail in its mouth, does the essay come full circle?

Stage Four, Editing

Many people confuse editing, which is primarily concerned with punctuation and grammar, described in the chart below with revision, which entails the more analytical, organizational, and content concerns described above.

Key Point: The stages are not to be interpreted rigidly. Editing of grammar and punctuation goes in the revision stage and in the publishing stage; so, too, changes in organization may take place during editing. The stages are steps, operations, and guidelines, not formulas.

Stage Five Formatting and Publishing

Preparing the essay to submit for an assignment or for a publication is largely attending to the details of its visual appearance and to those of the conventions of punctuation, spacing, quotations, and documentation of sources.

Many of these details depend upon which of the 4-5 major style manuals is required by your teacher/instructor, or the publication for which you are writing. Where to place the title, where to put page numbers, the font style and font size to use, how to punctuate quotations, and how to entitle, organize, and punctuate sources (in the body of the paper-citations; at the end, the bibliography)—all of these depend upon whether you are using MLA, APA, etc. (these are described in the next section on research and documentation).

Quotations

Writers acknowledge sources they use as paraphrases, as summaries, and as exact quotations. All three cases require a citation next to them, and direct or exact quotations require punctuation.

In addition, to be effective quotations must be integrated into their surrounding text—both grammatically and contextually. By contrast, students often drop quotations into their papers without clarifying why they are using them, and/or, in a grammatical form that is inconsistent with the whole passage.

The following illustrates this typical weakness:

> *Dicey, the major character in* The Homecoming *gets to know Gram better in a long conversation. She learns that Gram has good qualities. "I kept those promises, love, honor, and obey. Even when I didn't want to, I kept them." Gram is creating trust.*

Note: It's not clear, although the reader surmises it must be, that these are Gram's words; and the writer has not provided the context which gives them full meaning as the following revision does:

> *Dicey, the major character in* The Homecoming *gets to know Gram better in a long conversation. She learns that Gram has good qualities. For instance, she discovers Gram's sense of loyalty when Gram reports how despite the abuse of her husband, she stayed with him: "I kept those promises, love, honor, and obey. Even when I didn't want to, I kept them." As she confides the uncomfortable detail of her life, Gram both reveals her character and creates trust between herself and Dicey.*

Another example of a non-integrated quotation:

> *To be most effective, do only one thing at a time. Working on multiple tasks takes away from your ability to function at your maximum. "The brain is a sequential processor, unable to pay attention to two things at the same time." (Medina: 93).*

Again, the passage lacks context; it also lacks any introduction. In contrast, the following revision introduces the quotation and its relevance to the main point:

> *To be most effective, do only one thing at a time. Working on multiple tasks takes away from your ability to function at your maximum. Neurologists provide a physiological basis for the importance of focus; as Medina explains, "The brain is a sequential processor, unable to pay attention to two things at the same time." (93).*

Quotation Length–There are two main points to emphasize in terms of quotation length:

1. They should be as short as possible: Students typically use too many and too long. Basically, quotations should be used only when a paraphrase or a summary (preferred) cannot capture the special language of the quotation

2. According to MLA guidelines, any quotation longer than four lines is indented one inch from the left, double spaced along with the rest of the essay, and does not have quotation marks (unless they are internal to the quoted passage). For other formats consult APA, the Chicago Manual, or the documentation manual required by your instructor.

> **Teaching Tip:** Show students how to use ellipses to eliminate unnecessary words from a lengthy quotation.

RESEARCH: METHODS AND MATERIAL

Selecting an effective research subject. As with any writing assignment, perhaps more so because you will be spending time searching and reading, pick a topic that interests you.

Then focus on **narrowing to a manageable scope**. Most school and college essays are relatively limited 3-5 pages, or 10-15 pages; it is therefore crucial to select a research topic that can be adequately covered within these limits.

Like the thesis statement, the research focus is not the subject; rather it's the slant, the position, or the approach to the subject which you are taking. Accordingly, the research focus is not general and vague, but specific and concrete.

The research should be designed to answer questions—your research question. Take for instance the question posed in the table below: What is the history of the welfare system? Are we asking about the welfare system worldwide? Is there one worldwide welfare system? Does it have the same history across countries? You can see the problem—it is a very broad topic! But look at a narrower question: What is the history of AFDC in the U.S. welfare system? Now that is certainly a research project that can be done. Note that the question will determine what kind of essay you will be writing—in this case it would be an **expository essay**.

Table 7.6 Narrowing the Research Question

	Essay Purpose	Broad Question	Narrower Question
Welfare System	Expository: Inform readers of history.	What is the history of welfare system?	What is the history of AFDC in the US welfare system?
Welfare System	Argumentative: Welfare recipients should get more benefits.	Are welfare benefits enough to live on?	What cash, housing, and health benefits do single parents on AFDC receive?

Evidence based questions are those for which research materials are available. Steer away from topics that are speculative: Is there life on other planets? Will books on tape make real books extinct?

Major Research Sources

Primary Sources are original, firsthand materials such as diaries, letters, autobiographies, journals, legislation, novels, and poems.

Secondary Sources are materials written about primary sources. Literary criticism, for instance, is typically a secondary source about an author's novel, poem, or whole body of work. History books are secondary sources based on interpreting and arranging primary materials.

Documentation

A quotation, an idea, a paraphrase, or a summary from another source must be documented—that is, the writer needs to identify very specifically where the reader can find the source.

In an essay there are two locations for documentation:

- At the end where all the sources consulted for the essay are listed. The Bibliography comes at the end of the paper. It identifies all the materials you used in developing the paper, even if you didn't quote them.
- Citations: in the body of the paper after the quotation, summary, or paraphrase.

These two locations are cross-referenced. When, for instance, there is a quotation in the body of the paper, the citation gives only part of the identification—a page number and usually the author, too. But the full identification is in the endnotes called "Works Cited" or "References," or "Bibliography," etc.

Documentation Format

Whether you call that final listing "Works Cited," or "References," and how you will make the citations, and many other details of how you present information (the order) depends totally on the documentation format that the teacher, or the publisher requires. In secondary and in undergraduate education, three formats are generally used, and these are attached to the various disciplines:

- *The Modern Language Association (MLA) Handbook for Writers of Research Papers*: humanities, literature, and the arts
- *Publication Manual of the American Psychological Association (APA)*: psychology and social sciences
- *The Chicago Manual of Style*: history and humanities

Research Plan and Methods

Time and Organization: Professional writers often have fairly extensive time to write their books, but even they have constraints on time. Students have even greater need to manage time. This is a good reason for students to focus as soon as possible, to take quality notes, to prepare for the documentation requirements from the start of the process, and to conduct the actual research as efficiently as possible.

Important Definitions

Abstracts are summaries generally of articles. These can help you decide whether the article is suitable for your research. Many databases (see below) contain abstracts.

Full texts are the complete article, and some databases contain these as well as abstracts.

Periodicals are magazines, newsletters, journals, and unlike books, they are published at regular intervals, e.g., monthly, biannually, etc.

Index: when not referring to a book's index, these are collections of source material, organized by subject. They identify where the researcher can locate them.

Databases are collections of sources (some general; some specialized subjects) that can be accessed. Depending on the particular database (see below), they will provide information on where to find sources, provide abstracts, provide full-texts–or all three.

Researching: The Action

Where to research: Resisting the temptation to rely solely on on-line resources is important for many reasons. Perhaps the most important is that libraries still have many more research materials than exist on-line, and, even more important, they have live persons with sophisticated knowledge and skills to help you find the best materials, and to save time in doing so. Think of the reference librarian as your friend.

The **Library** uses either the Dewey Decimal or the Library of Congress system to organize its book holdings. One can browse subject areas according to these organizations.

The **Library of Congress** organizes with 20 areas of study and the alphabet:

A, General Studies;
B, Philosophy, Psychology, Religion;
C, Auxiliary Sciences of History: archaeology, geology;

D, History;

E&F, History, America;

G, Geography;

H, Social Science;

K, Law;

L, Education;

M, Music

N, Fine Arts;

P, Language and Literature;

Q, Science;

R, Medicines Agriculture;

T, Technology;

U, Military Science;

V, Naval Science;

Z, Bibliography, Library Science

Dewey System has ten major headings

000 General Studies	500 Natural Sciences
100 Psychology and Philosophy	600 Useful Arts
200 Religion	700 Fine Arts
300 Social Sciences	800 Literature
400 Language Arts	900 History, Biography

The reference librarian can save much time by pointing the researcher to the best available resources. Students should be prepared to explain very clearly what they are working on and what they are looking for. Suggest that they take a copy of the assignment with them and encourage them to ask questions.

Method: From Background to Specifics

In general, research proceeds from general materials that provide the context, and then, gets increasingly specific. The materials also range from general to specific and specialized. Indexes, Guides to, and Databases are available in libraries, on CD-ROM, and as Electronic Databases.

However, the vast majority of research materials are still in libraries, and many of the best electronic or CD-ROM sources are very expensive and most practical to access through the library's subscription. Of course, the number and kind of electronic databases will vary library by library.

The following is a small sampling of the kind of research materials available. There are specialized indexes and guides to almost any subject one can think of from coin collecting, to railroads, to costumes....

Subject Guide to Books in Print: An excellent general guide to see how much has been written on a subject.

The Readers Guide to Periodical Literature 1900-present: Indispensable for articles, journals.

The Supplementary Index. 1979- Covers material not in the above and especially in smaller and specialized topic such as the environment, women.

Poole's Index to Periodic Literature

The New York Times Index 1951

New Encyclopedia Britannica in 3 parts is widely regarded as the classic and most authoritative.

Collier's Encyclopedia (24 volumes)

Encyclopedia Americana: especially for American persons and topics.

Biographic References:

- **Webster's New Biographical Dictionary.** 1983. Good for historical personages.
- **Who's Who in America**. 1899 to present. There are also specialized versions of this series covering Black Americans, American women....

Specialized Biographic References:
- **Dictionary of Literary Biography.** 1978-
- **Oxford Companion to American Literature.** 1983.
- **Oxford Companion to English Literature.** 1985.
- **MLA International Bibliography.** 1921

Almanacs, Yearbooks, News Digests

- Information Please Almanac. 1947-present
- Statistical Abstracts of the United States. 1878-Present (CD–ROM, 1987-)

- World Almanac and Book of Facts. 1868-Present (CD–ROM, Microsoft Bookshelf)

History

America: History and Life. 1964- Index and abstracts
Historical Abstracts. 1955 index and abstracts, worldwide, not in America

Psychology

Psychological Abstracts 1927 CD-ROM
PsychLIT

Education

Education Index
Physical Education Index

Social Sciences

Social Science Index
Index to Periodical Articles by and about Blacks
Criminal Justice Abstracts

Government Publications

Index to US Government Publications
Cumulative Subject Index to the Monthly Catalog of US Publications

Oxford English Dictionary (also on CDROM)

NetLibrary: 100,000 books available for download

ARTstor: an online resource with many digitalized art images

AP Photo Archive: great source for photographs

Electronic Databases: Libraries will provide access to a variety of databases, which ones and how many will depend upon the library. Some data bases cover a wide range of disciplines and subjects; some focus on one. The most popular are:

- Infotrac
- EBSCO
- ProQuest: has both summaries and full texts
- JStor: academic journals in several fields including arts and sciences, business
- Science Direct: Medicine, technology, and science; also a college student edition
- Lexis-Nexis: law, business and public records
- ProQuest Historical: Includes full text articles from major newspapers
- Factiva: specializes in business news

The most popular specialized databases are:

ERIC Education
MEDLINE Medicine
MLA Language and Literature
PsychINFO Psychology

Search Techniques

Keyword. In searching catalogues, indexes, and databases, it's important to try different terms because systems can vary in how they categorize a subject. For instance, if you are doing research on the Women's Suffrage Movement, try that term but also try "Women's History" or "Women's Movement." If you are researching the emancipation of the slaves in the US, try emancipation not proclamation, try abolition. If you are doing research on drugs, try narcotics, pharmaceuticals.

Boolean Search. Though Internet servers vary in how they organize searches, the so-called Boolean system is most used:

- Use quotation marks around a subject or phrase which must appear: "Lincoln Biography" you are looking for stories of his life, not his addresses.
- Use AND or + to search for items that contain both subjects and phrases: Lincoln AND Civil War, or Addiction + Prevention.

- Use not or (–) if you want to exclude topics often associated with your main subject: Lincoln NOT Biography, or Addiction-Prevention.
- Wildcard, usually an asterisk to get a range of spelling and terms: psycholog* will pick up psychology, psychologist, psychological, etc., or wom*n will pick up women, woman

> **Teaching Tip:** Consider giving students a structured assignment—a field trip on their own to a real library. Design the assignment to guide students to key research tools and to consulting with the reference librarian.

Practice Test 1

Praxis ParaPro Assessment
0755 & 1755

1. (A) (B) (C) (D)
2. (A) (B) (C) (D)
3. (A) (B) (C) (D)
4. (A) (B) (C) (D)
5. (A) (B) (C) (D)
6. (A) (B) (C) (D)
7. (A) (B) (C) (D)
8. (A) (B) (C) (D)
9. (A) (B) (C) (D)
10. (A) (B) (C) (D)
11. (A) (B) (C) (D)
12. (A) (B) (C) (D)
13. (A) (B) (C) (D)
14. (A) (B) (C) (D)
15. (A) (B) (C) (D)
16. (A) (B) (C) (D)
17. (A) (B) (C) (D)
18. (A) (B) (C) (D)
19. (A) (B) (C) (D)
20. (A) (B) (C) (D)
21. (A) (B) (C) (D)
22. (A) (B) (C) (D)
23. (A) (B) (C) (D)

24. (A) (B) (C) (D)
25. (A) (B) (C) (D)
26. (A) (B) (C) (D)
27. (A) (B) (C) (D)
28. (A) (B) (C) (D)
29. (A) (B) (C) (D)
30. (A) (B) (C) (D)
31. (A) (B) (C) (D)
32. (A) (B) (C) (D)
33. (A) (B) (C) (D)
34. (A) (B) (C) (D)
35. (A) (B) (C) (D)
36. (A) (B) (C) (D)
37. (A) (B) (C) (D)
38. (A) (B) (C) (D)
39. (A) (B) (C) (D)
40. (A) (B) (C) (D)
41. (A) (B) (C) (D)
42. (A) (B) (C) (D)
43. (A) (B) (C) (D)
44. (A) (B) (C) (D)
45. (A) (B) (C) (D)
46. (A) (B) (C) (D)

47. (A) (B) (C) (D)
48. (A) (B) (C) (D)
49. (A) (B) (C) (D)
50. (A) (B) (C) (D)
51. (A) (B) (C) (D)
52. (A) (B) (C) (D)
53. (A) (B) (C) (D)
54. (A) (B) (C) (D)
55. (A) (B) (C) (D)
56. (A) (B) (C) (D)
57. (A) (B) (C) (D)
58. (A) (B) (C) (D)
59. (A) (B) (C) (D)
60. (A) (B) (C) (D)
61. (A) (B) (C) (D)
62. (A) (B) (C) (D)
63. (A) (B) (C) (D)
64. (A) (B) (C) (D)
65. (A) (B) (C) (D)
66. (A) (B) (C) (D)
67. (A) (B) (C) (D)
68. (A) (B) (C) (D)
69. (A) (B) (C) (D)

70. (A) (B) (C) (D)
71. (A) (B) (C) (D)
72. (A) (B) (C) (D)
73. (A) (B) (C) (D)
74. (A) (B) (C) (D)
75. (A) (B) (C) (D)
76. (A) (B) (C) (D)
77. (A) (B) (C) (D)
78. (A) (B) (C) (D)
79. (A) (B) (C) (D)
80. (A) (B) (C) (D)
81. (A) (B) (C) (D)
82. (A) (B) (C) (D)
83. (A) (B) (C) (D)
84. (A) (B) (C) (D)
85. (A) (B) (C) (D)
86. (A) (B) (C) (D)
87. (A) (B) (C) (D)
88. (A) (B) (C) (D)
89. (A) (B) (C) (D)
90. (A) (B) (C) (D)

PRACTICE TEST 1 (0755 & 1755)
ParaPro Assessment

TIME: 2½ hours
90 multiple-choice questions

READING

Read the following paragraph, then answer questions 1 and 2.

Gina has a beautiful flower garden she planted herself. It seems like everything she plants flourishes. She really has a green thumb.

1. The phrase *has a green thumb* is an example of

    (A) a detail about Gina's gardening ability.
    (B) comparing and contrasting.
    (C) a figure of speech.
    (D) placing a term in context.

2. Which strategy would you suggest to a student who was unaware of the meaning of the word *flourish*?

    (A) Suggest the student look at the word in context.
    (B) Suggest the student re-read the word.
    (C) Suggest the student sound out the word.
    (D) Suggest the student make his best guess.

Read the following letter, then answer questions 3 through 6.

Dear Isabel,

Do you remember the bees we saw last week? We were scared of them. They came by our fresh peach sundaes so we killed them.

I just learned something about bees in school today. Did you know that without bees we would not have all of the fruits, vegetables, and other plants that we have today. Bees help pollinate plants. This is important because if the plants are not pollinated, seeds are not made. If seeds are not made, new plants will not grow. I'd sure hate to give up juicy peaches, sweet cherries, and messy watermelon!

I learned that bees are in trouble. There is a tiny mite, a member of the spider family that kills baby bees. Other bees are killed by pesticides, the chemicals used to kill bad insects. There used to be enough bees to pollinate farmers' crops. Now some farmers have to pay a beekeeper to bring thousands of bees to the field to pollinate the plants.

Sincerely, Jade

3. The author's purpose in writing is most probably

    (A) to inform Isabel that they shouldn't have killed the bees.
    (B) to explain why killing the bees was not a good idea.
    (C) to persuade Isabel not to use pesticides.
    (D) to inform Isabel about mites that kill baby bees.

4. The main idea in paragraph two is NOT that

   (A) bees help pollinate plants.
   (B) Jade learned about the importance of bees.
   (C) Jade learned that without bees we wouldn't have many fruits and vegetables.
   (D) Jade will learn to put up with bees.

5. Which question should the paraprofessional ask to help students read this passage?

   I.   Ask students to write questions about bees as they read.
   II.   Ask students what they would like to know about bees.
   III. Ask students if they've ever received a letter.
   IV.   Ask students if they know what the word *pollinate* means.

   (A) II only
   (B) III and IV
   (C) I only
   (D) II and IV

6. In paragraph two, how does Jade present her information to Isabel?

   (A) Jade compares and contrasts what she's learned about bees.
   (B) Jade's sentences all declare her support for bees.
   (C) Jade is attempting to persuade Isabel in this paragraph.
   (D) Jade provides examples as to why bees are important.

Read the following passage, then answer question 7 and 8.

Kali and Koko

It was dusk. The blue-black sky was star-sprinkled and clear. Kali and Koko raced down the path. Jenny put the horses into the warm, musky barn, then turned to call her two companions.

She heard excited barking where the path met the woods at the far cor-ner of the property. She leaned against the fence and called again. The only response was far-off barking. They've cornered something, she thought. "Kali! Koko! NOW!" Jenny warned.

She heard two yelps and then silence. Slowly a strong, recognizable stench wafted through the air. Jenny's eyes began to burn and she held her nose. She jumped the fence quickly as the two hairy animals ran toward her.

"You two! she groaned. "It looks like you've earned yourselves a few days out in the fresh air."

7. The author of the passage implies that

   (A) Kali and Koko are dogs.
   (B) Kali and Koko were in trouble with their owner.
   (C) the dogs were sprayed by a skunk.
   (D) the dogs will spend the night with the horses.

8. Which strategy is best to help students infer what is happening in the story?

   (A) Tell students that as they read, they should make predictions about what is happening in the story.
   (B) Tell students they will make some conclusions about what they read.
   (C) Tell students to write down a detail from the text and make a conclusion.
   (D) Tell students to look for clues and draw conclusions based on what happens and what the character says.

Read the following passage, then answer questions 9 and 10.

The Atmosphere

The atmosphere is the mixture of gas molecules and other materials surrounding the earth. It is made mostly of the gases nitrogen (78%), and oxygen (21%). Argon gas and water (in the form of vapor, droplets, and ice crystals) are the next most common things. There are also small amounts of other gases, plus many solid particles, like dust, soot and ashes, pollen, and salt from the oceans.

9. The primary purpose of the passage is to

    (A) tell the reader what the atmosphere is made up of.
    (B) explain that the atmosphere is mostly nitrogen.
    (C) tell the reader the common components of the atmosphere.
    (D) explain how complicated the atmosphere is.

10. How could the paraprofessional use this paragraph to help students locate details that support the main idea?

    (A) Tell students to look for transitional language using words like *the next most...*, and *there are also....*
    (B) Tell students that details are fact-based.
    (C) Explain that the main idea is in the first sentence and details follow.
    (D) Tell students details always support the author's purpose.

Read the following passage, then answer question 11.

Friday's game against the Wild Ones tallied up another loss for the pathetic Dogs. They were terrible. Raymond made a perfect shot from half-court to bring the Dogs score to 12 at the end of the quarter. Shepard scored four three-pointers in the final quarter. The previously winning Dogs should quit turning tail and go on the attack if they have any hope of making the playoffs.

11. All of the sentences are opinions EXCEPT for

    I.   Friday's game against the Wild Ones tallied up another loss for the pathetic Dogs
    II. They were terrible.
    III. Raymond made a perfect shot from half-court to bring the Dogs score to 12 at the end of the quarter.
    IV. Shepard scored four three-pointers in the final quarter.

    (A) I and II
    (B) II only
    (C) III and IV
    (D) IV only

Read the following passage, then answer questions 12 and 13.

A Cry for Peace
by Chief Joseph

Tell General Howard I know his heart. What he told me before, I have it in my heart. I am tired of fighting. Our chiefs are killed. Looking-Glass is dead; Ta-Hool-Shute is dead. The old men are all dead. It is the young men who say yes or no. He who led on the young men is dead. It is cold, and we have no blankets; the little children are freezing to death. My people, some of them, have run away to the hills, and have no blankets, no food. No one knows where they are—perhaps freezing to death. I want to have time to look for my children, and see how many of them I can find. Maybe I shall find them among the dead.

Hear me, my chiefs! I am tired; my heart is sick and sad. From where the sun now stands I will fight no more forever.

12. Which of the following would you suggest students do to establish the author's purpose for writing?

I. Tell students to ask themselves why the author is writing the text.

II. Tell students to compare and contrast what the author says about his people.

III. Tell students to give examples from the text to support their opinion.

IV. Tell students to think about how one sentence connects with another to support their opinion.

(A) I and III
(B) I only
(C) III and IV
(D) II only

13. The passage is primarily concerned with

(A) giving examples of the suffering of Chief Joseph's people.

(B) stating an argument for passing on his legacy to the young men of the tribe.

(C) telling why he will no longer battle with the military.

(D) telling the reader why there must be peace.

Read the following passage, then answer question 14.

My grandmother's face looked peculiar as we walked into the house. It was kind of pinched together, the way my little cousin Fernando's looked whenever he was hurt and about to cry. But I couldn't imagine Grace crying. Anyway, what was there to cry about?

14. A student is having trouble understanding the word *peculiar*. Which is the best choice for the paraprofessional to suggest the student use to understand the word *peculiar*?

I. Reread the sentence slowly and make predictions about the meaning of the word.

II. Compare and contrast Grace's face to Fernando's.

III. Ask the student why the author uses the word to describe Grace's face.

IV. Read on to see if the author provides more clues and information.

(A) IV only
(B) II and IV
(C) I only
(D) II and III

Read the following passage, then answer questions 15 and 16.

At one time, gray wolves lived all over the United States. After the settlement of the Europeans in the U.S., the wolf population quickly became endangered. By the 1930's wolves were gone from most of the west, including Yellowstone National Park. Some wolves were killed because they ate livestock. Others moved to avoid living near people. In the 1990's wolves returned to the western United States and Yellowstone. Some wolves were brought back to parks and wild regions by rangers and scientists. Some wolves moved from Canada back to Yellowstone. Scientists and wolf supporters are watching the progress of the wolf populations. They hope the wolf will no longer be classified as an endangered or threatened species.

15. Which of the following questions should a paraprofessional ask students to help them determine the main purpose of the passage?

(A) What details does the author give you that tell what the passage is about?

(B) What does the word *endangered* mean in the passage?

(C) What does the author imply in the passage about gray wolves?

(D) What does looking at the first and last sentence in the passage tell you about gray wolves?

16. How does one sentence connect to another in the passage?

(A) Each sentence builds a case for persuading the reader to support research about gray wolves.

(B) Each sentence builds on facts about gray wolves to explain why they became endangered.

(C) Each sentence is an argument for why wolf populations should be built up.

(D) Each sentence ties back to the topic sentence.

Read the following passage, then answer question 17.

Survival from *Kaffir Boy*
by Mark Mathabane

To prevent us from starving and to maintain a roof over our heads, my mother began running around the township *soliciting* money with which to pay the rent and to buy food, but very little came of it. A few people tried to help; but in the main, black people were burdened with their own survival.

17. The author most probably uses the word *soliciting* to mean

I.   take and acquire.
II. accumulate.
III. offering.
IV. stealing.

(A) III and IV
(B) I only
(C) II and III
(D) II only

Study the following bar chart, then answer questions 18 and 19.

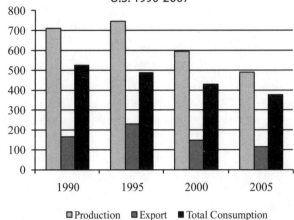

Cigarette Production, Exports, and Domestic Consumption
U.S. 1990-2007

Source: Centers for Disease Control and Prevention, www.cdc.gov

18. A student does not understand how to read the chart. Which question can the paraprofessional ask the student to help him read the chart?

(A) What is the purpose of this chart?
(B) What do the bars of the chart represent?
(C) What is the timespan covered in the chart?
(D) What is the chart asking of the reader?

19. According to the chart the United States

I.   has increased cigarette production from 1995-2005.
II. has exported fewer cigarettes from 1995-2005.
III. has decreased consumption from 1995-2005.
IV. has decreased production from 1995-2005.

(A) II only
(B) I only
(C) II and III
(D) I and IV

Read the following passage from a history text-book then answer questions 20 through 23.

The First People in America

Some ancient people may have crossed a land bridge that joined Asia and North America during the last Ice Age. The Ice Age was a time of extreme cold that lasted for thousands of year. Glaciers trapped so much water that ocean levels dropped. A bridge of land, now called Beringia, appeared where the Bering Strait is now. When the earth grew warm again, the glaciers melted and flooded Beringia. Some scientists who hold this theory believe the earliest Americans arrived 12,000 years ago. Other scientists believe humans came to the Americas much earlier. They have found artifacts in South America that tests show to be 30,000 years old. These scientists believe that people came to the Americas by many routes, over thousands of years. Some came by boat, sailing short distances from island to island. This theory may also change as scientists find more evidence of ancient America.

20. Which strategies would the paraprofessional suggest students use prior to reading this passage?

    (A) Skim and scan the text for important ideas
    (B) Read the title, scan the first and last sentence, look at graphics
    (C) Ask questions of the text before reading and look at graphics
    (D) Scan the text for unfamiliar words and put them into context, look at graphics

21. Which is the LEAST effective reading strategy you would use to understand the topic?

    (A) What point is the author trying to make?
    (B) What do I already know about this topic?
    (C) What books have I read about this topic?
    (D) What is the author trying to teach me?

22. In order to pronounce the word *Beringia*, it is important to know

    I.   how to sort consonants and vowels.
    II. phonemic awareness.
    III. that a consonant usually follows a noun in a word.

    (A) I and II
    (B) II only
    (C) I and III
    (D) III only

23. Which strategies should the paraprofessional tell students to use in order to decode the word *glacier*?

    (A) Slow down and reread.
    (B) Read sentences before and after the word.
    (C) Make a prediction about the word and read on.
    (D) Use a thesaurus to look for antonyms for the word.

Read the following informational text passage, then answer questions 24 through 27.

An Owl in the House
by Alice Calaprice

A few years ago I did something that I probably shouldn't have done, but to my mind I didn't have much of a choice, really. I adopted a wild animal—a baby great horned owl—after I found it buried in the snow in the Vermont woods near my home.

I am a zoologist and naturalist. That means I study animals that live in the wild. I know very well that wild animals should usually be left to fend for themselves, and that many die an early death in the process. This is the way nature intended it to be. It is unkind to force a wild animal into captivity.

Tampering with nature's ways causes the natural system of interdependence of all wild animals and plants to become unbalanced. In addition, most wild animals die when they leave their natural habitat and food supply. Despite this knowledge, I felt a moment of kinship with the owlet and instinctively reached out to protect it. I could not leave it there to die.

24. Which question would the paraprofessional ask students about the reading to check their understanding of the text?

(A) How did you like the text?
(B) What was the text about?
(C) Do you agree with the author's decision? Why? Why not?
(D) What is the author's profession?

25. *Tampering* is an example of a word with a

(A) prefix.
(B) affix.
(C) long vowel sound.
(D) suffix.

26. In order to stay focused as you read, you should

(A) predict what will happen to the owlet.
(B) slow down as you read.
(C) read the title of the story.
(D) take a short break from the reading.

27. The word *kinship* is an example of a

(A) simile.
(B) synonym.
(C) compound word.
(D) prefix.

28. Students are writing synonyms for the word *good* in their word notebooks to describe a happy moment in their lives. Which of the following are the best examples of synonyms for good?

I.   profit, benefit, gain
II. satisfactory, adequate, outstanding
III. marvelous, excellent, first-rate
IV. bad, poor, satisfactory

(A) I and II
(B) I and III
(C) III only
(D) IV only

Use the Table of Contents below to answer question 29.

29. On which page or pages would a person be most likely to find information evaluating the literature?

(A) pages 45-48
(B) page 45
(C) page 9
(D) pages 9-25

30. Why should children be taught to use graphic organizers as a method of organizing data during an inquiry?

(A) It discourages the practice of copying paragraphs out of the source book.
(B) It helps children to see similarities and differences across sources.
(C) Graphic organizers look good to parents.
(D) It provides the students an opportunity to use a word processor.

MATHEMATICS

31. Which one of the following is best translated as "the quotient of 5 and 4 added to the product of 2 and 3"?

(A) $\dfrac{5}{4} \times (2 + 3)$

(B) $5 \times 4 + \dfrac{2}{3}$

(C) $\dfrac{5}{4} + 2 \times 3$

(D) $5 \times 4 - \dfrac{2}{3}$

32. What is the mean for a group of 20 numbers in which seven of them are 3's, nine of them are 6's, and the rest of them are 10's?

(A) 9.25
(B) 7.67
(C) 6.33
(D) 5.75

33. The following bar chart describes the results of a survey taken for the favorite ice cream flavor for 120 individuals. The only available choices were vanilla, chocolate, strawberry, and mocha. (V = Vanilla, C = Chocolate, S = Strawberry, M = Mocha)

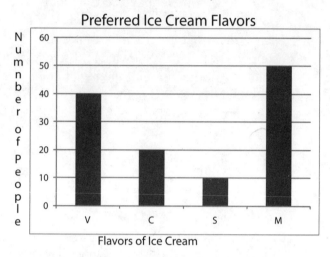

Preferred Ice Cream Flavors

What percent of ALL people surveyed favored vanilla OR strawberry?

(A) 50%
(B) 41.6%
(C) 33.3%
(D) 30.%

34. Each adult resident of the town of Peoplefine was surveyed to determine the efficiency of the mayor. The categories were "Excellent," Very Good," Average," and "Poor."

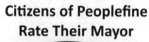

Citizens of Peoplefine Rate Their Mayor

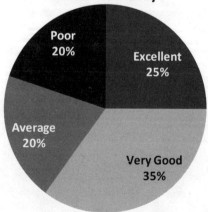

Using the pie chart, if a combined total of 1440 residents rated the mayor as either "Excellent" or "Very Good," how many adult residents are there?

(A) 2400
(B) 2800
(C) 3200
(D) 3600

35. Which one of the following statements is NOT correct?

(A) $-1.62 < -2.32$
(B) $16 \geq 16$
(C) $0 < 0.88$
(D) $-\dfrac{2}{3} > -\dfrac{3}{2}$

36. Which one of the following is equivalent to $\dfrac{87}{93}$?

(A) $\dfrac{25}{31}$

(B) $\dfrac{26}{33}$

(C) $\dfrac{29}{31}$

(D) $\dfrac{31}{33}$

37. What is the volume of a rectangular box whose length is 5 inches, width is 4 inches, and height is 9 inches?

(A) 81 cubic inches
(B) 90 cubic inches
(C) 162 cubic inches
(D) 180 cubic inches

38. A pair of shoes is being sold for 18% off its normal selling price of $96. What is the sale price?

(A) $90.82
(B) $84.67
(C) $78.72
(D) $72.57

39. What is the value of $2^3 \times 5^2$?

(A) 60
(B) 80
(C) 150
(D) 200

40. What is the name associated with a triangle whose sides are 5, 7, and 7?
(A) Equilateral
(B) Scalene
(C) Perpendicular
(D) Isosceles

41. The perimeter of a rectangle is 27 feet. If the length is 8 feet, what is the width?

(A) 3.375 feet
(B) 5.5 feet
(C) 6.75 feet
(D) 11 feet

42. Jerry has kept a log of the number of projects he has completed at work for a six-month period. This data is represented in the line graph below.

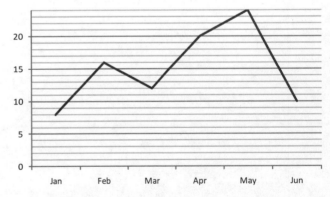

Number of Projects January - June

During which period of time was there an increase each month in the number of projects that Jerry completed?

(A) From January to April
(B) From February to May
(C) From March to May
(D) From April to June

43. A morning workshop begins at 8:45 AM and ends at 11:05 AM. In terms of hours, what is the length of this workshop?

    (A) $3\frac{2}{3}$

    (B) $2\frac{3}{4}$

    (C) $2\frac{1}{3}$

    (D) $2\frac{1}{6}$

44. What is the value of x in the following equation?

    $7x - 15 = 2x + 30$

    (A) 9
    (B) 7
    (C) 5
    (D) 3

Consider the line segment shown below and answer question 45.

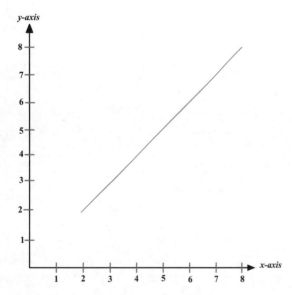

45. Which one of the following points does NOT lie on this line segment?

    (A) (2,2)
    (B) (4,3)

(C) (5,6)
(D) (8,5)

46. What is the median for the following group of numbers?

    18, 35, 15, 25, 13, 20

    (A) 18
    (B) 19
    (C) 20
    (D) 21

47. Rebecca drives for three hours at a rate of 40 miles per hour, then drives two hours at a rate of 50 miles per hour. What is her average rate in miles per hour?

    (A) 44
    (B) 45
    (C) 46
    (D) 47

48. The length of a fence is 4 yards and 2 feet. What is this length in inches?

    (A) 216
    (B) 200
    (C) 184
    (D) 168

49. A student wrote the incorrect answer zero for the calculation $25 + 15 \div 5 - 2 \times 4$. What mistake did the student most likely make?

    (A) Dividing 15 by 5, then subtracting 2.
    (B) Adding 25 and 15, then dividing by 5.
    (C) Subtracting 2 from 5, then multiplying by 4.
    (D) Multiplying 2 by 4, then subtracting from 5.

50. Which one of the following would be the best way to introduce the meaning of "mode" to a class?

    (A) Write a list of different numbers and ask the students to name the highest.
    (B) Write a list of the same number repeated ten times.

(C)   Write a list of different numbers and ask the students to subtract the lowest from the highest.

(D)   Write a list of different numbers for which one of the numbers is repeated more often than any of the others.

51.   A student claimed that every right triangle is isosceles. Which one of the following could represent the sides of a triangle that would be a counterexample to this claim?

(A)   6, 6, 6
(B)   5, 5, 8
(C)   4, 5, 6
(E)   3, 4, 5

52.   A student decides to calculate her average for five exams. Her average for the first four exams is 90 and her score on the fifth exam is 100. The student states that her average for all five exams is $\frac{90 + 100}{2} = 95$. What is the instructor's best response?

(A)   Tell the student that her calculation is completely correct.

(B)   Tell the student that her average for all five exams is actually higher than 95 because it is a weighted average.

(C)   Tell the student that her average for all five exams is actually lower than 95 because it is a weighted average.

(D)   Tell the student that she would have had a higher average if she had scored 100 on the first test.

53.   If Larry walks at the rate of 5 miles per hour, what is his rate in feet per minute?

(A)   88
(B)   300
(C)   440
(D)   1048

54.   A class problem is to fill in the missing blank for the proportion $\frac{2}{3} = \frac{\_\_}{72}$. What strategy would work best?

(A)   Divide 72 by 2, then multiply that quotient by 3.

(B)   Divide 72 by 3, then multiply that quotient by 2.

(C)   Subtract 3 from 72, and then add that number to 2.

(D)   Subtract 2 from 72, and then add that number to 3.

55.   A student is asked to change 5.12 hours to minutes. He proceeds to multiply 5.12 by 60 to get 307.2 as his answer. What is the BEST advice that his teacher should give him?

(A)   He should first change .12 to a number of hours.

(B)   He should first multiply 5 by 60.

(C)   No advice is necessary. The student's method is correct.

(D)   He should first divide 5 by .12.

56.   One particular problem in a student's homework is to find the original price of a dress if it was discounted by 20% and was subsequently bought for $100. The student calculated $100 divided by 0.80 to get her answer. How should her teacher correct this answer?

(A)   No correction is needed. The student's method is correct.

(B)   She should have divided $100 by 0.20.

(C)   She should have multiplied $100 by 0.80.

(D)   She should have multiplied $100 by 0.20, then add that number to $100.

57.   A substitute teacher is teaching a class how to find the area of a geometric figure. The majority of the class states that the rule is just to multiply length by width. What is this substitute teacher's BEST response?

(A)   The area is never equal to the product of length and width.

(B) The class is correct. The area of a geometric figure is always length times width.

(C) The area is equal to length times width only for specific figures.

(D) The area is always the sum of the lengths of the figure.

58. A teacher asks the class to explain how two geometric figures are similar but not identical. Which one of the following students' explanation is BEST?

(A) Kathleen says that all corresponding angles are equal and the corresponding sides are in proportion.

(B) Sam says that all corresponding sides are equal and the corresponding angles are in proportion.

(C) Melinda says that if two figures are similar, then they must be identical.

(D) Rocky says that only triangles can be similar.

59. A teacher writes seven different numbers on the blackboard. These numbers are not in any special order. Students are asked how to find the median. One student says that the middle number, namely the fourth number, must be the median. What underlying principle is this student ignoring?

(A) None. The student's answer is correct.

(B) The numbers must be arranged in order.

(C) The numbers must be integers.

(D) The median may not exist.

60. Ms. Roberts is teaching a Math Fundamentals class. Today's topic deals with the rules for rounding off numbers to specific places. She asks the class to round off 0.4492 to the nearest tenth. Four different students offer an answer with an explanation. Which one of the four students offers the correct answer and the correct explanation?

(A) The first student says that the correct answer is 0.4 because the digit 2, which is in the last place to the right, is less than 5.

(B) The second student says that the correct answer is 0.5 because the digit 9 is higher than 5.

(C) The third student says that the correct answer is 0.4 because the digit 4, which is in the hundredths place, is less than 5.

(D) The fourth student says that the correct answer is 0.5 because the number is first rounded off to the nearest hundredth as 0.45. Then this decimal is rounded off to the nearest tenth.

WRITING

61. Which of the following are correct assessments of these four sentences?

I. Although the band played expertly, they left the stage looking dejected because the audience did not clamor for an encore.

II. Each of the performers left his/her instrument in place, walked to the stage apron, looked directly at the audience, and took a low, slow bow.

III. How young children's computer and video game usage are effecting their ability to read needs to be carefully studied.

IV. Martin Luther King used many biblical quotations that gave resonance to his speeches; consequently, he is an excellent role model who demonstrates how illusion can add to the power of a talk or text.

(A) I shows incorrect comma usage; II violates pronoun agreement

(B) II is non-parallel construction; IV is incorrectly punctuated

(C) III has an incorrect word usage; IV also has an incorrect word usage

(D) III has an incorrect possessive case; I shows incorrect comma usage

62. Which of the following is a simple sentence?

    (A) Charles Dickens, the great 19th century novelist, published his novels one chapter at a time for an audience always hungering for the next episode and, therefore, more than willing to pay a shilling or two for each installment.

    (B) The battle was long, and the warriors returned exhausted to camp.

    (C) They won even though they played poorly.

    (D) Since the law forbidding cell phone use went into effect, automobile accidents have decreased significantly.

63. Which of the following sentences has either an incorrect comma usage or is lacking a comma where one is needed?

    (A) Whoever can claim to be without faults please come up upon the stage and judge our actions.

    (B) Both the law and longstanding custom allow dissent and, in some ways, actually encourage it.

    (C) In late autumn before the arrival of storms and snow, nature puts on a spectacular show, using the trees as brushes to paint the blue sky with rainbow colors.

    (D) Those who are virtuous will prosper, and this is as it should be.

64. Which of the following is incorrect in its punctuation of a quotation?

    (A) The Cherokee Indians called their forced migration "the Trail of Tears"; I consider it a "national tragedy."

    (B) Every evening when my grandfather visited my childhood home, he would ask, as if oblivious to all the noise we kids were making, "Isn't anyone home"?

    (C) It was Thomas Jefferson himself who said, "Eternal vigilance is the price of liberty."

    (D) The newest historian on the Cuban Missile crisis of 1962 reveals that JFK clearly experienced the bizarre possibility of unleashing nuclear weapons, and exclaimed out loud, "Oh, my God, this cannot be!" (Ross 20).

65. Which of the sentences below is NOT correct in pronoun agreement?

    (A) The team attributes its victory to weeks of grueling practice.

    (B) Somebody in the crowd is calling for an ambulance.

    (C) The jury is ready to announce its verdict on this case involving so many important precedents.

    (D) Every one of the ideas presented in the lecture are further developed on the university's web site.

66. Which of the following has an error in verb agreement?

    (A) It's a shame that there is no limits on the noise pollution in residential neighborhoods.

    (B) The leaders of the Senate are all lawyers.

    (C) Despite the hours of planning, the committee failed to deliver its reports.

    (D) There is a lack of funds to carry out the improvements in the district.

67. Which choice accurately identifies all the underlined sections (note some may be partially correct)?

The senators and representatives$_I$, all of them elected officials$_{II}$, worked diligently$_{III}$ to meet $_{IV}$ the promises they had made to their constituencies $_V$.

    (A) compound subject II. Pronouns III. Adverb IV. Infinitive V. Prepositional phrase

    (B) compound subject II. Appositive III. Adverb IV. Infinitive V. Prepositional phrase

    (C) compound subject II. Appositive III. Adjective IV. Gerund V. Prepositional phrase

(D) subject II. Prepositional phrase III. Adverb IV. Infinitive V. Prepositional phrase

68. Select the choice that correctly identifies all the underlined words and phrases.

Poor _I writing _{II} seriously handicaps students, making it extremely _{III} difficult to achieve _{IV} their _V career goals.

(A) Adverb I. Subject II. Adverb III. Infinitive IV. 3rd Person Pronoun, objective case. V.

(B) Adjective I. Gerund II. Adverb III. Verb Complement IV. Possessive Pronoun V.

(C) Adjective I. Gerund II. Adverb III. Infinitive IV. Possessive Pronoun V.

(D) Adverb I. Present Progressive Verb II. Adverb III. Infinitive IV. Possessive Pronoun V.

69. All of the following have an error in word usage EXCEPT

(A) Pollution generated by all types of power plants—coal nuclear, waster-effects air quality to some degree.

(B) The new principal, Dr. Brooks, graduated summa cum laude from Boston University.

(C) Martin Luther King used many Biblical quotes which added resonance to his speeches.

(D) In the past, writers use to publish their novels in serial form, chapter by chapter.

70. Which of the following statements is accurate?

I. As the defendant was intoxicated at the time of the accident, the jury's verdict was harsher than normal even though it was the defendant's first offense.

II. Contrary to expectations, and to the disappointment of many, Grace Ross lost the election to Vivian Rios, who is a relative newcomer on the political scene of our town.

III. In the interests of public safety, we must ban cell phone use by drivers; the accident linkage is just too compelling.

IV. The use of cell phones in automobiles is indisputable dangerous, and it is our responsibility as public servants to ban this practice.

(A) Both sentences I and II are complex sentences correctly punctuated.

(B) Sentence I is the only simple sentence.

(C) Sentence I and IV are compound sentences.

(D) Sentence III is a complex sentence.

71. Which statement accurately identifies the following sentences?

I. While he held the Office of Secretary, the department's protocols were rigorously maintained to the admiration of all the staff.

II. With all her vast experience and know-how, she, nonetheless, failed to convince the interviewers of her merits.

III. Real citizens are few and far-between, but Ramona White is one of them.

IV. However well educated he is, his rude, aggressive manner alienates the scholarly community and undermines his success.

(A) Sentence II is a complex sentence, and III is a compound sentence.

(B) Sentence I is a compound sentence and IV is complex.

(C) I is a complex sentence, and II is a simple sentence

(D) III and IV are complex sentences.

72. The word that refers to a verb and its related words in a clause or sentence is a

(A) verb clause.
(B) noun clause.
(C) predicate.
(D) postulate.

73. Which statement regarding the underlined sections is accurate?

To the uninitiated members _I of the class _{II} of 2012, the President's words of disdain seemed far removed from fairness _{III} because, not understanding their context $_{IV}$, they attributed negative tones to what was to the initiated members a humorous, playful jab at the typical foibles $_V$ of youth.

(A) I, II, III, IV, V are all prepositional phrases.

(B) I, II, III, are prepositional phrases, and IV and V are not.

(C) I, II, III, and V are prepositional phrases, and IV is not.

(D) I, II, IV, and V are prepositional phrases, and III is not.

74. Which of the sentences contains a common usage error?

I. Given how much good she had done for the organization, President Obama's highly complementary words to introduce her cannot be considered exaggeration.

II. To advise is one thing, but to provide council laced with threats is an abuse of the therapist's power.

III. The current economic crisis effects everyone, but no one more so than the working poor.

IV. In the Homecoming, four children are abandoned and must undertake a journey further than any of them had ever imagined they would have to go,

(A) I only

(B) II only

(C) III and IV

(D) All of them

75. Which of the following underlined clauses is a restrictive clause that allows no commas around it?

(A) The pit bulls that live down the street ran past my window, with their owner frantically running after them.

(B) Three of my favorite dogs which are possible choices are labs, shepherds, and huskies.

(C) The women who may now be justly called leaders behaved with a calm assurance that soothed the agitated crowd.

(D) Still waters which may run deep may be stagnant and polluted.

76. Which of the following requires at least one comma?

(A) The trip to Bermuda goes to the competitor who scores the least points.

(B) Three symptoms that indicate the possibility of infection are inflammation, fever, and pain.

(C) Whoever has the courage to take an unpopular stand has the qualities of a leader, rather than a mere politician.

(D) Ex-President Jimmy Carter who won the Nobel Peace Prize last year has recently written a book urging that the U.S. take a more balanced approach to the Middle East crisis.

77. An independent clause

(A) must have at least one dependent clause.

(B) contains a subject and a verb but is not necessarily a complete thought.

(C) is not necessarily a complete thought.

(D) can be connected to either dependent clauses or to another independent clause.

78. A complex sentence is a sentence

(A) that has at least two dependent clauses.

(B) that contains several ideas.

(C) that has at least one dependent clause and an independent clause.

(D) with two or more independent clauses.

79. Which of the following is the best thesis statement for a five-page research paper?

(A) History provides many clues to the origin of war amongst human beings.

(B) Experience is the best teacher.

(C) Recent research directly links cigarette smoking to lung cancer and respiratory disease such as emphysema.

(D) Advertising is the cause of eating disorders.

Read the passage below and answer question 80.

My nephew is only five years old, but he is amazing. He reads a lot. He also is always giving speeches on some interesting topic. I don't know how he comes up with so much! I also notice, however, that the children I babysit for are interesting. Their mother reads to them every night. Even though one of them is only three and the other is four and a half, both of them have great vocabularies and, like my nephew, they seem to know a lot. I think this reflects the benefits of reading to children when they are very young because I know that my nephew's mother also used to read to him even when he was before one year old. Educators are now beginning to urge parents to read to their children because this lays the foundation for the ability to read and to master language. My nephew would be an excellent subject for a case study.

80. The paragraph suffers from which of the following problems:

I.   The paragraph lacks a unifying topic statement

II. The paragraph needs more transitional phrases to connect sentences.

III. The paragraph needs more development, and there are a few grammatical errors

IV. The paragraph erroneously places the topic statement as the conclusion

(A) I only
(B) I and III only
(C) I and II only
(D) II and III only

Read the passage below and answer question 81.

The floors, originally oak hardwood, had several layers of lime green and orange paint covering them. We had first to scrape the paint off with hand tools on our hands and knees. You can imagine how our backs felt after three days of this tortuous work but that was only the start. Then came the sanding with the electric rotor that weighs about 200 pounds. Just getting it home from the rental store was worth one day of exhaustion. Let's skip the ordeal of getting the sandpaper properly wound around the drum of the machine. That ordeal was minor against the challenge of holding this 200 pound machine with a revved up engine roaring to gouge its way across the floor in rein. Next came the walls. These had three layers of ghastly flowered decorated wall paper...10 rooms. But I'll spare you the fatigue for the moment. Suffice it to say: buying a fixer-upper is not all fun and profits!

81. Which of the following sentences is the BEST topic sentence?

(A) Old houses have many surprises for their new owners.
(B) Sweat equity can turn an old house into a grand profit.
(C) Taking on the restoration of the old house was like signing up for a year of hard labor.
(D) Old houses bring problems galore with them.

82. All of the following are laws of organization for both paragraphs and essays EXCEPT

(A) development.
(B) transition.
(C) unity.
(D) coherence.

83. Complete the following sentence. The law of unity applies to

    (A) paragraphs and to the order of their sentences.
    (B) both paragraphs and essays and to maintaining focus on the main idea.
    (C) essays and their thesis statements.
    (D) both paragraphs and essays and to their organizational strategies.

84. In the following paragraph, what is the topic sentence?

    "My man that cannot be cut." "What is it?" The correct answer determined whether the traveler who found himself in the court of the Tahitian King would live or die. In this case, the traveler was clever and after a few minutes of thought, goaded by his desire to survive, he answered: "shadow," and so he was free to continue on his way. In the annals of many people throughout the world, we find accounts of riddles, and we might recall the fairy tale of Rumplestiltskin that many of us read as children. There the dwarf challenges the princess to discover his name. These episodes, however, illustrate that word games, particularly riddles, were not always the play of children; rather, in earlier civilizations, they were contests liken war whose outcome spelt life or death. We recall, for instance, how Oedipus saves himself from being devoured by the Sphinx, the fate of all others who had failed, by correctly answering the riddle that had stumped others: "who is it that walks on four legs at dawn, on two legs during the day, and on three legs in the evening?" Oedipus, noble in arms, proves himself sharp in wit and intelligence, for he answers, "Man" and explains how he crawls at first, walks on two legs in adulthood, and as an old man walks with a cane, his third leg. The Sphinx is thwarted and enraged that she has lost her dinner, but Oedipus is allowed to continue on what we know is a tragic journey to situation that is a riddle of a different sort but one no less challenging and no less consequential for the Greek hero who has given his name to the Freudian original sin—the Oedipus complex. Riddles are very serious business!

    (A) Riddles are serious business!
    (B) These episodes, however, illustrate that word games, particularly riddles, were not always the play of children; rather, in earlier civilizations, they were contests liken war whose outcome spelt life or death
    (C) There is no topic sentence; rather we find a list of examples
    (D) In the annals of many people throughout the world, we find accounts of riddles, and we might recall the fairy tale of Rumplestiltskin that many of us read as children.

85. Which of the following sentences is the most effective thesis statement for an expository essay?

    (A) The media is biased and narrow.
    (B) Slavery was a major pillar of the South's economy in the century before the Civil War.
    (C) The death penalty is morally wrong and should be abolished.
    (D) Single parent households are not as beneficial as households with two parents.

86. Which of the statements below accurately assesses the following paragraph?

    When Elizabeth Cady Stanton and Susan B. Anthony paired up to fight the New York lawmakers, Anthony was the one who collected the 10,000 signatures to convince the lawmakers to allow women the vote. Her contributions to the suffragettes often involved speaking in public and touring. Indeed, we can safely say that she was in the "advertising business selling" the suffragettes. Also, she traveled all through the United States even when she was old and fragile, and she took many courageous actions on behalf of women's rights. Appropriately, she is the first woman to be pictured on a US coin. Because of all her contributions, she is ranked as one of the most honored of all American feminists.

(A) The paragraph suffers from weak development

(B) The paragraph needs many more transitional devices to make it coherent.

(C) The paragraph needs a stronger topic statement to pull it together.

(D) The paragraph lacks unity; one or the supporting sentences has wandered from the main point.

87. Which of the following statements most effectively characterizes the following paragraph?

The relationship between Susan B. Anthony and Elizabeth Cady Stanton began on May, 1851 at an anti-slavery meeting at Seneca Falls. The meeting was the beginning of an extraordinarily productive partnership and lifelong friendship. Anthony and Stanton's common objective was to achieve women equality in the United States. Stanton wrote all the speeches, and Anthony delivered them: "Stanton forged the fire bolts that Anthony fired to the world." They formed the National Women's Loyal League during the Civil War, to pass the 13th amendment. The point of this league was to abolish slavery. Later they formed another league, The National Woman's Suffrage League. The league worked for equal pay and property rights for women. Both these women also became proponents of the 14th amendment. It was designed to grant rights to all African-Americans in the United States. In the final analysis, their partnership embraced a large view of women's rights and extended to those of other oppressed groups,-notably the Black slaves.

(A) weak development and lacks a topic statement

(B) lacks a conclusion and a topic sentence

(C) lacks unity and development

(D) poor coherence: needs sentence variety and transitional phrases

88. Which of the statements following the paragraph accurately assesses it?

Susan B. Anthony and Elizabeth Cady Stanton published a newspaper called The Revolution. Thanks to Edward Train, a wealthy merchant who helped them fund it, they served the women's cause because the publication created a forum, focus, and direction. Later on, they formed the National Women's Suffrage Association together, which still exists today. Another of their contributions was the book which they both wrote called *A History of Women Suffrage*, in which they explained the lowly status of females in life and how the suffragette movement changed the attitude of society towards women. Although they had extremely different personalities and lifestyles, they formed an everlasting bond. In 1902, when Stanton died, her daughter sent a letter to Anthony telling her the news. After this Anthony said to Stanton's daughter "It seems impossible that the voice is stilled which I have loved to hear for more than 50 years." Anthony was left alone, but even without her partner, she continued her work for women suffrage until the day she died. The irony in the end was that they themselves never had the chance to vote because the 19th amendment was ratified after their deaths.

(A) The paragraph lacks unity.
(B) The paragraph lacks development.
(C) The paragraph lacks coherence.
(D) The paragraph lacks a conclusion.

89. Which of the following statements accurately assesses the following paragraph?

Teachers should take steps to stop students from cheating on examinations. To begin with teachers should stop using tests that they've given before. Inevitably, these "used goods" are found and distributed by the student underground. A copy of last year's examination is somehow smuggled out of the exam room, so a clique of kids has all the questions before the exam. Teachers should also be careful during the testing period. For instance, they should keep a good distance between students, separating every one by at least one chair. Furthermore, sitting in the rear of the classroom gives the teacher a bird's-eye view that prevents the long necked from stretching their eyes onto their neighbors' papers, and the note passers can be seen. Finally, teachers need to enforce penalties for cheating. Anyone caught must get an

automatic zero; those caught more than once must be expelled from the course with a failing grade on their transcripts. Cheating is so unfair to the honest students that teachers are duty-bound to implement very specific methods to insure its prevention.

(A) The paragraph lacks a conclusion.
(B) The paragraph needs more transitional phrases to connect the sentences.
(C) The paragraph shows a classification form of development which makes the main idea very clear.
(D) The paragraph lacks unity.

90. Which of the following activities are considered part of the prewriting phase of the writing process?

(A) delimiting the topic, point of view, organizational format, audience for the piece
(B) determining the length of the piece, genre, audience for the piece
(C) choosing the theme, point of view, choice of specific vocabulary to be used
(D) delimiting the topic, choice of theme, length of the piece

ANSWER KEY FOR PRACTICE TEST 1 (0755 & 1755)

1. (C)	28. (C)	55. (C)	82. (B)
2. (A)	29. (D)	56. (A)	83. (B)
3. (B)	30. (B)	57. (C)	84. (A)
4. (D)	31. (C)	58. (A)	85. (B)
5. (C)	32. (D)	59. (B)	86. (C)
6. (D)	33. (B)	60. (C)	87. (D)
7. (C)	34. (A)	61. (C)	88. (A)
8. (D)	35. (A)	62. (A)	89. (C)
9. (A)	36. (C)	63. (A)	90. (A)
10. (A)	37. (D)	64. (B)	
11. (D)	38. (C)	65. (D)	
12. (A)	39. (D)	66. (A)	
13. (D)	40. (D)	67. (B)	
14. (A)	41. (B)	68. (C)	
15. (D)	42. (C)	69. (B)	
16. (B)	43. (C)	70. (A)	
17. (B)	44. (A)	71. (C)	
18. (A)	45. (C)	72. (C)	
19. (C)	46. (B)	73. (C)	
20. (B)	47. (A)	74. (D)	
21. (C)	48. (D)	75. (A)	
22. (B)	49. (B)	76. (D)	
23. (B)	50. (D)	77. (D)	
24. (C)	51. (D)	78. (C)	
25. (D)	52. (C)	79. (C)	
26. (B)	53. (C)	80. (C)	
27. (C)	54. (B)	81. (C)	

PRACTICE TEST 1 (0755 & 1755): PROGRESS CHART

Reading Skills and Knowledge   ____/18

1	2	3	4	5	6	7	8	9	10	11

12	13	14	15	16	17	18

Application of Reading Skills and Knowledge to the Classroom   ____/12

19	20	21	22	23	24	25	26	27	28	29

30

Mathematics Skills and Knowledge   ____/18

31	32	33	34	35	36	37	38	39	40	41

42	43	44	45	46	47	48

Application of Mathematics Skills and Knowledge to the Classroom ____/12

49	50	51	52	53	54	55	56	57	58	59

60

Writing Skills and Knowledge   ____/18

61	62	63	64	65	66	67	68	69	70	71

72	73	74	75	76	77	78

Application of Writing Skills and Knowledge to the Classroom   ____/12

79	80	81	82	83	84	85	86	87	88	89

90

Detailed Explanations of
Answers for Practice Test 1

Praxis ParaPro Assessment
(0755 & 1755)

READING

1. (C)

The correct answer is (C). The passage, *"has a green thumb,"* is an example of a figure of speech. A figure of speech creates an image or picture in the reader's mind. Figures of speech use language in a non-literal way.

2. (A)

The correct answer is (A). Re-reading, sounding out, and best guesses are not viable strategies for figuring out unknown words. Writers often leave clues before and after using an unknown word to provide context clues for the reader.

3. (B)

The correct answer is (B). An author's purpose is the reason why they are writing the text. It is the big picture they're attempting to get across to the reader. (A), (C), and (D) all help support the author's purpose, which is (B).

4. (D)

The correct answer is (D). The main idea in a text ties everything together. (D) could be a consequence of what Jade learned about bees, but it is not the main idea. (A) is a detail. (B) is a consequence. (C) is the closest to being the main idea.

5. (C)

The correct answer is (C). Having students question and think about the text as they write supports reading comprehension. (A) would be acceptable if it was phrased, "Ask students what they know about bees." rather than "... what they'd like to know."

6. (D)

The correct answer is (D). Jade provides examples to support her argument as to why bees should not be killed. Jade is attempting to persuade (C) her friend, but Jade's organization of the passage is done by using solid examples to support her argument.

7. (C)

The correct answer is (C). While Kali and Koko are dogs (A) and at one point in trouble with their owner (B), the conclusion drawn as to what happens to the dogs is inferred more than the previous two responses. (D) is conjecture.

8. (D)

The correct answer is (D). To infer, readers look for clues from the author about settings, plot, characters, and intentions. Readers draw conclusions from the clues and adds their own background knowledge to make inferences.

9. (A)

The correct answer is (A). The author is telling the reader many things. However, the primary purpose of the passage is to explain what the atmosphere is made of.

10. (A)

The correct answer is (A). When authors give details, particularly several details, they often use transitional language to list the details. It's a roadmap of sorts for the reader.

11. (D)

The correct answer is (D). Facts can be proved. Opinions are statements that reflect a person's beliefs. They should be supported with facts, but are not based in fact. (B) is strictly an opinion. (A) and (C) are a mix of fact and opinion.

12. (A)

The correct answer is (A). While (B) is also correct, asking why an author is writing a piece *along with* supporting examples makes for a stronger answer.

13. (D)

The correct answer is (D). Although Chief Joseph does give examples of his people's suffering (A), he makes no argument (B) for passing on his legacy. We assume the list he provides are the reasons for no longer fighting (C) with the military. However, due to the destruction of his tribe, his overall purpose in writing is a plea for peace.

14. (A)

The correct answer is (A). The author provides clues as to the meaning of *peculiar,* in the next sentence when she compares her grandmother's face to her cousin Fernando's. "*It was kind of pinched...the way...Fernando/s looked whenever he was hurt and about to cry.*" Reading on to see if the author provides clues in context is an important reading strategy that is applied to many genres.

15. (D)

The correct answer is (D). Details (A) may help you get a notion of what the passage is primarily about, but it will be an incomplete picture. Knowing the word *endangered* doesn't get at the focus of the piece. We're not looking for inferences (C) in the response. In this particular passage the author clearly states in the first and last sentence what the focus of the passage is.

16. (B)

The correct answer is (B). This is primarily a fact-based passage. The author uses facts to explain first why the wolf population decreased, and then reports as to why, in more recent years, wolves have increased their population. There is nothing in the passage about research (A) and there isn't a discussion as to why the wolf population should be built up. *Contradict* means to go against, which is not the case regarding each sentence and its relation to the topic sentence (D).

17. (B)

The correct answer is (B). Mark's mother tried to *acquire* money for rent and food and would *take* money offered to her to do so. She was not offering or stealing money.

18. (A)

The correct answer is (A). Asking the student to identify the purpose of the chart is a 'big picture' question that goes to why the chart was created. What does the author or creator of the chart hope to do with the information on the chart? (D) is also a good question but not as focused as (A).

19. (C)

The correct answer is (C). From 1995-2005 the United States has exported fewer cigarettes AND decreased consumption of cigarettes. (B) is incorrect.

20. (B)

The correct answer is (B). When previewing a text, particularly informational text, there are a number of clues the reader is given to get a sense of what the text is about. While skimming and scanning is a good strategy (A), there is more involved with previewing a reading. Asking questions is important as well (D) but reading the title, the first and last sentences and examining the graphics is a more thorough approach.

21. (C)

The correct answer is (C). While you may have background knowledge about the topic, all authors have their own purpose for writing and their own understanding of the topic. The reader is trying to learn a particular author's purpose for writing and that may conflict with what you already know.

22. (B)

The correct answer is (B). The goal is to teach phonemic awareness, an understanding of the relationship between sounds and symbols. A consonant doesn't necessarily follow a noun in a word (D). Sorting consonants and vowels is one aspect of phonemic awareness (A and C).

23. (B)

The correct answer is (B). Reading sentences or phrases around the unfamiliar word's often gives students clues as to the words meaning. A thesaurus gives synonyms but is not always available.

24. (C)

The correct answer is (C). Asking a student how they like a text will elicit little in the way of understanding. Asking a student what the text is about is a basic comprehension question. When you ask a student about their opinion and require the evidence to support it, the student must have a deeper understanding of the text in order to respond.

25. (D)

The correct answer is (D). The *–ing* ending is a suffix. Affixes are prefixes and suffixes.

26. (B)

The correct answer is (B). Often, slowing down helps a reader stay on track. Racing through ones reading means a reader is not thinking and making meaning of the text.

27. (C)

The correct answer is (C). Compound words combine two base words with different meanings to form a new word. *Kin* means family. *Ship* as a noun is a sea vessel and *to send* is a verb. *Kinship* means you have a close relationship with someone.

28. (C)

The correct answer is (C). *Profit, benefit* and *gain* (A) are all synonyms for good, but they are nouns. In this context, the word *good* is used as an adjective, which describes something. *Satisfactory, adequate, outstanding* are synonyms and adjectives for *good*, but are combined under (A) making them incorrect.

29. (D)

The correct answer is (D). The entire Chapter 2, pages 9-25, contains a discussion of the literature review.

30. (B)

Asking children to complete a graphic organizer as they research an issue helps them keep organized, see connections, and pull together what they can then use in some interesting and meaningful way.

MATHEMATICS

31. (C)

The correct answer is (C). *Quotient* means *division* and *product* means *multiplication*. Thus, 5 should be divided by 4 and 2 should be multiplied by 3.

32. (D)

The correct answer is (D). The mean is found by adding all numbers, then dividing by the number of numbers. Thus, the mean equals $\frac{(7)(3) + (9)(6) + (4)(10)}{20} = \frac{115}{20} = 5.75$

33. (B)

The correct answer is (B). A total of 50 people (40 + 10) favored either vanilla or strawberry ice cream. To find the percent we divide 50 by 120 and multiply by 100 percent.

$$\frac{50}{120} = .416 \text{ then } .416 \times 100\% = 41.6\%$$

34. (A)

The correct answer is (A). The combined percent of respondents who rated the mayor as Excellent (25%) or Very Good (35%) is 60% which represents 1440 residents. We can find the total number of respondents by dividing 1440 by 60%. First convert the percentage to a decimal (.60). Then $\frac{1440}{0.60} = 2400$.

35. (A)

The correct answer is (A). The number −1.62 is larger than −2.32, because it lies further to the right on the number scale.

36. (C)

The correct answer is (C). Divide the numerator and denominator by 3. $87 \div 3 = 29$ and $93 \div 3 = 31$. Thus, $\frac{87}{93} = \frac{29}{31}$.

37. (D)

The correct answer is (D). The volume is the product of the length, width, and height. So the volume is $(5)(4)(9) = 180$.

38. (C)

The correct answer is (C). The sale price is $100\% - 18\% = 82\%$ of $96. Then $(0.82)(\$96) = \$78.72$.

39. (D)

The correct answer is (D). $2^3 = 2 \times 2 \times 2 = 8$ and $5^2 = 5 \times 5 = 25$. Then $(8)(25) = 200$.

40. (D)

The correct answer is (D). If two sides of a triangle have the same length, the triangle is isosceles.

41. (B)

The correct answer is (B). The perimeter is 2 lengths + 2 widths. Let w represent the width. Then, $(8)(2) + 2w = 27$. This equation simplifies to $16 + 2w = 27$. So $2w = 11$, from which $w = 5.5$

42. (C)

The correct answer is (C). From March to April, the number of projects increased from 12 to 20. Also, from April to May, the number of projects increased from 20 to 24.

43. (C)

The correct answer is (C). From 8:45 AM to 10:45 AM represents 2 hours. From 10:45AM to 11:05 AM represents 20 minutes, which is $\frac{20}{60} = \frac{1}{3}$ hour. The total time is $2\frac{1}{3}$ hours.

44. (A)

The correct answer is (A). Subtract $2x$ from each side to get $5x - 15 = 30$. Next, add 15 to each side to get $5x = 45$. Finally, divide 45 by 5 to get 9.

45. (C)

The correct answer is (C). The point $(5, 6)$ lies above this line segment.

46. (B)

The correct answer is (B). Arranged in order, the numbers are 13, 15, 18, 20, 25, 35. The median is the average of the third and fourth numbers. So the median is $(18 + 20) \div 2 = 19$.

47. (A)

The correct answer is (A). The average rate is determined by dividing the total distance by the total time. The total distance is $(3)(40) + (2)(50) = 220$ miles, and the total time is 5 hours. Then $220 \div 5 = 44$ miles per hour.

48. (D)

The correct answer is (D). 4 yards = (4)(36) = 144 inches, and 2 feet = (2)(12) = 24 inches. Thus, the length is 144 + 24 = 168 inches.

49. (B)

The correct answer is (B). By adding 25 and 15, then dividing by 5, the result would be 40 ÷ 5 = 8. Then 8 − 2 × 4 = 8 − 8 = 0.

50. (D)

The correct answer is (D). The mode represents the number or numbers that occur most frequently. Initially, it would be best for the teacher to give an example in which there is only one mode.

51. (D)

The correct answer is (D). Since $3^2 + 4^2 = 5^2$, this is an example of a right triangle. It is not isosceles because no two sides have the same length.

52. (C)

The correct answer is (C). The student's actual average for all five exams is $\dfrac{(90)(4) + (100)(1)}{5} = 92$. Thus, her average is lower than 95.

53. (C)

The correct answer is (C). To answer the question you must know how many feet are in a mile the answer to which is 5,280 feet. Therefore, five miles per hour is equivalent to (5)(5280)

which equals 26,400 per feet per hour To calculate the feet per minute, divide 26,400 by 60.

26,400/60 = 440 feet per minute

54. (B)

The correct answer is (B). To solve for the missing numerator, divide 72 by 3 to get 24. Then multiply 24 by 2 to get the correct missing numerator of 48.

55. (C)

The correct answer is (C). The student's method is correct. To change hours to minutes, multiply the number of hours by 60.

56. (A)

The correct answer is (A). The student's method is correct. If an item is discounted 20%, then the purchase price will be 100% − 20% = 80% of the original price. This means that if the purchase price is known, the original price can be found by dividing the purchase price by 80%.

57. (C)

The correct answer is (C). In rectangles and squares, the area is the product of the length and the width. This method for finding the area is not correct for other geometric figures.

58. (A)

The correct answer is (A). By definition, two geometric figures are similar if all corresponding angles are equal and all corresponding sides are in proportion.

59. (B)

The correct answer is (B). The median of a group of seven numbers is the fourth number, provided that the numbers are arranged in either ascending or descending order.

60. (C)

The correct answer is 0.4. When rounding off to the nearest tenth, first look at the digit in the hundredths place. If this digit is less than 5, leave alone the digit in the tenths place.

WRITING

61. (C)

The correct answer is (C) The correct word is *affecting* in III and *illusion* in IV. I is correct with its comma after the introductory phrase and no comma before the dependent clause that comes at the end of the sentence; II is correct as each is singular in number and the items in the series are parallel.

62. (A)

The correct answer is (A). It has one independent clause and a string of prepositional phrases and participial phrases. There are no dependent clauses, necessary to a complex sentence. (B) is a compound sentence with a FANBOYS; (C) is a complex sentence as is (D).

63. (A)

The correct answer is (A) because the sentence needs a comma after the beginning dependent clause. (B) is correct as it surrounds the parenthetical phrase with commas; (C) is correct in placing a comma after the introductory phrase and before the adverbial phrase at the end.(D) correctly punctuates a compound sentence.

64. (B)

The correct answer is (B): the quotation marks should come after the question mark because it is a direct quotation of President John F. Kennedys. The other sentences correctly place quotation marks after periods and before a semicolon as in (A).

65. (D)

The correct answer is (D) which is the incorrect usage. The verb *are* is 3rd person plural, but the pronoun is an indefinite pronoun that is singular, just as (B) correctly demonstrates with *somebody* and *is*, in agreement both singular, 3rd person. Note, too, that (A) and (C) show correct verb/pronoun and verb agreement. *Jury* and *team* are collective nouns that are treated as singular in number.

66. (A)

The correct answer is (A) which incorrectly uses the 3rd person singular verb *is*; it should use 3rd person plural *are* to fit the subject complement of *there*. The subject of (B) is plural, *leaders*, as is the verb *are*. *Committee* is a collective noun, hence singular as is its verb *failed*, and the pronoun *its*. (D) is another example of a subject complement after a linking verb (like A), but it correctly uses a singular verb *is* in agreement with *lack*, - singular in number.

67. (B)

The correct answer is (B). All of the others have at least one error.

68. (C)

The correct answer is (C): the opening adjective describes the gerund (verb made into noun).

69. (B)

The correct answer is (B): *principal* is the correct alternative to *principle*. (A) should be *affects*; (C) should be *quotation*; (D) should be *used to*.

70. (A)

The correct answer is (A): both have dependent clauses, *even though...*; *who is...*IV is a compound sentence; III is also a compound sentence. There are no simple sentences.

71. (C)

The correct answer (C): I begins with dependent clause and is complex; II. Is a simple sentence with one subject and verb, two prepositional phrases, and an infinitive; III is a compound connected with FANBOYS; IV is a complex opening with a dependent clause.

72. (C)

The correct answer is (C). The predicate expresses what the subject does, experiences, or is; it includes all the words related to the verb. For example, in the sentence *The fish swims,* the predicate is simply *swims*. However, in the sentence *The partygoers celebrated wildly for a long time,* the predicate is *celebrated wildly for a long time.* Of course, the noun clause (B) and the verb clause (A) do not necessarily relate to the verb and its related words in a sentence. A postulate (D), or axiom, is a statement or a theory that one can use to prove other statements or other theorems.

73. (C)

The correct answer is (C): *understanding* is not a preposition. All of the others are prepositional phrases.

74. (D)

The correct answer is D, all of them: I requires *complimentary*; II needs the correct *counsel* as it is a noun; III. requires the verb *affects*; and IV the adverb *farther.*

75. (A)

The correct answer is (A) because we need to know which pit bulls the sentence refers to. All the others should have commas around them because they are non-restrictive clauses, providing extra information that is not necessary to the meaning.

76. (D)

The correct answer is (D): *who...last year* is a non-restrictive clause, not necessary to the main meaning.

77. (D)

The correct answer is (D). (A) is incorrect—a dependent clause would create a complex sentence but is not necessary to an independent clause. (B) is incorrect because to stand alone, it must meet the 3rd criterion and be a complete thought.

78. (C)

The correct answer is (C), which is the definition of a complex sentence. (A) is incorrect—we need only one. (B) is not about structure and (D) defines a compound sentence.

79. (C)

The correct answer is (C). It is specific and its purpose is to provide the scientific evidence supporting cigarette smoking as a cause of lung cancer and emphysema. (A) is both very broad (HISTORY) and not specific as to "origins"; (B) is much too general. Experience could be about anything from fixing a car to enduring a dangerous situation; (D) is also too broad—what kind of advertising? And too general: it may encourage eating disorders, but it is not the only cause.

80. (C)

The correct answer is (C). There is no one sentence that pulls together all of the points into one focus. Take, for example, *Early reading experience dramatically develops children's cognitive abilities* which could serve as a topic sentence. Further, the paragraph jumps from sentence to sentence without any transitional connectors. III is not to the point as the paragraph does provide many examples. Further, there are no punctuation or grammar errors; and IV is not correct. The last sentence does not focus the main idea.

81. (C)

The correct answer is (C). The key words in this selection are *the old house* and *hard labor*; and by examining the body of the paragraph, you find a list of hard labor details. Selection (A) is too vague. What are surprises? They could be ghosts, or a rodent infestation....Selection (B) is askew of the main topic; its key words *sweat equity* and *profit* are in the first instance, a very indirect allusion to the hard labor that the paragraph minutely describes, and in the second case, profit is not the topic of the sentences. Finally, (D) is, like (A), too vague to be an effective topic statement.

82. (B)

The correct answer is (B). Transition is a device for achieving coherence, that sense of flow that characterizes a coherent piece of writing. Development is one of the three laws, and it refers to providing enough information and explanation to deliver meaning to the reader. Unity is the quality of all parts supporting the main idea(s)—the supporting sentences, the topic statement of the paragraph, the thesis of the essay.

83. (B)

The correct answer is (B). (A) is partially right about coherence, but coherence also applies to both paragraphs and essays. (C) says too little; (D) refers to development, not to unity.

84. (A)

The correct answer is (A). Remember that the topic sentence can be anywhere in a given paragraph. We have only recommended that student writers place it first to aid in the development of unity. Each of the examples in the body of the paragraph are about how serious riddles have been in history, and this is exactly what (A) states. The other selections develop this main idea by providing examples and support for it.

85. (B)

The correct answer is (B). Note how specific it is: the writer will "educate" the reader on how slavery served the economy of the South in the 100 years before the Civil War that ended it. By contrast, (A) is far too broad—all the media, radio, press, television; and it is far too vague—what kind of bias? And, what does *narrow* mean?

86. (C)

The correct answer is (C). The body of the paragraph provides several examples of what Anthony accomplished as one of the partners in the Stanton/Anthony team, but the first sentence, which comes closest to being a topic sentence, does not express this point. What would work? One possibility would be: *While both women thought alike and contributed together to many major events, Susan B. Anthony nonetheless claims her own distinctive record of achievement, influence by Stanton for sure, but still uniquely Anthony's.* The paragraph is well developed—contrary to (A); it has many examples and they are very specific and clear. It also is coherent and uses many transitional devices to achieve this. (D) is off-base because while there is unity—all of Anthony's achievements—no sentence pulls it together into sharp focus.

87. (D)

The correct answer is (D). Note how most of the sentences are simple sentences, and these are strung together without transitions to connect

them. The paragraph does have a topic statement as its first and it does have a concluding sentence. Note how the first and last sentences are tied together with the word *partnership*. It is also well developed with many specifics of the partnership. (C) is incorrect not only because the paragraph shows sufficient development but also because it keeps to the main idea and therefore doesn't lack unity.

88. (A)

The correct answer is (A). Note how midway through, the paragraph shifts from their products to their personalities and lifestyles, breaking the unity. The fact that there is not an effective topic statement lays the groundwork for violating unity. Conversely, the paragraph does have sentence variety and many specifics.

89. (C)

The correct answer is (C). Note how the paragraph lists a series of action that the teacher can take to stop students from cheating. It is neither (A) nor (B) because the paragraph has an excellent conclusion and many transitional phrases.

90. (A)

These are all activities that writers typically engage in during the prewriting or planning phase of writing.

Practice Test 2

Praxis ParaPro Assessment
0755 & 1755

1. Ⓐ Ⓑ Ⓒ Ⓓ
2. Ⓐ Ⓑ Ⓒ Ⓓ
3. Ⓐ Ⓑ Ⓒ Ⓓ
4. Ⓐ Ⓑ Ⓒ Ⓓ
5. Ⓐ Ⓑ Ⓒ Ⓓ
6. Ⓐ Ⓑ Ⓒ Ⓓ
7. Ⓐ Ⓑ Ⓒ Ⓓ
8. Ⓐ Ⓑ Ⓒ Ⓓ
9. Ⓐ Ⓑ Ⓒ Ⓓ
10. Ⓐ Ⓑ Ⓒ Ⓓ
11. Ⓐ Ⓑ Ⓒ Ⓓ
12. Ⓐ Ⓑ Ⓒ Ⓓ
13. Ⓐ Ⓑ Ⓒ Ⓓ
14. Ⓐ Ⓑ Ⓒ Ⓓ
15. Ⓐ Ⓑ Ⓒ Ⓓ
16. Ⓐ Ⓑ Ⓒ Ⓓ
17. Ⓐ Ⓑ Ⓒ Ⓓ
18. Ⓐ Ⓑ Ⓒ Ⓓ
19. Ⓐ Ⓑ Ⓒ Ⓓ
20. Ⓐ Ⓑ Ⓒ Ⓓ
21. Ⓐ Ⓑ Ⓒ Ⓓ
22. Ⓐ Ⓑ Ⓒ Ⓓ
23. Ⓐ Ⓑ Ⓒ Ⓓ

24. Ⓐ Ⓑ Ⓒ Ⓓ
25. Ⓐ Ⓑ Ⓒ Ⓓ
26. Ⓐ Ⓑ Ⓒ Ⓓ
27. Ⓐ Ⓑ Ⓒ Ⓓ
28. Ⓐ Ⓑ Ⓒ Ⓓ
29. Ⓐ Ⓑ Ⓒ Ⓓ
30. Ⓐ Ⓑ Ⓒ Ⓓ
31. Ⓐ Ⓑ Ⓒ Ⓓ
32. Ⓐ Ⓑ Ⓒ Ⓓ
33. Ⓐ Ⓑ Ⓒ Ⓓ
34. Ⓐ Ⓑ Ⓒ Ⓓ
35. Ⓐ Ⓑ Ⓒ Ⓓ
36. Ⓐ Ⓑ Ⓒ Ⓓ
37. Ⓐ Ⓑ Ⓒ Ⓓ
38. Ⓐ Ⓑ Ⓒ Ⓓ
39. Ⓐ Ⓑ Ⓒ Ⓓ
40. Ⓐ Ⓑ Ⓒ Ⓓ
41. Ⓐ Ⓑ Ⓒ Ⓓ
42. Ⓐ Ⓑ Ⓒ Ⓓ
43. Ⓐ Ⓑ Ⓒ Ⓓ
44. Ⓐ Ⓑ Ⓒ Ⓓ
45. Ⓐ Ⓑ Ⓒ Ⓓ
46. Ⓐ Ⓑ Ⓒ Ⓓ

47. Ⓐ Ⓑ Ⓒ Ⓓ
48. Ⓐ Ⓑ Ⓒ Ⓓ
49. Ⓐ Ⓑ Ⓒ Ⓓ
50. Ⓐ Ⓑ Ⓒ Ⓓ
51. Ⓐ Ⓑ Ⓒ Ⓓ
52. Ⓐ Ⓑ Ⓒ Ⓓ
53. Ⓐ Ⓑ Ⓒ Ⓓ
54. Ⓐ Ⓑ Ⓒ Ⓓ
55. Ⓐ Ⓑ Ⓒ Ⓓ
56. Ⓐ Ⓑ Ⓒ Ⓓ
57. Ⓐ Ⓑ Ⓒ Ⓓ
58. Ⓐ Ⓑ Ⓒ Ⓓ
59. Ⓐ Ⓑ Ⓒ Ⓓ
60. Ⓐ Ⓑ Ⓒ Ⓓ
61. Ⓐ Ⓑ Ⓒ Ⓓ
62. Ⓐ Ⓑ Ⓒ Ⓓ
63. Ⓐ Ⓑ Ⓒ Ⓓ
64. Ⓐ Ⓑ Ⓒ Ⓓ
65. Ⓐ Ⓑ Ⓒ Ⓓ
66. Ⓐ Ⓑ Ⓒ Ⓓ
67. Ⓐ Ⓑ Ⓒ Ⓓ
68. Ⓐ Ⓑ Ⓒ Ⓓ
69. Ⓐ Ⓑ Ⓒ Ⓓ

70. Ⓐ Ⓑ Ⓒ Ⓓ
71. Ⓐ Ⓑ Ⓒ Ⓓ
72. Ⓐ Ⓑ Ⓒ Ⓓ
73. Ⓐ Ⓑ Ⓒ Ⓓ
74. Ⓐ Ⓑ Ⓒ Ⓓ
75. Ⓐ Ⓑ Ⓒ Ⓓ
76. Ⓐ Ⓑ Ⓒ Ⓓ
77. Ⓐ Ⓑ Ⓒ Ⓓ
78. Ⓐ Ⓑ Ⓒ Ⓓ
79. Ⓐ Ⓑ Ⓒ Ⓓ
80. Ⓐ Ⓑ Ⓒ Ⓓ
81. Ⓐ Ⓑ Ⓒ Ⓓ
82. Ⓐ Ⓑ Ⓒ Ⓓ
83. Ⓐ Ⓑ Ⓒ Ⓓ
84. Ⓐ Ⓑ Ⓒ Ⓓ
85. Ⓐ Ⓑ Ⓒ Ⓓ
86. Ⓐ Ⓑ Ⓒ Ⓓ
87. Ⓐ Ⓑ Ⓒ Ⓓ
88. Ⓐ Ⓑ Ⓒ Ⓓ
89. Ⓐ Ⓑ Ⓒ Ⓓ
90. Ⓐ Ⓑ Ⓒ Ⓓ

TIME: 2½ hours
90 multiple-choice questions

READING

Read the passage below and answer questions 1 through 3.

Robots Will Never Replace Humans
by Rosa Velasquez

In movies and science fiction novels, we've seen many kinds of talking robots. They are always smart and well behaved and walk like people. That creature, however, simply doesn't exist in the real world. Even a baby less than two years old can do three things no robot can: recognize a face, understand a human language, and walk on two legs. If they can't do everything a person can, then robots will never replace humans.

Robots do have their place, however. They can perform certain tasks, such as building car bodies in factories and stacking boxes for shipping. These kinds of jobs they do very well. And it is the dangerous and boring tasks that robots do best – those jobs that no person enjoys. During the 1960's the first industrial robots lifted a piece of metal from a conveyor belt, drilled a hole in it, and returned it to the conveyor belt. Before, human workers would perform the same task hour after hour, sometimes feeling like little more than robots themselves.

1. Students are learning about fact and opinion. Which statement is LEAST helpful for helping students understand the difference between fact and opinion?

   (A) A fact is a statement that can be proved.
   (B) An opinion must be supported with facts and details.
   (C) An opinion can be proved with facts and details.
   (D) A fact is a statement that is known to be true.

2. Which of the following is a statement of fact rather than an expression of opinion?

   (A) "They are always...and walk like people."
   (B) "Robots do have their place, however."
   (C) "These kinds of jobs they do very well."
   (D) "During the 1960's...a piece of metal... returned it to the..."

3. The paraprofessional asks the students, "What do you think the author's attitude is regarding robots?" Which response from the students shows the best understanding of the text?

   (A) disdain for the idea of robots replacing humans
   (B) understanding as to why robots could replace humans
   (C) authority regarding the replacement of humans with robots
   (D) understanding that there is an argument for replacing humans at times with robots

Read the passage below and answer questions 4 through 6.

From *Orphan Train Rider*
by Andrea Warren

More than 200,000 children rode "orphan trains" in this country between 1854 and 1930. They were part of a "placing out" program created to find homes for children who were orphans or whose parents could not take care of them.

Most of the riders came from New York or other large cities in the East. The trains brought groups of them to other parts of the country where they were lined up in front of crowds of curious onlookers. Interested families could then choose the child they wanted. Within a week a child could go from living in an orphanage or on city streets to living in a Midwestern farmhouse or village. Many children found parents who loved them and took care of them; others never felt at home with their new families. Some were mistreated.

There is not much time left for orphan train riders to tell their stories. Those still alive are now elderly. Some will not talk about their experiences because they feel ashamed of being a "train kid" or because they did not find a happy home at the end of their ride.

4. The passage is primarily concerned with recording the

    I.   history of the children who rode orphan trains.
    II. conditions of the children who rode orphan trains.
    III. attitudes of the children who rode orphan trains.
    IV. history of an unusual occurrence in history.

(A) II and III
(B) II and IV
(C) I and II
(D) I and IV

5. The paraprofessional asks the students for details that support the main idea. Which response from the students is most accurate?

    (A) "The trains brought groups...where they were lined up...curious onlookers."
    (B) "Interested families...the child they wanted."
    (C) "Some were mistreated."
    (D) "Some will not talk...they did not find...of their ride."

6. The author says, "Many children found parents who loved them and took care of them; others never felt at home with their new families. Some were mistreated." The author says this is most likely in order to

    (A) show how one sentence is related to another.
    (B) provide an example of the orphan riders experience.
    (C) contradict the claim that orphan train riders were mistreated.
    (D) present information that is both fact and opinion.

Read the passage below and answer questions 7 and 8.

I Have a Dream excerpt by
Dr. Martin Luther King, Jr.

I say to you today, my friends, so even though we face the difficulties of today and tomorrow, I still have a dream. It is a dream deeply rooted in the American dream.

I have a dream that one day this nation will rise up and live out the true meaning of its creed: "We hold these truths to be self-evident, that all men are created equal."

I have a dream that one day on the red hills of Georgia, the sons of former slaves and the sons of former slave owners will be able to sit down together at the table of brotherhood.

I have a dream that one day even the state of Mississippi, a state sweltering with the heat of injustice, sweltering with the heat of oppression, will be transformed into an oasis of freedom and justice.

I have a dream that my four little children will one day live in a nation where they will not be judged by the color of their skin but by the content of their character. I have a dream today."

7. The paraprofessional asks students what they believe is the author's purpose in writing the speech. The LEAST acceptable response is

(A) Martin Luther King, Jr.'s desire to publicly state his dream.
(B) Martin Luther King, Jr.'s dream of racial equality.
(C) Martin Luther King, Jr.'s desire for world peace.
(D) Martin Luther King, Jr.'s wish for everyone to be judged for their character.

8. Martin Luther King, Jr. uses the phrase, "We hold these truths to be self-evident, that all men are created equal" to

I.   contradict the idea that racism is acceptable.
II.   compare and contrast notions of racial equality in the U.S.
III. provide an example of how stated principles of this country are not honored.
IV. assert both facts and opinions regarding racial equality.

(A) I and IV
(B) II and III

(C) II only
(D) III only

Read the scenario below and answer questions 9 and 10.

Reality Check/Some Things to Ponder

If we could shrink the earth's population to a village of precisely 100 people, with all the existing human ratios remaining the same, it would look something like the following:

There would be:

57 Asians
21 Europeans
14 from the Western Hemisphere, both north and south
8 Africans

52 would be female
48 would be male

70 would be non-white
30 would be white

70 would be non-Christian
30 would be Christian
89 would be heterosexual
11 would be homosexual

6 people would possess 59% of the entire world's wealth and all 6 would be from the United States.

80 would live in substandard housing
70 would be unable to read
50 would suffer from malnutrition
1 would be near death; 1 would be near birth
1 (yes, only 1) would have a college education
1 would own a computer

9. The paraprofessional asks the class what the author implies about Americans from this passage. Which response is most accurate?

(A) Americans have the most wealth and the fewest people on the planet.

(B) Americans have the highest rate of literacy and the best health care.

(C) Americans have the most wealth and the highest rate of literacy.

(D) Americans have an obligation to help people from other countries.

10. Which response is LEAST important regarding the author's purpose in writing this passage?

(A) As a whole, Americans are more privileged than many people in the world.

(B) Americans are part of a diverse world.

(C) Everyone in the world should have health care.

(D) Many Americans might be surprised by what the author says.

Read the poem below and answer questions 11 through 13.

Those Winter Sundays
by Robert Hayden

Sundays too my father got up early
and put his clothes on in the blueblack cold,
then with cracked hands that ached
from labor in the weekday weather made
banked fires blaze. No one ever thanked him.

I'd wake and hear the cold splintering, breaking.
When the words were warm, he'd call,
and slowly I would rise and dress,
fearing the chronic angers of that house,

Speaking indifferently to him,
who had driven out the cold
and polished my good shoes as well.
What did I know, what did I know
of love's austere and lonely offices?

11. Which is the LEAST effective reading strategy you can use to make meaning of the poem?

(A) predicting what will happen

(B) making a connection to one's own experience

(C) rereading the poem

(D) using a dictionary for unknown words

12. Which word foundation strategy would the paraprofessional use to help students pronounce the word *chronic*?

(A) easy consonants

(B) consonant second sounds

(C) finding the word in the dictionary

(D) long vowels

13. *In-* in the word *indifferently* changes the meaning of the first line in the last stanza by

(A) indicating that the speaker is not different from his father.

(B) showing that the speaker had a lack of interest in his father.

(C) changing the speaker's attitude about his father.

(D) showing how his feelings changed over time.

14. The first three letters, *lab*, in *labor* are an example of a

(A) compound word.

(B) consonant blend.

(C) root word.

(D) rhyming word.

15. For a science project, students must alphabetize their vocabulary terms. The proper order for alphabetizing is

(A) photosynthesis, physical properties, physical matter, plantlet.

(B) photosynthesis, physical matter, physical properties, plantlet.

(C) plantlet, photosynthesis, physical matter, physical properties.

(D) photosynthesis, physical matter, physical properties, plantlet.

16. Which is NOT the best explanation for the term *homonym*?

(A) words that share the same meaning but are spelled differently

(B) words that must be used in context in order to be understood

(C) words that share the same sound but are spelled differently

(D) words that sound the same, have different meanings, and usually different spellings

17. Using phonics helps students learn

(A) the definition of words.

(B) to pronounce words correctly.

(C) the relationship between letters and sounds.

(D) to comprehend their reading.

18. "When I was a teenager, I *contradicted* almost everything my mother said to me." Which is the LEAST effective strategy or strategies for helping students understand the word, *contradict*?

I. Teach students to use a thesaurus
II. Teach students root words and affixes
III. Teach students to ask the paraprofessional
IV. Teach students to use a dictionary

A. I only
B. III and IV
C. II and IV
D. I and III

Read the scenario below and answer questions 19 and 20.

Exam Directions

DIRECTIONS: Write an opinion essay about banning student cell phone use at schools. First, read the prompt below. Then, decide how you feel and offer support for your opinion. Proofread your work. Before handing in your paper, make sure you've written your name in the top right hand corner. You have until the end of the period to finish the essay. Place the completed essay in the basket on my desk.

Prompt: Some public schools have made it a rule that students leave or turn off their cell phones at school. How do you feel about banning student cell phone use? Write an essay stating your opinion. Support it with 3-4 convincing reasons.

19. Which is the LEAST effective suggestion for helping students read directions?

(A) Model previewing the directions and the writing prompt.

(B) Model looking for key words in the directions.

(C) Model reflecting on what is known about taking other exams.

(D) Model asking questions that begin with *what, when, where, how* and why.

20. The last task the student should do is

(A) place the essay in the basket on the teacher's desk.

(B) write his name in the upper right hand corner.

(C) reread his essay.

(D) check the time that is left.

Read the diary below and answer questions 21 and 22.

The Diary of Latoya Hunter
by Latoya Hunter

September 12, 1990

Dear Diary,

The dreaded Freshman Day is drawing near. I can see into the deranged minds of the 8th and 9th graders. They can't wait. I've heard rumors that they attack kids in the hall. I wonder if that could be true. Are they that cruel? I feel there will be a lot of fights between freshmen and seniors. I hope I won't be in any of them. The thing is, I know the kind of people they'll be aiming for. They are the quiet ones, like the ones who aren't into the crowd, the kids who don't act like animals on the street. That's the kind of person I am. That's how I'll leave J.H.S. 80. I'm not about to change to fit in their dead-in-an-alley crowd. I intend to make something of myself. Life is too precious to waste.

21. The paraprofessional is working with students on making predictions about the text. The paraprofessional asks students what they think will happen to Latoya in school. Which student response shows the best understanding of the clues so far?

(A) Latoya will be popular and receive good grades.
(B) Latoya will probably help other students avoid trouble.
(C) Latoya may get extra credit for keeping a diary.
(D) Latoya may have confrontations with bullies, but stay out of trouble.

22. Which question could the paraprofessional ask a student who doesn't know what the word *deranged* means?

(A) What do you know about what happens to a new person in school?
(B) Where does the word appear in the sentence?
(C) What clues appear if you read on in the paragraph?
(D) What do you know about the use of affixes?

Read the poem below and answer question 23.

In moving-slow he has no Peer.
You ask him something in his ear;
He thinks about it for a Year;

And, then, before he says a Word
There, upside-down (unlike a Bird)
He will assume that you Have Heard

23. The passage above can be used for demonstrating

I. long vowel patterns.
II. short vowel sounds.
III. easy consonants.
IV. effective rhyme schemes.

(A) I and IV
(B) III and IV
(C) II only
(D) IV only

slack[1] ■adj. 1 not taut or held tightly in position; loose. 2 (of business or trade) not busy; quiet. 3 careless, lazy, or negligent. 4 W. Indian lewd or promiscuous. 5 (of a tide) neither ebbing nor flowing. ■n. 1 the part of a rope or line which is not held taut. 2 (**slacks**) casual trousers. 3 informal a period of inactivity or laziness. ■v. 1 loosen (something, especially a rope). 2 (**slack** off/up) decrease in intensity or speed. 3 Brit. informal work slowly or lazily. 4 slake (lime).
– PHRASES **cut someone some slack** N. Amer. informal allow someone some leeway in their conduct. **take** (or **pick**) **up the slack** improve the use of resources to avoid an undesirable lull in business.
– DERIVATIVES slacken v. slackly adv. slackness n.
– ORIGIN OE slæc 'inclined to be lazy, unhurried', of Gmc origin.

slack[2] ■n. coal dust or small pieces of coal.
– ORIGIN ME: prob. from Low Ger. or Du.

24. A student does not understand the meaning of the word *slack* as it is used in the sentence, "The man's mouth went *slack* as he grabbed his chest, collapsed on the floor, and fainted." Using the dictionary excerpt, which definition should the student use to understand the word *slack* in the context of the sentence?

(A) adj. definition. 1
(B) v. definition. 1
(C) n. definition. 1
(D) n. definition. 3

25. "Since the student had worked throughout the semester with so much energy and drive, the teacher decided to *give her some slack* on her final quiz." In the context of the term's definition, *give her some slack* most nearly means

(A) make the student work harder than she had during the semester.

(B) make the student work just as hard as she had during the semester.

(C) allow the student the option of dropping one of her grades.

(D) allow the student the option of not taking the quiz.

26. Which strategy would the paraprofessional use to help a student figure out the meaning of the word *meek* in the following sentence?

> Was she (the overseer's wife) a *meek*, obedient little woman, or someone like Mrs. Cutler, who would rule him as he ruled the girls under his watchful eye?

(A) Tell students that there are context clues before and after unknown words that help them figure out the word.

(B) Tell students to look for words that are similar and different from the unknown word to help decode unfamiliar words.

(C) Tell students an understanding of synonyms and root words will help them figure out the word.

(D) Tell students to sound out the word and then use antonyms to help them figure out the word.

27. In the classroom, the paraprofessional would use rhyming to

(A) help students learn consonant sounds.

(B) help students learn vowel and consonant sounds.

(C) help students learn vowels in single syllable words.

(D) help student learn the initial sound of a syllable.

Read the poem below and answer questions 28 and 29.

The Rider
by Naomi Shihab Nye

A boy told me if he roller-skated fast enough his loneliness couldn't catch up to him.

the best reason I ever heard for trying to be a champion.

What I wonder tonight pedaling hard down King William Street is if it translates to bicycles.

28. Which question is the LEAST effective for checking student understanding of the poem?

(A) Did you enjoy the poem?

(B) What is your reaction to this poem?

(C) What is the message the author conveys to the reader?

(D) Did this poem mean anything to you?

29. What feelings do you infer from the author of the poem?

(A) The author would like to be a champion bike rider.

(B) The author understands the feelings expressed by the roller-skater.

(C) The author is interested in keeping her feelings to herself.

(D) The author has difficulty expressing her feelings.

30. Which word from the following passage is the clearest example of a word with the long *a* sound?

There are plenty of activities you can become involved in at school. For example, yesterday I went to the gym and shot baskets with my friends. Tomorrow, I'm applying for the Academic Decathalon team. My friend, Gina, plans on trying out as well.

(A) activities
(B) baskets
(C) Gina
(D) yesterday

MATHEMATICS

31. What is the area of a triangle with a base of 14 and a height of 9?

(A) 126
(B) 92
(C) 63
(D) 46

32. What is the median for the following group of numbers?

7, 8, 10, 12, 16, 16, 17, 20

(A) 13
(B) 14
(C) 15
(D) 16

33. One inch is approximately 2.54 centimeters. How many centimeters are equivalent to 8 inches?

(A) 25.20
(B) 20.32
(C) 10.54
(D) 3.15

34. Which one of the following groups of numbers has TWO modes?

(A) 2, 3, 4, 5, 5, 6, 7, 9
(B) 3, 4, 4, 4, 5, 5, 5, 5
(C) 4, 7, 7, 8, 8, 8, 9, 9
(D) 5, 5, 5, 7, 7, 9, 9, 9

35. Consider the following sequence of four numbers: 4, 12, 36, 108. If this pattern were to continue, which of the following would be the next number?

(A) 160
(B) 324
(C) 432
(D) 972

36. Look at the following table of values for x and y:

x	4	6	8	10	12	14	16
y	30	28	26	24	22	20	18

Which one of the following sets of statements is COMPLETELY correct?

(A) As x increases, y increases. The sum of each pair of x and y values is 34.
(B) As x increases, y increases. The difference of each pair of x and y values remains the same.
(C) As x increases, y decreases. The difference of each pair of x and y values remains the same.
(D) As x increases, y decreases. The sum of each pair of x and y values is 34.

37. Growing Strong Hospital surveyed the marital status of each of their employees. Review the results in the pie chart on the next page and answer the following question.

General Hospital's Marital Survey Results

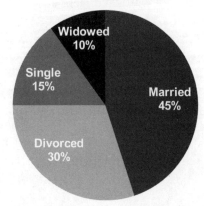

There are 1440 employees who are either divorced (30%) or widowed (10%). What is the total number of employees?

(A) 2880
(B) 3200
(C) 3600
(D) 4800

38. Which one of the following represents the sides of an equilateral triangle?

(A) 10, 15, and 15
(B) 11, 13, and 16
(C) 12, 12, and 12
(D) 13, 17, and 21

39. What is the value of $2 \times 3^3 \times 5$?

(A) 270
(B) 210
(C) 150
(D) 90

40. In a group of ten people, six of them each weigh 135 pounds, three of them each weigh 180 pounds, and one weighs 90 pounds. What is the mean weight of all 10 people?

(A) 144 pounds
(B) 140 pounds
(C) 135 pounds
(D) 131 pounds

41. Which one of the following numbers lies between $\dfrac{9}{16}$ and $\dfrac{2}{3}$?

(A) $\dfrac{17}{24}$

(B) $\dfrac{29}{48}$

(C) $\dfrac{27}{48}$

(D) $\dfrac{13}{24}$

42. What is the value of x in the equation $4x - 20 = 36$?

(A) 4
(B) 6
(C) 10
(D) 14

43. If 1 kiloliter equals 1000 liters and 1 deciliter equals 0.1 liters, then 5 kiloliters equals how many deciliters?

(A) 500
(B) 5,000
(C) 50,000
(D) 500,000

44. From last week to this week, the price of gasoline has dropped by 12%. If the price of gasoline this week is $2.40 per gallon, what was the price per gallon last week to the nearest cent?

(A) $2.73
(B) $2.69
(C) $2.58
(D) $2.52

45. Consider the positive portion of the xy-coordinate plane, shown below.

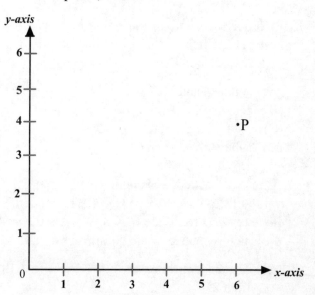

What are the coordinates of point Q if it is placed 2 units to the right and 3 units down from point P?

(A) (4, 7)
(B) (4, 1)
(C) (8, 7)
(D) (8, 1)

46. The volume of a sphere is given by the formula $V = \frac{4}{3}\pi r^3$, where r is the radius. What is the volume of a sphere whose radius is 5?

(A) $\dfrac{1000\pi}{3}$

(B) $\dfrac{500\pi}{3}$

(C) $\dfrac{100\pi}{3}$

(D) $\dfrac{50\pi}{3}$

47. Which one of the following is the closest approximate value of 6.2342×999?

(A) 62
(B) 623
(C) 6,230
(D) 62,300

48. In order to calculate the value of $60 - 2 \times (4 + 1)^2$, which of the following would NOT be a correct step?

(A) adding 4 and 1
(B) squaring 5
(C) multiplying 2 by 25
(D) subtracting 2 from 60

49. A teacher asked a student to calculate the value of $25 - 18 + 6 \div 3 \times 4$. The student's first step was to divide 6 by 3. What is the appropriate response of the paraprofessional?

(A) The student should have first subtracted 18 from 25.
(B) The student's first step is correct.

(C) The student should have first multiplied 3 by 4.
(D) The student should have first added 18 to 6.

50. A student needs to convert 7.25 miles to yards. She knows that there are 1760 yards in one mile. First, she proceeds to multiply 1760 by 7, then she divides 1760 by 0.25, then adds these values to get an answer of 19,360. How should the paraprofessional help this student?

(A) In her second step, the student should have multiplied 1760 by 0.25.
(B) The student should have simply divided 1760 by 7.25.
(C) In her last step, the student should have subtracted the two values.
(D) Congratulate her—the student's method and answer are correct.

51. A student claimed that whenever an altitude is drawn from a vertex angle of a triangle, the opposite side is bisected. Which one of the following would represent a type of triangle that would be a counterexample to this claim?

(A) scalene triangle
(B) isosceles triangle
(C) equilateral triangle
(D) It is impossible to find a counterexample.

52. Which one of the following would be the best example for a teacher to explain an application of a pie chart?

(A) The trend of a company's monthly profit over a period of six months.
(B) The comparison of the top three types of traffic violations for a town.
(C) The projection of auto sales next year, based on an auto company's sales this year.
(D) The categories that show their respective percents of a monthly budget.

53. A student was asked to convert $\frac{2}{3}$ into an equivalent fraction with a denominator of 24. Which one of the following is the correct pro-

cedure for finding the numerator of this equivalent fraction?

(A) Divide 24 by 2, then multiply this quotient by 3.
(B) Multiply 2 by 3, then divide this product into 24.
(C) Divide 24 by 3, then multiply this quotient by 2.
(D) Subtract 3 from 24, then add this difference to 2.

54. A student needs to present an example of a geometric figure whose area and perimeter are equal. To which of the following forms should a paraprofessional guide the student?

(A) a square with a side of 4
(B) any equilateral triangle
(C) a rectangle with a length of 5 and a width of 10
(D) a regular pentagon with a side of 2

55. Ms. Rohrbach is teaching a statistics class. She asks her students to give an example of a group of numbers for which the mean equals the mode. Four students volunteer an answer. Which one of them is correct?

(A) Kenny suggests the numbers 2, 4, 8, 16, and 32.
(B) Linda suggests the numbers 3, 5, 5, 5, and 7.
(C) Nicky suggests the numbers 5, 6, 7, 8, and 9.
(D) Melissa makes the claim that it is not possible for the mean to equal the mode for any group of numbers.

56. Mr. Vigil is teaching a beginning geometry class. He assigns a problem to work through in class, in which the students must explain the meaning of a diagonal of a geometric figure. Which one of the following is the best explanation?

(A) any line segment that joins two vertices
(B) a part of the figure that lies completely within the interior

(C) a part of the figure that has two endpoints
(D) a line segment that joins two non-adjacent vertices

57. Tonya is a student who is trying to solve the equation $6x - 7 = 4x + 9$ for x. Which one of the following is a correct step for Tonya to use in solving?

(A) Add 9 to each side.
(B) Add 7 to each side.
(C) Multiply each side by the sum of the four numbers.
(D) Simplify the right side to $13x$.

58. A student asks a paraprofessional to explain how to find the median of a group of 10 numbers. Which one of the following is the BEST response?

(A) The median is the most common number.
(B) The median is the fifth number.
(C) After the numbers are placed in ascending order, the median is the average of the fifth and sixth numbers.
(D) After the numbers are placed in ascending order, the median is the fifth number.

59. Marc is a student who is trying to DISPROVE the claim that if a side of a triangle is opposite a 70° angle, then it must be the largest side. Which one of the following examples could Marc use for the measures of all three angles?

(A) 30°, 70°, and 80°
(B) 50°, 60°, and 70°
(C) 60°, 65°, and 70°
(D) 45°, 45°, and 90°

60. An algebra class is beginning to study word problems. The teacher writes the following statement on the blackboard: "Seven less than ten times a number equals the number." Cassandra, a student, offers the following algebraic response: $7 - 10x = x$. How should this equation be changed to make her response correct?

(A) No change is necessary.

(B) $7x - 10 = x$

(C) $10 - 7x = x$

(D) $10x - 7 = x$

WRITING

61. Which statement below most accurately describes the following sentence: *As time passes, we all develop feelings that are deeper and more complex than those of our youthful days*.

    (A) The sentence is a compound-complex sentence.

    (B) The sentence is a simple sentence with several phrases.

    (C) The sentence is a complex sentence with one independent and two dependent clauses.

    (D) The sentence is complex with one independent and one dependent clause.

62. Which of the following statements most accurately identifies the following sentences?

    I.   A compound sentence includes at least two independent clauses linked by a coordinating conjunction or by a semi-colon.

    II. A compound sentence connects ideas of relatively equal weight.

    III. A compound sentence expresses more complicated ideas than a simple sentence, but less complicated than a complex-compound sentence.

    IV. A compound sentence is incorrectly punctuated if the two independent clauses are separated by a comma.

    (A) I, II, III are accurate statements.

    (B) I, II and IV are accurate.

    (C) I, III, and IV are accurate.

    (D) All are accurate.

63. Which one of the following statements correctly describes the underlined segments in the above sentence?

To his credit_I, Abraham Lincoln, <u>who was the 16th President of the US_II</u>, resisted the pressure <u>of the Southern Colonies_III</u>, <u>whose economies were dependent upon slavery_IV</u>, and <u>he became the champion of emancipation_V</u>.

    (A) I and III are prepositional phrases, and V is a dependent clause.

    (B) II and IV are both dependent clauses, and V is an independent clause.

    (C) II is a dependent clause whose information is necessary to the meaning.'

    (D) I, III, and IV are dependent clauses that make this a complex sentence.

64. All of the following statements about the research process are accurate EXCEPT:

    (A) It is important to select a topic of interest about which a substantial amount has been written.

    (B) Selecting a topic that is controversial is required.

    (C) Researching in a library as well as on the Internet is important to an effective outcome.

    (D) The writer should know the documentation style required before beginning the research process.

65. Which statement would completely edit or correct the following sentences?

My wife's father used to argue that instead of restoring the Hall the town fathers should have razed it and erected a discount store in its place. But he was a man of many opinions most of them outrageous and in any case the hall by then a mere shell caught fire years ago and burned to its foundations. (Richard Russo, **Bridge of Sighs**, NY:2007, 12)

    (A) comma after *Hall* and after *razed it*; a comma after *outrageous*; commas around *by then a mere shell*

    (B) comma after *argue*; a comma after *razed it*; comma around *most of them outrageous*; commas around *by then a mere shell*

(C) comma after *Hall*; commas around *in any case*; commas around *most of them outrageous* commas around *by then a mere shell*

(D) comma after *erected*; comma after *outrageous*; a comma around *by then a mere shell*

66. Which of the following sentences contains a non-restrictive clause that needs commas around it to indicate it is not necessary to the main meaning?

(A) The theory of evolution <u>which still is controversial</u> was discovered by both Darwin and Wallace, but it was not published until 1859.

(B) The law students <u>who plagiarized their papers</u> were summarily dismissed from school.

(C) The physicists <u>that created the atomic fission necessary to developing the first bomb</u> worked in an underground lab at the University of Chicago.

(D) <u>Behaving without respect</u> is simply unacceptable in this institution: It will not be tolerated.

67. All of the following sentences have either a misplaced or a dangling modifier EXCEPT:

(A) John went out to see Andrew wearing only his shirts and a t-shirt

(B) Speaking loudly and angrily, I wondered who would tolerate this behavior.

(C) *Psycho* is a terrifying film about a crazed son directed by Alfred Hitchcock

(D) Dressed in a gown and decked out in diamonds and pearls, I entered the ballroom feeling like a princess.

68. Which of the following has an error in pronoun case?

(A) We all placed bets on who the next champion would be.

(B) Does anyone in this room know who wrote *For Whom the Bell Tolls*?

(C) We all want to know who he thinks he is.

(D) To who shall we give the recommendation letter?

69. All of the following show correct parallel structure EXCEPT:

(A) The Romans loved art, sports, and warfare.

(B) Either do your homework, or you are preparing to fail.

(C) Loving good food, cultivating the arts, and supporting the public good, Stephen Benet proved to be a model of the cosmopolitan citizen.

(D) Neither your family nor your friends can save you from defeat without your own effort and commitment.

70. All of the following contain a fragment EXCEPT:

(A) The school had five cases of swine flu last week. Which is why it is closed this week.

(B) As a result of his failure to study. John failed his chemistry test.

(C) Sandra completed the essay section of the examination in record time. She being a speed typist.

(D) Of the five hundred marathon racers over fifty years old, Sandra finished first. She deserves her pride!

71. Which of the following sentences demonstrates a comma splice type of run-on sentence?

(A) The commander in chief, although only twenty-nine years old, holds more medals and honors than most retired military personnel.

(B) FDR and Eleanor Roosevelt are amongst the most famous historical personages of modern times—reputations they both deserve.

(C) Hurricane Katrina shocked America in many ways, the worst perhaps was the degree of unpreparedness on behalf of our government agencies.

(D) For all their fierce appearance and behavior in Nazi war films, Dobermans are generally placid and gentle dogs.

72. Which of the following statements accurately describes the following sentences?

I.   Ann was shocked by her friend's betrayal; and ended the relationship right on the spot.

II.   The day was dark and gloomy; however, nothing was going to deter us from hiking.

III. The three dates to chose from are Monday, April 22nd; Wednesday, the 23rd; or Saturday, the 26th

IV.   The snow piled up very quickly; and we were forced to leave.

(A) I and IV show correct semi-colon usage

(B) I and II show correct semi-colon usage

(C) II and III show correct semi-colon usage

(D) II and IV show correct semi-colon usage

73. Which of the following choices does NOT contain errors in the use of capitalization?

I.   The *terminator* is one of the biggest successes in film history.

II.   Joe Biden, the Vice President, has been taking a back seat for two months now.

III. Farah Fawcett struggled with dignity against the colon cancer that took her life.

IV.   The Admirals presented President Obama with a medal of honor aboard the battleship, avenger.

(A) I and II have capitalization errors. The rest are correct.

(B) I and III have capitalization errors. The rest are correct.

(C) I and IV have capitalization errors. The rest are correct.

(D) All have capitalization errors.

74. All of the following statements are correct EXCEPT:

(A) A dependent clause can function as a noun, an adjective, or an adverb.

(B) A verbal phrase can be a gerund, an infinitive, or a present participle.

(C) A dependent clause can stand on its own in special circumstances.

(D) Another word for sentence is independent clause.

75. Which of the following statements is CORRECT?

(A) A gerund is a verb phrase ending in *ing*; it generally functions as a noun.

(B) A phrase is a synonym for a clause.

(C) Correlative conjunctions do not require parallel construction.

(D) There are four kinds of sentence: declarative, interrogative, imperative, narrative.

76. A sentence fragment is

(A) an independent clause that stands on its own and begins with a capital letter and ends with a terminal punctuation such as a period.

(B) a dependent clause or phrase incorrectly punctuated to look like a sentence.

(C) a phrase that contains a subject and a predicate that that expresses a thought.

(D) a group of words punctuated with an initial capital and a terminal period, question mark, or exclamation point.

77. All of the following sentences contain a verbal phrase or clause EXCEPT:

(A) Sensing that there was something wrong, Eloise called home before starting off.

(B) The researchers are having a good day and expect results very soon.

(C) Troy was intending to study but the annoying music prevented him from doing so.

(D) To err is human; to forgive is divine.

78. All of the following are possessive-form errors EXCEPT:

(A) The store lost it's liquor license after selling beer to two minors.

(B) The boys's names were inscribed on the trophy wall.

(C) Susan B. Anthony's and Elizabeth Cady Stanton's families were Abolitionists.

(D) Dr. Smith's and Dr. Trek's office is on the first floor.

79. Similes and metaphors are

(A) language tools that are used to connect independent clauses to compound sentence types.

(B) figures of speech that assist meaning by showing the similarities between unlike things.

(C) laws of paragraph and essay development.

(D) figures of speech that separate denotative from connotative meanings.

80. Which of the following is NOT a method of development?

(A) arranging ideas or stories in a logical order

(B) providing examples to help explain the main idea

(C) using figurative language such as similes and metaphors

(D) giving a definition

81. Which of the statements accurately assesses this paragraph?

Eating disorders are epidemic amongst young women. Studies done in the last ten years reveal that 10% of teenagers in the U.S. are suffering from anorexia or bulimia. A huge number are spending their energy fretting over weight and dieting—often hurting their health from poor nutritional these women are victims of stereotyping; Girls think they need to be skinny to be liked. But skinny' is not even a reality. The role models they see on TV cause these unrealistic expectations.

I. The paragraph has grammar and word errors.

II. The paragraph lacks a topic statement.

III. The paragraph suffers from abstract language.

IV. The paragraph lacks unity.

(A) II and III

(B) I and II

(C) III and IV

(D) I and IV

82. All of the following sentences contain a figure of speech EXCEPT:

(A) The look in his eyes was as cold and distant as an arctic snowfield.

(B) Karen is the perfect slave in her marriage.

(C) Dublin, the glowing white pit-bull, is the king of the pack and master of the harem.

(D) Logan, the pit-bull mix, is brown speckled, and while not as strikingly handsome as Dublin, he is the real leader and most desired.

83. All of the following are names of documentation guidelines for research and essays EXCEPT:

(A) *The Guide to Periodical Literature*

(B) *The Modern Language Association (MLA) Style*

(C) *The Chicago Manual of Style*

(D) *The American Psychological Association (APA) Guide*

84. Coherence is

(A) along with unity and development, one of the laws of organization in writing.

(B) the quality of both paragraphs and essays that creates the feeling of flow.

(C) organization that involves the arrangement and order of the ideas of both paragraphs and essays and uses connectors between the sentences.

(D) an identification of what different parts do and their functions.

85. Which of the following thesis statements is the most effective for an argumentative essay?

(A) It is extremely important to take steps to address global warming as soon as possible.

(B) Scientists have provided evidence for three major causes of global warming.

(C) Contrary to critics who refuse to accept its reality, science provides compelling evidence that global warming exists and that we must implement policies that will reduce its impact.

(D) Global warming needs to be described along with evidence of its impact provided and widely disseminated in all media.

86. Which of the following choices accurately describes the *development strategies* in the paragraph below?

I discovered today that a seemingly small event can make a big difference. This morning I left or camp—finally, after months of excited waiting. My two best friends, Myra and Cory, and I had been dreaming and planning for this since the beginning of the school year. We had two big hikes planned on our days off from the rest of the campers, and for these strenuous but rewarding peak climbs we had prepared for 6 months, getting ourselves into tip-top shape, taking First Aid classes, and learning how to use serious terrain maps and compasses. We were anticipating adventure, and challenge, and proving our worth. You can imagine then how crestfallen I was when settling into our cabin, I unpacked my duffle bag to discover that I had not packed my hiking boots. It was like a bad dream, but it was real, and it was decisive. No hiking boots, no hike for me. The trails high up above timberline were still deep with snow, and even before reaching them, the terrain was rocky and treacherous. I was so dejected; I went into a dazed, stupefied tor-

por. Myra was the first person I let in as I felt her arms around me, and her voice comforting me. She told me how much she would miss me on the trails. Cory, however, jut sat across from me on her bunk, no touches or words of comfort, but with a steady, unflappable look, and a slight elfish smile, she said, "No problem, Stef, you and I are going to use my boots. We'll flip a coin to see who goes first, but I am really happy that I'll be able to finish this mystery I've been reading." I protested half-heartedly, but to no avail, and the truth is the sick despair in my stomach evaporated, my spirit lifted, and in the front lobe of my head, the thinking part of the brain, I suddenly understood the difference between real and superficial, between sympathy and empathy, between a friend and a best friend.

I. Descriptive
II. Narrative
III. Classification
IV. Cause and effect
V. Contrast

(A) I and III
(B) II and V
(C) III and IV
(D) I and II

87. All of the following statements are accurate EXCEPT:

(A) An expository essay's objective is to inform and educate.

(B) A narrative essay or paragraph tells a story.

(C) A descriptive essay uses specific and concrete language to describe a person, event, or thing.

(D) An argumentative essay describes the terms of a controversial topic.

88. All of the following groups of words are specific and concrete EXCEPT:

(A) blue, sour, scratchy, ragged
(B) excellence, courage, love, quality, loud

(C) creamy, grating, skimpy, red-hot, hoarse

(D) hairy, blotched, saw-toothed smile, straw-harried, raspy

89. In which of the following research sources are abstracts and full texts most likely to be found?

(A) a periodical index

(B) a database

(C) encyclopedias and almanacs

(D) the Dewey decimal system

90. Which is the most effective topic statement for the paragraph?

Thumb through the magazine section of any newsstand and you will find numerous glossy covered magazines targeted to a teenage audience. Pick up any one of these, and you'll find photo after photo of young boys and girls—median age about 16, but some as young as twelve—maybe even eleven years old. But all of them are very consciously dressed and meticulously fashionable—even the cut-offs and jeans have flash and the aura of "the expensive." All of them also are sometimes subtly, sometimes egregiously, but always posing to accentuate their sexuality. The girls bend at their waists, showing off their twelve-year-old "cleavage;" or they're flopped over a chair with their precocious butts provoking lascivious fantasies; or, they are staring straight at the camera, with naughty, "Lolita" pouts daring you to....The boys are never so provocative and indirect. They're usually standing straight with markedly vertical bodies and strong featured faces, or they're rough-housing and playing sports. But not the way we played when we were teens—not unself-conscious, rough and tumble jocks, but thirteen year olds peddling their masculinity—the masculinity their being groomed to fit, represent, and sell clothes with.

(A) Magazines are using children to advertise clothes.

(B) Magazines for the teenage audience use children, portraying them as sexual objects, and creating definitions of femininity and masculinity as well as selling their products.

(C) Magazines for teenagers are exploiting them at very young ages, both girls and boys, as children in earlier times never were.

(D) Readers can find soft pornography in the pages of magazines targeted to teenagers.

ANSWER KEY FOR PRACTICE TEST 2 (0755 & 1755)

1. (C)	24. (B)	47. (C)	70. (D)
2. (D)	25. (D)	48. (D)	71. (C)
3. (D)	26. (B)	49. (B)	72. (C)
4. (A)	27. (B)	50. (A)	73. (D)
5. (A)	28. (A)	51. (A)	74. (C)
6. (B)	29. (B)	52. (D)	75. (A)
7. (C)	30. (D)	53. (C)	76. (B)
8. (D)	31. (C)	54. (A)	77. (B)
9. (A)	32. (B)	55. (B)	78. (C)
10. (A)	33. (B)	56. (D)	79. (B)
11. (D)	34. (D)	57. (B)	80. (A)
12. (A)	35. (B)	58. (C)	81. (D)
13. (B)	36. (D)	59. (A)	82. (D)
14. (C)	37. (C)	60. (D)	83. (A)
15. (D)	38. (C)	61. (C)	84. (C)
16. (B)	39. (A)	62. (B)	85. (C)
17. (C)	40. (A)	63. (B)	86. (D)
18. (C)	41. (B)	64. (B)	87. (D)
19. (C)	42. (D)	65. (C)	88. (B)
20. (A)	43. (C)	66. (A)	89. (B)
21. (D)	44. (A)	67. (D)	90. (B)
22. (C)	45. (D)	68. (D)	
23. (C)	46. (B)	69. (B)	

Reading Skills and Knowledge _____/18

1	2	3	4	5	6	7	8	9	10	11

12	13	14	15	16	17	18

Application of Reading Skills and Knowledge to the Classroom _____/12

19	20	21	22	23	24	25	26	27	28	29

30

Mathematics Skills and Knowledge _____/18

31	32	33	34	35	36	37	38	39	40	41

42	43	44	45	46	47	48

Application of Mathematics Skills and Knowledge to the Classroom _____/12

49	50	51	52	53	54	55	56	57	58	59

60

Writing Skills and Knowledge ____/18

61	62	63	64	65	66	67	68	69	70	71

72	73	74	75	76	77	78

Application of Writing Skills and Knowledge to the Classroom ____/12

79	80	81	82	83	84	85	86	87	88	89

90

Detailed Explanations of Answers for Practice Test 2

Praxis ParaPro Assessment (0755 & 1755)

READING

1.　(C)

The correct answer is (C). An opinion *cannot* be proved. It would be a fact if it could be proved. (A), (B), and (D) would all help students understand how facts and opinions are defined.

2.　(D)

The correct answer is (D). The remaining statements are the opinions of the author. Statements using judgmental words such as *always* (A) are often opinions.

3.　(D)

The correct answer is (D). Despite the author's seeming lack of support for robots, the writer understands that an argument can be made for their use in some situations.

4.　(D)

The correct answer is (D). Mention of the conditions and attitudes (A) of the children who rode orphan trains are details. (B) and (C) are partially correct. The author is concerned with recording the history of people who may not live much longer.

5.　(A)

The correct answer is (A). This response identifies specifically who the author is talking about. It ties back to author purpose, recording the history of these individuals.

6.　(B)

The correct answer is (B). The author provides an example that attempts to be balanced in its discussion of the experiences of orphan train riders. The passage does not show how one sentence relates to another (A). Nor does it contradict the claim that orphan train riders were mistreated, since it states that they were within the passage.

7.　(C)

The correct answer is (C). The LEAST acceptable response is Dr. King's desire for world peace. Although Dr. King probably dreamed of world peace, in this particular passage of the speech, his dreams focus on racial equality (B) and the desire that his children, and others, be judged for who they are rather than on their skin color (D). Additionally, the reason a person makes a speech is to share his ideas and opinions with others. It is a form of public discourse.

8.　(D)

The correct answer is (D). Dr. King quotes this phrase to condemn publically those who would not honor one of the primary principles of the American government cited in the Declaration of Independence. He is attempting to persuade people to honor a guiding principle of American society.

9.　(A)

The correct answer is (A). The text states directly that 6 people out of 100 would possess

59% of the world's wealth and those people would be from the United States. The reader must look at the breakdown of Asians, Europeans, people from the northern and southern hemisphere, and Africa to surmise that Americans represent a minority compared to others who populate the planet. The other statements are assumptions based on opinions.

10. (A)

The correct answer is (A). In stating the author's purpose, the paraprofessional should be prepared for a different interpretation from her or his own. The text seems to imply that Americans are more privileged than many people in the world (A). It can also be said that in looking at the breakdown of who populates the world, Americans are part of a diverse world (B). Also, such specific data could be a revelation to many Americans (D). While the author may believe that everyone in the world should have health care, it is not stated or implied (C).

11. (D)

The correct answer is (D). Making meaning requires numerous reading strategies. Reading a poem several times is recommended to help make meaning. Using a dictionary to look up unknown words will help define a term or terms, but not aid in making meaning.

12. (A)

The correct answer is (A). To build fluency in reading, so that students read silently and aloud with greater ease, means they need a basic foundation in the varying sounds that consonants and vowels make. The letter 'c' is an easy consonant, one of several used most frequently in modern language.

13. (B)

The correct answer is (B). The prefix *in-* changes the meaning of the word as many prefixes do. Indifference means treating someone without concern or care. Knowing and using prefixes expand vocabulary. For this purpose, the writer uses the word to show how he treats his father.

14. (C)

The correct answer is (C). Knowledge of Greek and Latin root words expands our vocabulary and enables us to understand more modern English words. English shares many words with romance languages that also have their roots in Greek and Latin. This is an important teaching point for English Language Learners who speak Spanish.

15. (D)

The correct answer is (D). The rule in alphabetizing is to continue to the next letter until you come to the letter that comes next in the alphabet. This also applies when there is more than one word that's utilized as a single term.

16. (B)

The correct answer is (B). The other answers all share characteristics of homonyms. The most complete answer is (D).

17. (C)

The correct answer is (C). In some cases phonics will help students with their pronunciation (B). However, students must learn the relationships between letters and sounds because there are so many variations on the sounds letters make.

18. (C)

The correct answer is (C). The goal is to make students **independent** learners with skills and the knowledge to know where to find information.

19. (C)

The correct answer is (C). While accumulated knowledge about taking exams is helpful, the other responses are more specific. Asking who, what, when, where, why and how focuses the student on the task (D).

20. (A)

The correct answer is (A). Everything else needs to be done before the student turns in the essay.

21. (D)

The correct answer is (D). This response shows that the student understands the possibility that Latoya will get into trouble (possibly through connecting personal experiences to the text). The student also takes into account Latoya's perceptiveness about the people bullies go after. Latoya's statement at the end of the paragraph shows that she doesn't believe she will fall into that trap.

22. (C)

The correct answer is (C). Students may make some accurate guesses about what happens on the first day of school (A). However, encouraging students to read on (or in some cases reread the text) to see what clues are given is a more sophisticated practice that should become a habit.

23. (C)

The correct answer is (C). Rhymes are helpful to students in learning vowel and consonant sounds. In this case, the rhyme uses short vowel sounds. For early or less proficient readers, using single syllable words is the best way to begin.

24. (B)

The correct answer is (B). *Slack* describes the man's mouth. It is used as an adjective that describes a noun (the man's mouth). Although *loosen* seems like the right answer, or close, in this case *slack* is not a verb/action word. In (C) and (D), slack is used as a noun.

25. (D)

The correct answer is (D) Within the context of the sentence, the figure of speech, to *cut or give someone slack* means to allow some 'give' or leeway in their conduct or lighten their load. Another common way to say this is to, "*give someone a break.*"

26. (B)

The correct answer is (B). Writers often give synonyms in sentence or passage for a word that may be unfamiliar to students. They also may us an antonym to provide contrast for the unfamiliar word.

27. (B)

The correct answer is (B). Using vowel and consonant combinations for rhyming helps students with their pronunciation and expands student's vocabulary. For example, *ap* leads to words like *apple, caption, evaporate, capsul*e and *aptitude.*

28. (A)

The correct answer is (A). Answer (A) elicits a yes or no response. (B) isn't focused enough to elicit a specific response. (D) is also an unfocused question. Asking student what the message of the author is and their response lets you know whether or not they 'got it.' Be prepared for their response to differ from yours, however.

29. (B)

The correct answer is (B). Without saying specifically, "I know how that skater feels," the writer conveys that feeling in the last stanza in the lines "...what I wonder ... is if it translates to bicycles."

30. (D)

The correct answer is (D). A long vowel a is pronounced in the word, yesterday, just as it is pronounced when you recite the alphabet.

MATHEMATICS

31. (C)

The correct answer is (C). The area of a triangle is one-half the product of the base and the height. Thus, with a base of 14 and a height of 9, the area equals

$$\left(\frac{1}{2}\right)(14)(9) = \left(\frac{1}{2}\right)(126) = 63$$

32. (B)

The correct answer is (B). Arrange eight numbers in order, then the median is the average of the fourth and fifth numbers. Thus, the median equals.

$$\frac{12 + 16}{2} = 14.$$

33. (B)

The correct answer is (B). 8 inches = (8)(2.54) = 20.32 centimeters.

34. (D)

The correct answer is (B). Each of 5 and 9 is a mode since they both occur the most often.

35. (B)

The correct answer is (B). Starting with the second number, each number is three times the previous number. The fifth number in this sequence is (108)(3) = 324.

36. (D)

The correct answer is (D). Reading from left to right, the value of x increases from 4 to 16 and the value of y decreases from 30 to 18. Also, each pair of x and y adds up to 34.

37. (C)

The correct answer is (C).

1) The percent of employees who are either divorced or widowed is 40% (30% + 10%).

2) Since 40% = .40 we can rewrite the equation as 1440 = 0.4 × a, (1440 is 40% of what?).

3) Then we would divide both sides by 0.4: $\frac{0.4}{0.4}a = \frac{1440}{0.4}a$ which simplifies to

$$a = \frac{1440}{0.4}$$

4) Then, $a = 3600$.

Then the total number of employees is 1440 ÷ 0.40 = 3600.

38. (C)

The correct answer is (C). In an equilateral triangle, all three sides have the same length.

39. (A)

The correct answer is (A). $2 \times 3^3 \times 5 = 2 \times 3 \times 3 \times 3 \times 5 = 270$.

40. (A)

The correct answer is (A). The total weight of all ten people is $(6)(135) + (3)(180) + (1)(90) = 810 + 540 + 90 = 1440$ pounds. The mean weight is $1440 \div 10 = 144$ pounds.

41. (B)

The correct answer is (B). Change each fraction to a denominator of 48. Then $\frac{9}{16} = \frac{27}{48}$ and $\frac{2}{3} = \frac{32}{48}$. In order to find a number between these two fractions, we look for a fraction with a numerator between 27 and 32, with a denominator of 48. Thus, one such fraction is $\frac{29}{48}$.

42. (D)

The correct answer is (D). Add 20 to each side of the equation to get $4x = 56$. Then $x = 56 \div 4 = 14$.

43. (C)

The correct answer is (C). Since 1 deciliter equals 0.1 liters, we can rewrite it as 10 deciliters equals 1 liter. Then 5 kiloliters $= (5)(1000) = 5000$ liters. Finally, 5000 liters $= (5000)(10) = 50,000$ deciliters.

44. (A)

The correct answer is (A). Since the price dropped by 12% from last week to this week, the current price of $2.40 represents $100\% - 12\% = 88\%$ of last week's price. Thus, the price of gasoline last week was $2.40 \div 0.88 \approx \$2.73$.

45. (D)

The correct answer is (D). Point P is located at $(6, 4)$. Counting 2 units to the right changes the first coordinate to $6 + 2 = 8$. Counting 3 units down changes the second coordinate to $4 - 3 = 1$. Thus, the coordinates of point Q would be $(8,1)$.

46. (B)

The correct answer is (B). Using the formula given in the question, the volume is $\left(\frac{4}{3}\right)(\pi)(5^3) = \left(\frac{4}{3}\right)(\pi)\left(\frac{125}{1}\right) = \frac{500\pi}{3}$.

47. (C)

The correct answer is (C). Since the question asked for the closest approximate value, in this case, rounding to the nearest hundredth is the first best step; and 999 is very close to 1000. When multiplying a number by 1000, simply move the decimal point 3 places to the right. So, $(6.2342)(1000) = 6234.2$, which closely approximates 6230.

48. (D)

The correct answer is (D). To calculate $60 - 2 \times (4 + 1)^2$, the sequence of steps are as follows:

1) The first order of operations is to simplify the expressions inside the parenthesis; we begin by adding 4 and 1 to get 5.

2) The second order of operations is to simplify exponents, so square 5 to get 25.

3) Then complete multiplication and division from right to left, multiply 2 by 25 to get 50.

4) Finally, complete any addition and subtraction, 50 from 60 to get 10.

Therefore, subtracting 2 from 60 would not be a correct step.

49. (B)

The correct answer is (B). The student's first step is correct. The operation of multiplication or division, whichever comes first, must be performed. In this example, the division of 6 by 3 precedes the multiplication of 3 times 4.

50. (A)

The correct answer is (A). The student could have made the conversion to yards by either

(a) multiplying 1760 by 7.25, or by

(b) multiplying 1760 by 7, then multiplying 1760 by 0.25, then adding the results.

51. (A)

The correct answer is (A). In a scalene triangle, an altitude drawn from any vertex will not bisect the opposite side.

52. (D)

The correct answer is (D). A pie chart is used when showing how an entire amount is subdivided into each of its contributing parts. Each subdivision is a portion represented by a percentage or a number.

53. (C)

The correct answer is (C). To find the missing numerator, one method is to divide 24 by 3 to get 8. Then multiply 8 by 2 to get 16.

54. (A)

The correct answer is (A). Given a square with a side of 4 the perimeter and the area is 16.

55. (B)

The correct answer is (B). Linda's suggestion is correct because both the mean and mode equal 5. The mode is the most common number and the mean is the sum of these five numbers, divided by 5.

56. (D)

The correct answer is (D). By definition, a diagonal is a line segment that joins two non-adjacent vertices.

57. (B)

The correct answer is (B).

1) The first step is to simplify the equation: $6x + -7 = 4x + 9$

2) Reorder the terms: $-7 + 6x = 4x + 9$

3) Reorder the terms: $-7 + 6x = 9 + 4x$

4) Then we begin solving: $-7 + 6x = 9 + 4x$ for variable x.

5) Move all terms containing x to the left, all other terms to the right.

6) Add $-4x$ to each side of the equation: $-7 + 6x + -4x = 9 + 4x + -4$

7) Combine like terms:
$6x + -4x = 2x$
$-7 + 2x = 9 + 4x + -4x$

8) Combine like terms again:
$-4x + -4x = 0$ and
$-7 + 2x = 9 + 0$, and
$-7 + 2x = 9$

9) Add 7 to each side of the equation:
$-7 + 7 + 2x = 9 + 7$

10) Again, combine like terms:
$-7 + 7 = 0$ and
$0 + 2x = 9 + 7$ and
$2x = 9 + 7$

11) Combine like terms:
$9 + 7 = 16$ and
$2x = 16$

12) Divide each side by 2 and simplify:
$x = 8$

58. (C)

The correct answer is (C). The ten numbers should be placed in ascending (or descending) order. The median is the mean (average) of the two middle numbers, which are the fifth and sixth numbers.

59. (A)

The correct answer is (A). The largest side of any triangle is always opposite the largest angle. By using a triangle with angle measures of 30°, 70°, and 80°, the largest side must lie opposite the 80° angle. Note that answer choice (C) is wrong because the sum of the angles of any triangle must be 180°.

60. (D)

"Ten times a number" is written as $10x$. The expression "seven less than" means that 7 is subtracted FROM a quantity. The correct answer is therefore $10x - 7 = x$.

61. (B)

The correct answer is (C): there are two dependent clauses: *As time passes* and *...that are complex.* (A) is incorrect because there is only one independent clause.

62. (B)

The correct answer is (B) because III is incorrect. Sentence type has nothing to do with the quality of ideas and meanings; it is all about structure.

63. (B)

The correct answer is (B). I and III are prepositional phrases.

64. (B)

The correct answer is (B). A topic may be informational as in an expository essay; it need not be controversial unless the assignment is for an argumentative essay. All other statements are correct recommendations for a research project.

65. (C)

The correct answer is (C): after *Hall* because *instead of restoring the Hall* is introductory; commas around *in any case* because it is a parenthetical phrase; around *most ...outrageous,* because it an appositive, and *by then...shell* because it, too, is an appositive. (B) is incorrect: after *argue* would break the sentence, and after *razed it* would incorrectly separate the compound verb which (A) also incorrectly does. (D) incorrectly separates the verb from its predicate with its comma after *erected*.

66. (A)

The correct answer is (A) *which still is controversial* is not necessary to the meaning and thus should have commas around it. All of the others are necessary to their sentences' meanings and thus correctly do not use commas.

67. (D)

The correct answer is (D). (A) is confusing—a misplaced modifier: is John or Andrew *only wearing a t-shirt*? (B), *who was speaking angrily* (?)—a dangling modifier. (C), the son is not directed by Hitchcock, misplaced modifier. It is, of course, the movie that is directed by Alfred Hitchcock.

68. (D)

The correct answer is (D). *To* is a preposition and the pronoun must be in the objective, not the subjective case. To *whom* shall we give the recommendation letter?

69. (B)

The correct answer is (B). Correlative conjunctions (the twins) require parallel structures, but *do your homework* is an imperative (you) *do* in the present tense while *you are preparing* is declarative and the present progressive. *Either do your homework, or be prepared to fail.*

70. (D)

The correct answer is (D). Both sentences are complete, meeting the three criteria: subject, verb, and a complete thought. All the others have dependent clauses or phrases incorrectly standing alone as sentences: *Which is why... .*and *She being... .*and *As a result of... .*

71. (C)

The correct answer is (C). It is the only one with two independent clauses. To connect these requires either a semi-colon or one of the FANBOYS with a comma.

72. (C)

The correct answer is (C). In option II the semicolon links two independent clauses, forming a compound sentence; in III the semicolon separates items in series that have internal punctuation (commas). I does not have two independent clauses; rather it has a compound verb that is incorrectly separated by the semicolon. In IV, the semi colon is not necessary because one of the FANBOYS is linking the two independent clauses.

73. (D)

The correct answer is (D). In statement I, the name of films require capitalization *Terminator*; II, titles are not capitalized unless they precede the name: *Vice President Biden* but not *Biden, the vice president*; III, specific diseases require capitalization, *Colon Cancer*; Option IV, unless the title of a specific person, the title is not capitalized. Hence, *Admiral Drew Person* would be correct; but it should be *The admirals presented*; also in IV, the name of the ship needs capitalization—*Avenger*.

74. (C)

The correct answer is (C). A dependent clause by definition cannot stand on its own. If it is presented with a capital at the beginning and a terminal punctuation, it is a sentence fragment.

75. (A)

The correct answer is (A): *Dancing is a great stress reliever.* (B) is incorrect as it is critical to identify the difference between phrases and clauses. (C) is also incorrect, they do require parallel construction as in: *Either speak up and take the consequences, or be silent and don't complain.* (D) is also incorrect—narrative is not a sentence type; the missing fourth is an exclamatory sentence.

76. (B)

The correct answer is (B). (A) is the definition of a true sentence. (C) and (D) are too vague to serve as good descriptions.

77. (B)

The correct answer is (B). *Having* is the main verb of the sentence; it's not a verbal phrase. (A) has two: *sensing* and *starting off* both are gerunds, the first modifying *Eloise*, the second the object of the preposition *before*. (C) has two, *annoying* and *doing*, both gerunds. (D) has two infinitive phrases, *to err* and *to forgive*.

78. (C)

The correct answer is (C). Both members of the compound subject need the apostrophe *s* because they do not have the same family. Contrast this to *John and Mary's car was totaled.*

The car belongs to both of them; it is one car. (A) requires the possessive pronoun *its*. Possessive pronouns never use apostrophe *s*, (B) should be *boys'*; (D) again, the *office* is one that belongs to both; the possessive goes to the last member of the compound subject: *Dr. Smith and Dr. Trek's office... .*

79. (B)

The correct answer is (B). Both similes by the use of *like or as* and metaphors which do not use such specific connectors show the similarity between two things in order to make the message clearer or more powerful. *My day was one long nightmare.* The *day* and a *nightmare* are not the same, but the writer connects them to enhance the message of how very bad the day was.

80. (A)

The correct answer is (A)—this defines coherence. (B), (C), and (D) are all ways of providing strong development.

81. (D)

The correct answer is (D). Note the misuse of *nutritional*, the run-on (fused sentence) between *nutritional* and *these*, the incorrect capitalization of *girls* and the incorrect apostrophe on *skinny*. The topic sentence is the first one, but the paragraph fails to give it support—breaking unity with sentence 3. Otherwise the language is not abstract; in fact, it's concrete and specific.

82. (D)

The correct answer is (D). The first, (A), has a simile. (B) is a metaphor—the wife is compared to a slave. (C) is also a metaphor: a dog's magnificence is expressed by comparing him to a king and the head man in a harem.

83. (A)

The correct answer is (A), which is a research tool to find articles. The other three are, in fact, the three major documentation and style manuals.

84. (C)

The correct answer is (C). Note that it specifies the order of ideas and the use of transitions whereas the other two choices are very general.

85. (C)

The correct answer is (C). Note that it takes a specific position, a *must* or *should*, and it is on a controversial topic. It also specifically addresses and describes the evidence that critics deny. (A) does not take a position; it simply states a point, and it is very general. Address how? What steps? (B) is not a position; it could be the thesis for an expository essay but not for an argumentative one.

86. (D)

The correct answer is (D). The paragraph starts with a statement that it develops with a story (narrative) which includes a contrast between the behaviors of two friends.

87. (D)

The correct answer is (D). The argumentative essay does not just describe a controversial topic. It directs the student to investigate a topic, collect, generate, and evaluate evidence, and establish a position on the topic in a concise manner.

88. (B)

The correct answer is (B). Notice how all of the other selections contain many words that elicit the five senses. By contrast, all the words in (B) are "idea" words that need explanation.

89. (B)

The correct answer is (B). Periodical indexes will primarily provide the information necesary find articles; encyclopedias and almanacs are sources of factual information; and the general book stacks in a library, whether organized by the Dewey system or the Library of Congress system, are good for getting a very general view of books on a given subject.

90. (B)

The correct answer is (B). Note that its keywords are reflected in the body of the paragraph: portraying children as sexual objects, defining girls' and boys' sexuality, and selling products. (A) is far too general. *Using* how? (C) is too narrow and too general both, too general because *exploiting* is not specific as is using them as sexual objects, and too narrow because the point about earlier times is only one part of the development of the larger main idea. (D) is not the main point although it can be inferred. This instance of being related, but not directly relevant to the main idea, is an example of the kind of problems often found in students' topic statements.

Index

Praxis ParaPro Assessment

Index

S

NOTES

NOTES

NOTES

NOTES

NOTES

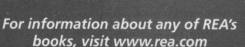